Cynthia Thayer

(517-355-3421

BROWNFIELDS REDEVELOPMENT

Programs and Strategies for Rehabilitating Contaminated Real Estate

Mark S. Dennison

Government Institutes
Rockville, MD

Government Institutes, Inc., 4 Research Place, Rockville, Maryland 20850, USA.

Library of Congress Cataloging-in-Publication Data

Dennison, Mark S.
        Brownfields redevelopment: programs and strategies for rehabilitating contaminated real estate / by Mark S. Dennison.
                p.   cm.
        Includes index.
        ISBN: 0-86587-579-0
        1. Industrial real estate--Environmental aspects--United States--Planning. 2. Hazardous waste site remediation--Government policy--United States. 3. Hazardous waste site remediation--Government policy--United States--States. 4. Brownfields--United States. 5. Brownfields--United States--States. 6. Real estate development--United States--Finance.   I. Title.
        HD257.5.D46   1997
        363.739'66'0973--dc21
                                                        97-40878
                                                        CIP

Printed in the United States of America

For Tracey,
who one day I hope will see
the aurora borealis with me

TABLE OF CONTENTS

Preface.. xix
About the Author... xxiii
Acknowledgments.. xxv

CHAPTER 1
U.S. EPA Brownfields Programs 1

Introduction 1
U.S. EPA Brownfield Initiatives.. 2
Removal of Sites from EPA's CERCLIS Database........................ 2
Brownfields Assessment Pilots 3
Brownfields Cleanup Revolving Loan Fund Demonstration
   Pilots 4
Prospective Purchaser Agreements 6
   1989 Guidance.. 6
   EPA Authority for Prospective Purchaser Agreement............. 7
   Purpose of the 1995 Guidance 8
   Criteria for Prospective Purchaser Agreements 8
      EPA Response Action Undertaken, Ongoing, or
         Anticipated 9
      Substantial Benefit to Agency... 11
      Site Operation Will Not Aggravate Existing
         Contamination or Interfere with EPA's Response
         Action 12
      Site Operation Will Not Pose Health Risks to the
         Community... 12
      Prospective Purchaser Is Financially Viable.................... 13
   Consideration 13
   Public Participation 14
   Model Prospective Purchaser Agreement 14
   Model Prospective Purchaser Agreement-Key Components .. 15

Comfort/Status Letters for Brownfield Properties 18
   Purpose of Policy Statement 19
   Sample Comfort/Status Letters 20
      No Previous Federal Superfund Interest Letter 21
      No Current Federal Superfund Interest Letter 22
      Federal Superfund Interest Letter 24
      State Action Letter 25
Policy on CERCLA Enforcement against Lenders and
  Government Entities 27
   Asset Conservation, Lender Liability, and Deposit Insurance
    Protection Act of 1996 28
Other Federal Initiatives 29
Brownfields National Partnership Action Agenda 29
Brownfields Showcase Communities 31
Empowerment Zone/Enterprise Community (EZ/EC) Program ... 32
   EZ/EC SSBG Funding 33
   Economic Development Initiative 34
   EZ/EC Strategic Plans 34
   EZ/EC Designations 35
   Baltimore, Maryland Empowerment Zone 36
Legislative Reforms 39

CHAPTER 2
State Brownfields Programs 45

Introduction 45
California's Brownfields Initiatives 49
   Voluntary Cleanup Program 53
   Expedited Remedial Action Program 55
   Prospective Purchaser Policy 57
Colorado's Voluntary Cleanup and Redevelopment Act 61
   Memorandum of Agreement with U.S. EPA 62
   Site Screening and Communication 63

Sites Listed on CERCLIS 65
Sites Not Listed on CERCLIS 65
Resources and Capabilities 67
Standards and Risk Analysis 68
Public Participation 68
Cleanup Verification 69
No Further Action Petition 70
Connecticut's Brownfields Redevelopment Programs 71
Voluntary Cleanup Program #1 - Public Act 95-183 71
Voluntary Cleanup Program #2 - Public Act 95-190 72
Comparison of Voluntary Cleanup Programs 74
Urban Sites Remediation Program 75
Neighborhood Revitalization Zones 76
Community Redevelopment Laws 76
Tax Increment Financing 77
Delaware's Voluntary Cleanup Program 78
VCP Site Eligibility 79
VCP Application and Agreement 80
VCP Site Investigation Process 82
Soil and Groundwater Screening Levels 82
Written Assurances 83
Illinois Site Remediation Program 84
Site Eligibility 84
Program Application and Service Agreement 85
Site Investigation and Remediation by Licensed Engineer 86
No Further Remediation Letter 87
Maryland's Brownfields Program 88
Voluntary Cleanup Program 89
Brownfields Revitalization Incentive Program 91
Lender Liability Relief 92
Minnesota's Voluntary Investigation and Cleanup Program 92
Program Improvements 94
Michigan's Brownfields Initiatives 95

Amendments to Michigan's Environmental Cleanup Law 98
Performance of Baseline Environmental Assessment 99
Liability Protections 100
Land Use-Based Cleanup Standards 101
Montana's Voluntary Cleanup Program 102
New Hampshire's Brownfields Program 103
Eligibility Criteria 104
Eligibility Determination 105
Liability Protection 105
Remedial Action and Certificate of Completion 106
New Jersey's Voluntary Cleanup Program 107
Liability Protection 108
Remediation Loans and Grants 109
Tax Abatement 110
New York's Brownfields Programs 110
Voluntary Cleanup Program 111
Environmental Restoration Projects Program 112
Ohio's Voluntary Action Program 113
Financial Assistance for VAP Remediations 116
Water Pollution Control Loan Fund (WPCLF) 116
Pollution Prevention Loan Program 117
Ohio Water Development Authority Loan Program 117
Brownfield Site Cleanup Tax Credit Program 118
Brownfield Grant Assistance Program 119
Competitive Economic Development Program 120
Oklahoma's Brownfields Program 120
Oregon's Voluntary Cleanup Program 123
Prospective Purchaser Agreements 124
Pennsylvania's Land Recycling Program 126
Uniform Cleanup Standards 126
Standardized Review Procedures 127
Releases from Liability 127
Financial Assistance 128

Texas Voluntary Cleanup Program 128
Vermont's Redevelopment of Contaminated Properties
    Program 130
Virginia's Voluntary Remediation Program 133
    Remediated Property Fresh Start Program 135
Washington's Independent Remedial Action Program 135
Wisconsin's Land Recycling Law 136
    Prospective Purchaser Protections 137

CHAPTER 3
Brownfields Redevelopment Strategies 141

Introduction 141
Brownfields Redevelopment Process 142
    Site Identification 142
    Initial Site Assessment or Phase I Investigation 142
    Economic Assessment 144
    Detailed Site Assessment or Phase II Investigation 146
    Project Development and Financing 146
    Cleanup Planning and Execution 147
    Redevelopment of the Site 147
Practical Considerations for Brownfields Projects 147
Performance of Environmental Site Assessments 147
    ASTM Standard E 1528: Transaction Screen Process 149
    ASTM Standard E 1527: Phase I Environmental
        Site Assessment 152
    Limitations on Use of ASTM Phase I Environmental Site
        Assessment 155
    Phase II Environmental Site Assessments 157
Environmental Risk Assessments 158
Public Participation 160
Liability Protections 160

CHAPTER 4
Brownfields Financing Tools... 163

Introduction 163
Direct Financing Strategies 163
Equity Participation... 164
Land Registration and Site Assessment Fees 166
Taxes 167
    Tax Increment Financing 167
    Real Estate Transfer Taxes.................................... 168
    Property Tax Abatement 169
    Tax Treatment of Brownfields Cleanup Expenses............... 170
Debt Financing 172
    Subsidized Low Interest Loans 172
    Revolving Loan Funds 173
    Bonds... 173
Grants 174
    EPA Brownfields Assessment Pilot Grants 174
    State Grant Programs 174
    Private/Nonprofit Grants 175
Indirect Strategies.. 176
Informational/Advisory Services 177
    Land Registry 177
    Brokering.. 177
    Regulatory Compliance Assistance........................ 178
Liability Assurances... 178
    No-Further-Action Letter 179
    Covenant Not to Sue 179
    Certificate of Completeness 180
    Liability Release... 180
Financial Assurances.. 181
    Loan Guarantees... 181
    Bond/Loan Insurance 181

CHAPTER 5
Brownfields Assessment Pilots **183**

Introduction 183
National Brownfields Assessment Demonstration Pilots 186
  Alabama 186
    Birmingham, AL 186
  Alaska 187
    Ketchikan Gateway Borough, AK 187
  Arizona 189
    Navajo Nation, AZ 189
    Tucson, AZ 189
  California 191
    Emeryville, CA 191
    Richmond, CA 191
    Sacramento, CA 192
    Santa Barbara County, CA 192
    Stockton, CA 194
  Connecticut 194
    Bridgeport, CT 194
    Hartford, CT 195
  Delaware 196
    Wilmington, DE 196
  Florida 198
    Dade County, FL 198
    Jacksonville, FL 199
    Tallahassee, FL 201
  Illinois 202
    Cook County, IL 202
    West Central Municipal Conference, IL 204
  Indiana 204
    Indianapolis, IN 204

Kansas 205
    Kansas City, KS and MO 205
Kentucky 205
    Louisville, KY 205
Louisiana 206
    New Orleans, LA 206
Maine... 206
    State of Maine 206
Maryland 208
    Baltimore, MD 208
Massachusetts.. 208
    Chicopee, MA 208
    Greenfield, MA 209
    Lawrence, MA 210
    Lowell, MA 211
    New Bedford, MA 211
    Worcester, MA.. 213
Michigan.. 213
    Detroit, MI.. 213
Minnesota.. 214
    Chippewa County/Kinross Township, MN...................... 214
    St. Paul Port Authority, MN.. 214
Missouri... 216
    St. Louis, MO.. 216
    Wellston, MO.. 216
New Jersey 218
    Jersey City, NJ.. 218
    Newark, NJ... 219
    Perth Amboy, NJ 220
    Trenton, NJ... 221
New York... 222
    Elmira, NY.. 222
    New York, NY 223

Niagara Falls, NY 224
Rochester, NY 225
Rome, NY 226
North Carolina 226
Charlotte, NC 226
Fayetteville, NC 227
High Point, NC 228
Ohio 229
Cuyahoga County, OH 229
Lima, OH 230
Oregon 230
Oregon Mill Sites, OR 230
Portland, OR 231
Pennsylvania 231
Bucks County, PA 231
Phoenixville, PA 233
Puerto Rico 234
Puerto Rico Industrial Development Company 234
Rhode Island 235
State of Rhode Island 235
South Carolina 236
Cowpens, SC 236
Tennessee 237
Knoxville, TN 237
Memphis, TN 238
Texas 239
Houston, TX 239
Laredo, TX 240
Vermont 240
Burlington, VT 240
Virginia 241
Cape Charles-Northampton County, VA 241
Richmond, VA 241

Washington 242
   Tacoma, WA 242
Wisconsin 242
   Northwest Regional Planning Commission, WI 242
Regional Brownfields Assessment Demonstration Pilots 244
   Alabama 244
      Prichard, AL 244
   California 244
      East Palo Alto, CA 244
      Oakland, CA 246
      San Francisco, CA 247
   Colorado 247
      Englewood, CO 247
      Sand Creek Corridor, CO 249
   Connecticut 249
      Naugatuck Valley, CT 249
      New Haven, CT 250
   Florida 250
      Clearwater, FL 250
      Gainesville, FL 251
      Miami, FL 252
      St. Petersburg, FL 253
   Georgia 253
      Atlanta, GA 253
   Idaho 254
      Panhandle Health District, ID 254
   Illinois 254
      Chicago, IL 254
      East St. Louis, IL 256
      State of Illinois 257
   Indiana 257
      Northwest Indiana Cities 257
      State of Indiana 258

Louisiana 259
    Shreveport, LA 259
Maine 259
    Portland, ME 259
Maryland 260
    Baltimore County, MD 260
Massachusetts 261
    Boston, MA 261
    Lynn, MA 262
    Somerville, MA 263
    Westfield, MA 264
Michigan 265
    Kalamazoo, MI 265
Minnesota 266
    Downriver Community Conference, MI 266
    State of Minnesota 266
Missouri 267
    Bonne Terre, MO 267
New Hampshire 268
    Concord, NH 268
New Jersey 268
    Camden, NJ 268
New York 269
    Buffalo, NY 269
Ohio 269
    Cincinnati, OH 269
Oklahoma 270
    Tulsa, OK 270
Pennsylvania 272
    Philadelphia, PA 272
    Pittsburgh, PA 272
South Dakota 273
    Sioux Falls, SD 273

Texas 273

    Dallas, TX 273

Utah 274

    Murray City, UT 274

    Ogden City, UT 274

    Provo, UT 276

    Salt Lake City, UT 276

    West Jordan, UT 277

Washington 277

    Bellingham, WA 277

    Duwamish Coalition, WA 278

    Puyallup Tribe of Tacoma, WA 278

Wisconsin 279

    Milwaukee County, WI 279

    Wisconsin Department of Natural Resources 279

CHAPTER 6
Brownfields Redevelopment Case Studies 281

Introduction 281

Case Study #1: Redevelopment for Industrial Use 282

    Avtex Fibers Site, Meadville, Pennsylvania 282

    Contamination Assessment 283

    Applicable Regulations 284

    Remedial Planning 285

    Land Use Planning Issues 286

Case Study #2: Redevelopment for Commercial Use 287

    Robinson Brick Company Site, Denver, Colorado 287

    Site History 287

    Applicable Cleanup Standards 289

    Remedial Planning 290

    Prospective Purchaser and Future Land Use of the Site 291

Case Study #3: Redevelopment for Residential Use................... 292
  Herndon Homes Site, Atlanta, Georgia................................ 292
  Contamination Assessment 293
  Applicable Regulations Governing Remediation.................. 293
  Remedial Planning 294
  Land Use Planning Issues 295
Comparison of the Three Projects... 296
Conclusions 297

APPENDICES

Appendix A - U.S. EPA Brownfield Program Contacts 299
Appendix B - State Brownfield Program Contacts 305
Appendix C - Model Prospective Purchaser Agreement 313
Appendix D - Sample EPA Comfort/Status Letters................... 327
Appendix E - CERCLA Enforcement against Lenders and
  Government Entities That Acquire Property Involuntarily...... 343
Appendix F - Brownfields Bibliography..................................... 351

Glossary.. 355
Index... 395

PREFACE

Past environmental policies created disincentives for the private cleanup of abandoned, underused industrial and commercial properties with actual or suspected contamination. Since both federal and state environmental cleanup laws generally imposed strict liability for cleanup on owners and operators of these contaminated brownfield sites—even though they did not cause or contribute to the contamination—prospective purchasers, developers, lenders, and local governments were discouraged from acquiring these properties for cleanup and productive reuse. Even where very low levels or no actual contamination was present, sites became stigmatized as brownfields simply because industrial uses were previously conducted on the property. The stigma attached to such properties made them especially difficult to lease, sell, or use as collateral due to serious concerns about potential environmental liability. The positive aspects of an old industrial or commercial site—its location and existing buildings, improvements, roads, and utilities—were frequently negated by the threat of environmental liability for cleanup costs. Lenders and other capital providers were reluctant to provide financing for brownfield redevelopment. Innocent purchasers shunned sites where the parties responsible for the contamination were bankrupt, insolvent, or couldn't be identified. Often, developers chose virgin land and suburban greenfields over contaminated urban sites.

Recognizing that this problem cannot continue to go unabated, government, business, and industry have taken affirmative steps to return brownfields to productive use. Recently, the U.S. EPA and many state government agencies have launched various practical initiatives to promote the rehabilitation and reuse of these properties. EPA's initiatives include delisting of sites from the National Priorities List, funding of brownfields assessment pilot projects, execution of prospective purchaser agreements, and issuance of comfort/status letters. Over 30 states have implemented programs to encourage the cleanup and redevelopment of brownfields. These state programs—called voluntary cleanup programs, brownfields programs, land recycling programs, and similar names—basically offer financial incentives and liability protections in exchange for voluntary investigation and cleanup of brownfield properties. Many states have created voluntary cleanup funds, grant programs, low-interest loan programs, tax breaks, and other economic incentives to assist brownfield project sponsors in their cleanup and redevelopment efforts. Importantly, under most programs, once cleanup is completed to the satisfaction of the state environmental agency, a participant in the voluntary cleanup program may be issued various liability protections and assurances, including a No-Further-Action letter, Certificate of Completion, or formal covenant not to sue.

These brownfields programs represent a shift in enviromental policy. Brownfields redevelopment is not driven by environmental cleanup and is not meant to be a substitute for cleanup under the federal and state Superfund programs. Rather, the impetus behind federal and state brownfields initiatives is primarily an economic one, aimed at economic revitalization of blighted urban areas that are saddled with abandoned or underused industrial and commercial properties. As such, the primary focus of federal and state brownfields programs is on accelerated cleanup and redevelopment of those sites that can be cleaned up and returned to productive, sustainable use in a relatively short period of time and that pose lesser degrees of financial and environmental risk to potential developers and investors.

Brownfields Redevelopment serves as a comprehensive guide to the programs and strategies that landowners, prospective purchasers, developers, investors, lenders, municipal government officials, and other parties must understand to carry out successful brownfield cleanup and redevelopment projects. In practical, easy-to-understand fashion, the book provides a framework for approaching the assessment, cleanup, redevelopment, and reuse of brownfields properties. Chapters 1 and 2 explain all of the federal and state programs that provide the regulatory process and economic stimulus for rehabilitating brownfields. Chapters 3 and 4 take the reader through each step of the brownfield redevelopment process, examine various practical considerations, and provide a discussion of different financing tools and liability assurances that can be used to support brownfields projects. Chapter 5 offers summaries of activities underway at each of the EPA's Brownfield Assessment Pilots. Finally, Chapter 6 gives real life case studies of three brownfield cleanup and redevelopment projects, providing an evaluation of applicable cleanup standards and appropriate remedial action for three different planned future uses of the property—industrial, commercial, and residential. The book also contains helpful reference tables to federal and state brownfield programs, checklists summarizing key points, and several useful appendices. It is hoped that this book will give project participants valuable information and helpful tools to assist them in meeting the challenges of brownfields redevelopment and reuse.

Mark S. Dennison

Westwood, New Jersey

ABOUT THE AUTHOR

Mark S. Dennison is an attorney and author of 16 books and over 100 articles dealing with environmental, land use, and real estate law issues. His books include *Wetland Mitigation* (Government Institutes 1996); *Pollution Prevention Strategies and Technologies* (Government Institutes 1995); *Environmental Reporting, Recordkeeping, and Inspections* (Van Nostrand Reinhold 1995); *Environmental Due Diligence for Lenders*, with R. Kenneth Keim and Philip W. Lee (Warren, Gorham & Lamont 1995); *Storm Water Discharges* (CRC Press 1995); *Hazardous Waste Regulation Handbook* (John Wiley & Sons 1994); *Understanding Solid and Hazardous Waste Identification and Classification* (John Wiley & Sons 1993); *Wetlands: Guide to Science, Law, and Technology*, with James F. Berry (Noyes Publications 1993).

Mr. Dennison is in private practice in Westwood, New Jersey, specializing in environmental, land use, real property, and zoning law. He is admitted to practice in New Jersey and New York. Mr. Dennison holds a B.A., *magna cum laude*, from the State University of New York (Oswego), an M.A. from Syracuse University, and a J.D. from New York Law School.

ACKNOWLEDGMENTS

I wish to express my appreciation to everyone who played a role in publication of this book. I thank the editorial and production staff at Government Institutes, especially my editor (now associate publisher), Alex Padro, for his never-ending enthusiasm and shared commitment to publication of a book of the highest quality. I must also give special thanks to Jack Riggenbach, Ron Fender, and Dan Hinds who who provided the valuable case studies found in Chapter 6.

Also, I wish to express my appreciation to the many helpful individuals working at different federal and state regulatory offices who answered my questions and provided copies of various forms, government documents, and regulations, including: Jean Koeninger, Arkansas Department of Pollution Control and Ecology; Sandra Karinen, California Environmental Protection Agency; Betsy Wingfield, Connecticut Department of Environmental Protection; Karl Kalbacher, Delaware Department of Natural Resources; Jim Metz, Maryland Department of the Environment; Claudia Kerbawy, Michigan Department of Environmental Quality; Kristin Lukes, Minnesota Pollution Control Agency; Carol Fox, Montana Department of Environmental Quality; Ronald Corcory, New Jersey Department of Environmental Protection; Jack McKeon, New York Department of Environmental Conservation; Michelle Thompson, Ohio Environmental Protection Agency; Rita Kottke, Oklahoma Department of Environmental Quality; Alan Kiphut, Oregon Department of Environmental Quality; Thomas Fidler, Pennsylvania Department of Environmental Protection; Charles Epperson, Texas Natural Resource Conservation Commission; George Desch, Vermont Department of Environmental

Conservation; Hassan Vakili, Virginia Department of Environmental Quality; and Harold Bucholz, Washington Department of Ecology.

Additional thanks goes out to family and friends who provided moral support and inspiration, especially Erin Carrather, Bobbie Waits, Keith Dennison, and Nikolai Andreivich Budinsky. Finally, my greatest appreciation is reserved for my dear Tracey, who is the constant source of joy in my life.

M.S.D.

BROWNFIELDS REDEVELOPMENT

Programs and Strategies for Rehabilitating Contaminated Real Estate

CHAPTER 1

U.S. EPA BROWNFIELDS PROGRAMS

Introduction

The term "brownfield" is used to describe abandoned, idled, or underused industrial and commercial property that has been taken out of productive use as a result of actual or perceived risks from environmental contamination. Communities across the country are faced with the challenge of cleaning up and redeveloping brownfields. The magnitude of the problem is formidable. For example, the City of Chicago has identified over 2,000 brownfields in its metropolitan area alone and the U.S. Government Accounting Office estimates that there may be as many as 650,000 brownfields sites throughout the United States.

Brownfields are often avoided by developers, businesses, lenders, and investors because of the uncertainties regarding environmental contamination. Developers are reluctant to risk liability for potential costs associated with hazardous waste assessment and cleanup, which may be imposed on current owners and operators of the property under the Comprehensive Environmental Response, Compensation, and Liability Act (CERCLA)—also known as Superfund—and parallel state hazardous waste cleanup laws, even though they did not cause or contribute to the existing contamination of the site. Lenders are likewise unwilling to participate in brownfields redevelopment projects due to the threat of environmental liability, the risk of bankruptcy by project sponsors, and devaluation of property used as loan collateral. This reluctance to rehabilitate brownfield properties has resulted in increased development of suburban greenfield areas, urban sprawl, and continuing economic and environmental blight in former industrial and commercial urban areas.

Various regulatory initiatives have been introduced at the federal and state government levels to reverse this trend and stimulate cleanup and reuse of brownfield sites. These initiatives offer economic opportunities and financial incentives to revitalize urban areas by bringing these abandoned or underutilized industrial and commercial properties back into productive and sustainable use. This chapter describes U.S. EPA and other federal programs and incentives for redevelopment of brownfield properties.

U.S. EPA Brownfield Initiatives

Against the backdrop of a more flexible approach to environmental protection,[1] on January 25, 1995, the U.S. Environmental Protection Agency (EPA) issued its "Working Draft of the Brownfield Action Agenda," which sets forth various initiatives to assist cities and private businesses in the redevelopment of brownfield sites.[2] The EPA's initiatives include removal of sites from the Comprehensive Environmental Response, Compensation and Liability Information System (CERCLIS) database, funding of brownfield assessment demonstration pilot projects, execution of prospective purchaser agreements, issuance of comfort/status letters for contaminated properties, and issuance of enforcement policy on the CERCLA liability of lenders and government entities that involuntarily acquire contaminated property. The EPA has taken significant steps toward implementation of each of these objectives.

---

[1]The New Generation of Environmental Protection: EPA's Five-Year Strategic Plan, EPA 200-B-94-002 (July 1994).
[2]The Working Draft of the Brownfields Action Agenda, U.S. EPA, January 25, 1995.

Removal of Sites from EPA's CERCLIS Database

On March 29, 1995, the EPA adopted new procedures for maintaining its Comprehensive Environmental Response, Compensation and Liability Information System (CERCLIS).[3] CERCLIS is the data base and data management system that EPA uses to track activities at sites considered for cleanup under CERCLA. The EPA rule announced the agency's decision to remove from CERCLIS those sites it decided do not warrant further evaluation under the Superfund program. The EPA is specifically including sites that the agency has given a designation of "No Further Response Action Planned (NFRAP)," to eliminate any possible disincentive to purchase, improve, redevelop, and revitalize sites related to inclusion on CERCLIS. Many of these NFRAP sites are not contaminated and others are currently being cleaned up by the states. EPA has already removed 25,000 NFRAP sites from the list of 38,000 sites included in CERCLIS.

Brownfields Assessment Pilots

Since September 1993, the U.S. EPA has awarded over 100 grants to states, cities, towns, counties, and American Indian Tribes for National and Regional Brownfields Assessment Demonstration Pilots. The EPA expects the pilot program to be instrumental in initiating nationwide brownfield redevelopment projects. National Pilots are awarded through a competitive application process under criteria developed by EPA Headquarters. Regional Pilots are selected by EPA Regions, which use their own selection criteria. These pilot grants, funded up to $200,000 each, will be used to support creative explorations and demonstrations of brownfield solutions. The objectives of the brownfield pilot program include:

- Increase the participation of interested parties in shaping the cleanup and productive reuse of contaminated sites;

- Stimulate a national search for innovative ways to overcome the current obstacles to the reuse of contaminated properties;

- Coalesce federal, state, and municipal efforts to examine new approaches to achieving cleanup and reuse; and

- Explore the potential for combining economic stimuli and prompt environmental cleanup to contribute to the achievement of environmental justice.

The pilots are expected to provide the EPA, states, municipalities, and communities with useful information and strategies as they continue to seek methods to promote a unified approach to site assessments, environmental cleanup, and redevelopment of brownfields. The ongoing activities of each of the brownfield assessment pilots are described in detail in Chapter 5.

Brownfields Cleanup Revolving Loan Fund Demonstration Pilots

As part of the EPA's Brownfields Initiatives, the EPA will be awarding Brownfields Cleanup Revolving Loan Fund (BCRLF) Demonstration Pilots to states, cities, towns, counties, territories, and Indian Tribes that meet certain eligibility criteria. A revolving loan fund is a variant of a bank bond, in which a sponsoring entity (in this case, the EPA) provides capitalization funds to a managing entity (e.g., a municipality) that are used to make loans for authorized purposes (brownfield cleanups). A revolving loan charges interest on the loans, generally at a low interest rate. This fund is termed revolving because it uses loan repayment (principal, plus interest) to make new loans for the same authorized purposes.

The EPA will award BCRLF pilots to test brownfields cleanup revolving loan fund models that facilitate coordinated public and private cleanup efforts at the federal, state, and local levels. From the BCRLF pilot funds, selected states, political subdivisions, and Indian Tribes may provide loans—but not grants—to public and private parties that have not contributed to contamination at the site(s) for the purposes of cleanup and redevelopment of sites that have already been assessed for contamination. Loan repayments provide a continuing source of capital for states, political subdivisions, and Indian Tribes to direct and facilitate brownfield site cleanups by providing additional loans to other eligible recipients for brownfield cleanups.

The BCRLF pilots are selected through an evaluation process. Eligible entities must demonstrate:

- An ability to manage a revolving loan fund and environmental cleanups;

- A need for cleanup funds;

- Commitment to creative leveraging of EPA funds with public-private partnerships and in-kind services;

- A clear plan for sustaining the environmental protection and related economic development activities initiated through the BCRLF program.

For EPA's 1997 fiscal year (FY97), only the 29 entities that were awarded National and Regional Brownfields Assessment Demonstration Pilots by September 30, 1995 were eligible to apply for the BCRLF demonstration pilot program. The 29 eligible entities must meet the EPA's threshold and evaluation criteria. There is no guarantee of an award. These pilots are funded up to $350,000; however, the size of the awards may vary depending on the proposed response to the evaluation criteria. The FY97 BCRLF demonstration pilots were awarded by EPA Headquarters. EPA Regional offices will award BCRLF pilots in future years.

Prospective Purchaser Agreements

Another key component of the EPA's Brownfields Initiative is the use of prospective purchaser agreements to encourage developers and investors to purchase, cleanup, and put contaminated properties to productive reuse. On June 21, 1995, the EPA issued long-awaited supplemental guidance on prospective purchaser agreements.[4] This new guidance document supersedes the agency's 1989 policy concerning agreements with prospective purchasers of contaminated property and is expected to give the EPA greater flexibility to consider agreements with covenants not to sue that would have substantial benefits to the community (e.g., through job creation or productive use of abandoned property), but also would be safe, consistent with site remediation, and still have some direct benefits to the agency.

1989 Guidance

In 1989, the EPA issued its original guidance regarding agreements with prospective purchasers of contaminated property.[5] Pursuant to the original guidance, the EPA basically considered issuing a covenant not to sue a prospective purchaser who agreed to perform work or to pay a certain portion of the cleanup costs at a given site.[6] Prospective purchaser agreements encouraged some people to purchase and develop contaminated sites where the fear of CERCLA liability might have posed a barrier. Prior to issuance of its revised criteria, the EPA had completed 17 Prospective

---

[4]Announcement and Publication of the Guidance on Agreements with Prospective Purchasers of Contaminated Property and Model Prospective Purchaser Agreement, 60 Fed. Reg. 34792 (July 3, 1995).

[5]Guidance on Landowner Liability under Section 107(a) of CERCLA, De Minimis Settlements under Section 122(g)(1)(B) of CERCLA, and Settlements with Prospective Purchasers of Contaminated Property, OSWER Directive No. 9835.9, 54 Fed. Reg. 34235 (Aug. 18, 1989).

[6]It is important to note that this covenant not to sue does not protect the purchaser from lawsuits brought by third parties.

Purchaser Agreements through the end of 1994.[7] In return for a covenant not to sue, prospective purchasers have paid cash consideration ranging in amounts as low as $6,000 and as high as $9 million. In addition to these cash payments, the EPA has accepted "in-kind" consideration, such as site investigation, transportation and disposal of hazardous substances, and performance of response actions at the site.[8]

EPA Authority for Prospective Purchaser Agreement

During the past few years, numerous prospective purchasers of contaminated property have requested that the EPA limit their CERCLA liability by offering covenants not to sue. Although Section 122 of CERCLA[9] empowers the EPA to enter into settlement agreements concerning CERCLA liability, including covenants not to sue and contribution protection, this authority only extends to agreements with potentially responsible parties (PRPs), as defined in Section 107(a) of CERCLA.[10] Since prospective purchasers are not yet owners or operators of contaminated property, they fall outside the contemplated reach of the statutory covenant not to sue. Thus, the basis for EPA's authority to enter into settlement agreements with prospective purchasers is derived from the U.S. Department of Justice (DOJ)'s inherent authority to settle matters for the United States. A prospective purchaser must have a mandatory consultation with the

---

[7]*See, for example,* 59 Fed. Reg. 60014 (Nov. 21, 1994) (Commodore Semiconductors Group Site, Norristown, PA.); 59 Fed. Reg. 41443 (Aug. 2, 1994) (Publicker Industries Site, Philadelphia, PA); 59 Fed. Reg. 34437 (July 5, 1994) (Peterson/Puritan, Inc. Site, Lincoln and Cumberland, RI); 58 Fed. Reg. 64766 (Dec. 9, 1993) (Atlantic Wood Preservers Site, Harmans, MD); 58 Fed. Reg. 64584 (Dec. 8, 1993) (Croyden TCE Site, Croyden, PA).

[8]*See* Malissa Hathaway McKeith and Nina Luban, "EPA Offers Innovative Vehicle to Cap Liability," Nat'l L.J. (Jan. 23, 1995) at B14.

[9]42 U.S.C. § 9622.

[10]42 U.S.C. § 9607(a).

Director of the EPA Regional Support Division, Office of Site Remediation Enforcement. Any agreement negotiated between the EPA and a prospective purchaser requires the express approval of the Department of Justice.

Purpose of the 1995 Guidance

The EPA has determined that prospective purchaser agreements might be both appropriate and beneficial in more circumstances than contemplated by its 1989 guidance. The 1989 guidance limited the use of these agreements to situations where the EPA planned to take an enforcement action, and where the agency received a substantial benefit, not otherwise available, from cleanup of the site by the purchaser.

The EPA now believes that it may be appropriate to enter into agreements resulting in somewhat reduced benefits to the agency. The new guidance authorizes use of prospective purchaser agreements, if the agreement results in either (1) a substantial direct benefit to the agency in terms of cleanup or funds for cleanup, or (2) a substantial indirect benefit to the community, coupled with a lesser direct benefit to the EPA. The new guidance is also applicable to persons who are prospectively seeking to operate or lease contaminated property.

Criteria for Prospective Purchaser Agreements

The 1995 guidance outlines several criteria that must be met before the EPA will consider entering into prospective purchaser agreements. These criteria are intended to reflect EPA's commitment to removing the barriers imposed by potential CERCLA liability while ensuring protection of human health and the environment. The EPA will consider the following five criteria when evaluating prospective purchaser agreements:

1. An EPA action at the facility has been taken, is ongoing, or is anticipated to be undertaken by the agency;

2. The Agency should receive a substantial benefit either in the form of a direct benefit for cleanup, or as an indirect public benefit in combination with a reduced direct benefit to EPA;

3. The continued operation of the facility or new site development, with the exercise of due care, will not aggravate or contribute to the existing contamination or interfere with EPA's response action;

4. The continued operation or new development of the property will not pose health risks to the community and those persons likely to be present at the site; and

5. The prospective purchaser is financially viable.

EPA Response Action Undertaken, Ongoing, or Anticipated

This criterion is meant to ensure that EPA does not become unnecessarily involved in purely private real estate transactions or expend its limited resources in negotiations, which are unlikely to produce a sufficient benefit to the public. EPA, however, recognizes the potential gains in terms of cleanup and public benefit that may be realized with broader application of prospective purchaser agreements. Therefore, this criterion has been expanded beyond the limitation in the 1989 guidance to sites where enforcement action is anticipated, to now include sites where federal involvement has occurred or is expected to occur.

When requested, the EPA may consider entering into prospective purchaser agreements at sites listed or proposed for listing on the National Priorities List (NPL), or sites where EPA has undertaken, is undertaking, or plans to conduct a response action. If the Agency receives a request for a prospective purchaser agreement at a site where EPA has not yet become involved, EPA will first evaluate the realistic possibility that a prospective purchaser may incur Superfund liability when determining the appropriateness of entering into a prospective purchaser agreement. This evaluation should clearly show that EPA's covenant not to sue is essential to remove Superfund liability barriers and allow the private party to cleanup and undertake productive use, reuse, or redevelopment of the site.

The EPA will consider the following factors when evaluating the appropriateness of entering into an agreement with a prospective purchaser at any site:

- Whether information regarding releases or potential releases of hazardous substances at the site indicates that there is a substantial likelihood of federal response or enforcement action at the site that would justify EPA's involvement in entering into the prospective purchaser agreement.

- Whether other available avenues (e.g., private indemnification agreements) may exist to sufficiently alleviate the threat of Superfund liability at the site without the need for EPA involvement. In most cases, EPA will decline to consider an agreement at a site that is currently undergoing cleanup through a state program, since future EPA activity at such a site is extremely unlikely.

Prospective purchaser agreements generally will not be appropriate at sites that are screened out using these criteria. For example, sites designated by EPA as No Further Response Action Planned (NFRAP) and removed from the CERCLIS will rarely be deemed appropriate for a prospective purchaser agreement.

Substantial Benefit to Agency

A cornerstone of the Agency's evaluation process under the 1995 guidance is the measurement of environmental benefit, in the form of direct funding, or cleanup, or a combination of reduced direct funding or cleanup and an indirect public benefit. The EPA believes that its past practice of limiting prospective purchaser agreements to those situations where substantial benefit was measured only in terms of cost reimbursement or work performed may have decreased the effectiveness of this tool.

Thus, the new guidance encourages a more balanced evaluation of both the direct and indirect benefits of a prospective purchaser agreement to the government and the public. EPA recognizes that indirect benefits to a community is an important consideration and may justify the commitment of the agency's resources necessary to negotiate a prospective purchaser agreement, even where there are reduced direct benefits to the agency in terms of cleanup and cost reimbursement. EPA may now consider negotiating prospective purchaser agreements that will result in substantial indirect benefits to the community as long as there is still some direct benefit to the agency.

Both direct and indirect benefits should be measurable to enable EPA to evaluate them effectively and to ensure they are substantial. Examples of indirect benefits to the community include measures that serve to reduce substantially the risk posed by the site, creation or retention of jobs, development of abandoned or blighted property, creation of conservation or recreation areas, or provision of community services (such as improved public transportation and infrastructure.) Examples of reduced but measurable benefits to EPA include partial cleanup or compensation.

Site Operation Will Not Aggravate Existing Contamination or Interfere with EPA's Response Action

EPA will not enter into an agreement if available information is insufficient for purposes of evaluating the impact of continued operation or new site development activities. Information that should be considered by the agency to evaluate the effect of these activities could include site assessment data and the Engineering Evaluation Cost Analysis (EE/CA) or remedial investigation/feasibility study (RI/FS), if available, and all other information relevant to the condition of the site.

If the prospective purchaser intends to continue the operations of an existing facility, the prospective purchaser should submit information sufficient to allow the agency to determine whether the continued operations are likely to aggravate or contribute to the existing contamination or interfere with the remedy. If the prospective purchaser plans to undertake new operations or development of the property, comprehensive information regarding these plans should be provided to EPA. If the planned activities of the prospective purchaser are likely to aggravate or contribute to the existing contamination or generate new contamination, EPA generally will not enter into an agreement, or will include restrictions in the agreement which prohibit those operations.

Site Operation Will Not Pose Health Risks to the Community

EPA believes it is important to consider the environmental implications of site operations on the surrounding community and to those likely to be present or have access to the site.

Prospective Purchaser Is Financially Viable

A settling party, including a prospective purchaser of contaminated property, should demonstrate that it is financially viable and capable of fulfilling any obligation under the agreement. In appropriate circumstances, EPA may structure payment or work to be performed to avoid or minimize an undue financial burden on the purchaser.

Consideration

As a matter of law, it is necessary for EPA to obtain adequate consideration when entering into a prospective purchaser agreement. In determining what constitutes adequate consideration, the agency will consider a number of relevant factors. Initially, the EPA will examine the amount of past and future response costs expected to be incurred at the site, whether there are other potentially responsible parties who can perform the work or reimburse EPA's costs, and whether there is likely to be a shortfall in recovery of costs at the site. EPA may then consider the purchase price to be paid by the prospective purchaser, the market value of the property, the value of any CERCLA lien on the property, whether the purchaser is paying a reduced price due to the condition of the property, and, if so, the likely increase in the value of the property attributable to the cleanup (e.g., compare purchase price or market price with the estimated value of the property following completion of the response action). Finally, EPA will consider the size and nature of the prospective purchaser and the proposed use of the site (e.g., whether the purchaser is a large commercial or industrial venture, a small business, a nonprofit or community-based activity).

The analysis of any benefits received by the agency also should contemplate any projected "windfall" profit to the purchaser when the government has unreimbursed response costs, and whether it is appropriate to include in the agreement some provision to recoup such costs. This analysis should be coupled with an examination of any indirect benefit that the EPA may receive (e.g., demolition of structures, implementation of institutional controls) in determining whether a prospective purchaser agreement provides a substantial benefit.

Public Participation

In light of EPA's new policy of accepting indirect public benefit as partial consideration, and the fact that the prospective purchaser agreements will provide contribution protection to the purchaser, the surrounding community and other members of the public should be afforded the opportunity to comment on the settlement, whenever feasible. Because settlements with prospective purchasers are not expressly governed by Section 122 of CERCLA, there is no legal requirement for public notice and comment. Whenever practicable, however, EPA intends to publish notices in the Federal Register and undertake other appropriate action to ensure that adequate notification of the agreement is given to all interested parties.

Model Prospective Purchaser Agreement

A significant final component of the 1995 guidance, not contained in the earlier guidance concerning agreements with prospective purchasers of contaminated property, is a model prospective purchaser agreement. The model agreement functions as a starting point for negotiations between the EPA and prospective purchasers. The key provisions of this model agreement are summarized here.[11]

---

[11]The model prospective agreement is reproduced in its entirety in Appendix C.

Model Prospective Purchaser Agreement - Key Components

Purpose: The purpose of the model agreement, as stated in Section I, is to settle and resolve the potential liability of the settling party for the Existing Contamination at the Property (subject to reservations and limitations contained in other sections of the Agreement), which would otherwise result from the settling party becoming the owner of the property. "Existing Contamination" is defined in Section II as "any hazardous substances, pollutants or contaminants, present or existing on or under the Site as of the effective date of this Agreement."

Payment: In consideration of and in exchange for the United States' Covenant Not to Sue in Section VIII, the settling party agrees to pay to EPA a specified sum within a set period of time from the effective date of the Agreement. A separate section may be added if the consideration is work to be performed.

Access/Notice to Successors in Interest: Commencing on the date that the settling party acquires title to the Property, the settling party must provide the EPA and all other persons performing response actions under EPA or state oversight, with an irrevocable right of access to the Property and to any other property to which access is required for the implementation of response actions at the Site. Within 30 days after the effective date of the Agreement, the settling party must record a certified copy of the Agreement with the county Recorder's Office, Registry of Deeds or other appropriate office. Thereafter, each deed, title, or other instrument conveying an interest in the Property must contain a notice stating that the Property is subject to the Agreement.

Due Care/Cooperation: The settling party must exercise due care at the Site with respect to the Existing Contamination and must comply with all applicable local, state, and federal laws and regulations. The settling party recognizes that the implementation of response actions at the Site may interfere with the settling party's use of the Property, and may require closure of its operations or a part thereof.

Certification: By entering into the Agreement, the settling party must certify, to the best of its knowledge and belief, that it has fully and accurately disclosed to EPA and the state all information known to the settling party and all information in the possession or control of its officers, directors, employees, contractors and agents which relates in any way to any Existing Contamination or any past or potential future release of hazardous substances, pollutants or contaminants at or from the Site and to its qualification for the Agreement. The settling party also must certify, to the best of its knowledge and belief, that it has not caused or contributed to a release or threat of release of hazardous substances or pollutants or contaminants at the Site. If the United States and the state determines that information provided by the settling party is not materially accurate and complete, the Agreement, within the sole discretion of the United States, will be rendered null and void.

Covenant Not To Sue: Subject to the Reservation of Rights in the Agreement, upon payment of the consideration specified in the Agreement, the United States and the state covenants not to sue or take any other civil or administrative action against the settling party for any and all civil liability for injunctive relief or reimbursement of response costs pursuant to Sections 106 or 107(a) of CERCLA, 42 U.S.C. § 9606 or § 9607(a) and applicable state law with respect to the Existing Contamination.

Reservation of Rights: The covenant not to sue set forth in Section VIII does not pertain to any matters other than those expressly specified in that section. The United States and the State reserves, and the Agreement is without prejudice to, all rights against the settling party with respect to all other matters, including but not limited to, the following:

- Claims based on a failure by the settling party to meet a requirement of the Agreement;

- Any liability resulting from past or future releases of hazardous substances, pollutants or contaminants, at or from the Site caused or contributed to by the settling party, its successors, assignees, lessees or sublessees;

- Any liability resulting from exacerbation of Existing Contamination by the settling party, its successors, assignees, lessees or sublessees; and

- Any liability resulting from the release or threat of release of hazardous substances, pollutants or contaminants, at the Site after the effective date of the Agreement, not within the definition of Existing Contamination.

Settling Party's Covenant Not To Sue: In consideration of the United States' Covenant Not To Sue in Section VIII of the Agreement, the settling party covenants not to sue and not to assert any claims or causes of action against the United States or the state, its authorized officers, employees, or representatives with respect to the Site or the Agreement. The settling party reserves, and the Agreement is without prejudice to, actions against the United States based on negligent actions taken directly by the United States, not including oversight or approval of the settling party's plans or activities, that are brought pursuant to any statute other than CERCLA or RCRA and for which the waiver of sovereign immunity is found in a statute other than CERCLA or RCRA.

Parties Bound/Transfer of Covenant: All of the rights, benefits and obligations conferred upon the settling party under the Agreement may be assigned or transferred to any person with the prior written consent of EPA and the state in its sole discretion. Prior to, or simultaneous with any assignment or transfer of the Property, the assignee or transferee must consent in writing to be bound by the terms of the Agreement, including but not limited to the certification requirement in the Agreement, in order for the Covenant Not to Sue in Section VIII to be available to that party.

Document Retention: The settling party agrees to retain and make available to EPA and the state all business and operating records, contracts, site studies and investigations, and documents relating to operations at the Property, for at least ten years, following the effective date of the Agreement, unless otherwise agreed to in writing by the Parties.

Contribution Protection: With regard to claims for contribution against the settling party, the parties to the Agreement agree that the settling party is entitled to protection from contribution actions or claims as provided by CERCLA Section 113(f)(2), 42 U.S.C. § 9613(f)(2) for matters addressed in the Agreement.

Comfort/Status Letters for Brownfield Properties

On January 30, 1997, the EPA issued a new policy statement, primarily designed to assist parties who seek to clean up and reuse brownfield properties.[12] EPA headquarters and regional offices often receive requests from parties for some level of comfort that if they purchase, develop, or operate on brownfield property, the EPA will not pursue them for the costs to clean up any contamination resulting from the previous use. The EPA hopes to provide a measure of "comfort" by helping an interested party to better understand the agency's potential or actual involvement at a brownfield site. However, the EPA intends to limit the use of such comfort to where it may facilitate the cleanup and redevelopment of brownfields, where there is the realistic perception or probability of incurring liability under CERCLA, and where there is no other mechanism available to adequately address the party's concerns. The new policy contains four sample comfort/status

---

[12.] 62 Fed. Reg. 4624 (Jan. 30, 1997)

letters that address the most common inquiries for information that the EPA receives regarding contaminated or potentially contaminated properties. While the sample comfort/status letters do not account for every possible situation, the EPA believes that the letters contained in this policy will address the most common requests for comfort. This policy is not a rule, and does not create any legal obligations. The extent to which the EPA applies the policy will depend on the facts of each case.

Purpose of Policy Statement

Uncertainty about potential contamination and/or CERCLA liability may prevent otherwise interested parties from purchasing or redeveloping brownfields. To allay the fear of potential federal pursuit of parties for cleanup of brownfields, the EPA may provide varying degrees of comfort by communicating the agency's intentions toward a particular piece of property. Comfort may range from a formal legal agreement containing a covenant not to sue, which releases a party from liability for cleanup of existing contamination, to agency policy statements regarding the exercise of the EPA's enforcement discretion as it relates to specific site circumstances or activities of a party.

Upon receiving a request from an interested party for information about a particular property, EPA regional offices may issue comfort/status letters, at their discretion, when there is a realistic perception or probability of incurring CERCLA liability and such comfort will facilitate the cleanup and redevelopment of a brownfield property, and there is no other mechanism available to adequately address the party's concerns. With the information provided by the EPA, the party inquiring about the property can decide whether the risk of EPA action is enough to forego involvement, whether to proceed as planned, whether additional investigation into site conditions is necessary, or whether further information from the EPA or other agencies is needed.

Sample Comfort/Status Letters

The EPA has developed four sample comfort/status letters to address the most common inquiries received regarding brownfield properties.[13] Each of the sample comfort letters is intended to address a particular set of circumstances and provide whatever information is contained within the EPA's databases. The sample letters are structured with opening and closing paragraphs applicable to all scenarios falling under that category of letter. EPA regional offices may then choose and combine the applicable substantive paragraphs to tailor the sample letter to address a party's particular request. The following is a brief summary of the sample letters:

1. *No Previous Federal Superfund Interest Letter:* This letter may be provided to parties when there is no historical evidence of federal Superfund program involvement with the property/site in question (i.e., site is not found in the CERCLA information system database, also known as the Comprehensive Environmental Response, Compensation, and Liability Information System or "CERCLIS");

2. *No Current Federal Superfund Interest Letter:* This letter may be provided when the property/site either has been archived and is no longer part of the CERCLIS inventory of sites, has been deleted from the National Priorities List ("NPL"), or is situated near, but not within, the defined boundaries of a CERCLIS site;

3. *Federal Superfund Interest Letter:* This letter may be provided at sites where the EPA either plans to respond in some manner or already is responding at the site. This letter is intended to inform the recipient of the status of the EPA's involvement at the property. Additionally, language is included to respond to requests regarding the

---

[13] *See* Appendix D for copies of each of the sample comfort/status letters.

applicability of a CERCLA policy, regulation, or statutory provision to a party or particular set of circumstances; and

4. *State Action Letter:* This letter may be provided when the state has the lead for day-to-day activities and oversight of a response action at the site (e.g., deferred sites.)

No Previous Federal Superfund Interest Letter

The No Previous Superfund Interest Letter introduces and explains the purpose of CERCLIS and may be sent when the property described by the interested party is not located in active or archived CERCLIS records. The purpose of the letter is to inform the recipient that, to the best of the EPA's knowledge, the property described in the request has never been addressed under the Superfund program, nor are there current plans to do so. EPA Regions, generally, should not interpret a request for a No Previous Superfund Interest Letter as notification that the site should be entered into CERCLIS.

Because the EPA does not have any information about the property, the letter does not express any opinion as to possible contamination at the property or appropriate usage of the property. Additionally, the EPA is not in a position to determine what obligations are associated with ownership or operation of the property under any present or future environmental or other federal, state, or local statute, regulation, or principle of common law. The interested party is encouraged to contact the appropriate state agency for further information regarding the state's intentions toward the property. EPA Regions are encouraged to check with other program offices to determine whether any enforcement action is planned or ongoing and, if so, coordinate within their region before deciding how and when to respond to the inquiry.

No Current Federal Superfund Interest Letter

The No Current Superfund Interest Letter is intended to address properties:

- That have been archived and removed from the CERCLIS inventory of Superfund sites;

- Where either all or part of a National Priorities List (NPL) site has been deleted following EPA's deletion policies (See "Deletion from the NPL," 40 C.F.R. § 300.425(e), or "Partial Deletion of Sites Listed on the National Priorities List," 60 Fed. Reg. 55466 (Nov. 1, 1995)); or

- Situated in the vicinity of, but currently not considered part of, the CERCLIS site (e.g., is adjacent to the site).

The purpose of the letter is to let the recipient know that the EPA does not anticipate taking any (or additional) response action under the Superfund program (which could include enforcement action if a Potentially Responsible Party ("PRP") search and/or cost recovery action has been completed), and the basis for its decision. The letter also refers the party to additional sources of information, such as the EPA's administrative record and the appropriate state agency.

The No Current Superfund Interest Letter is divided into three sections. Section I addresses archived properties and describes the conditions under which the EPA archives a site, the EPA's policy towards these sites, and the circumstances under which the agency would revisit an archived site. This section of the letter provides comfort by conveying that the EPA's expectation, based upon current information, is not to take further steps to list the site on the NPL or to take any other CERCLA response action.

The EPA archives a site when the site assessment event, removal event, or enforcement activity has been completed.

CERCLIS is updated to reflect the archiving of the property. EPA will archive a site if:

- No contamination was found at the site;

- The site, while contaminated, neither met the criteria for inclusion on the NPL, nor required any EPA response action; or

- Contamination was removed quickly without the need to place the site on the NPL, and EPA has completed its cost recovery action for the site.

EPA Regions should select one of the reasons, described above and in the sample letter, for its decision to archive the property and add it to the opening and closing paragraphs.

Section II of the letter focuses on sites deleted from the NPL and properties located in the vicinity of a CERCLIS site. Paragraphs (a) and (b) of Section II address inquiries regarding full or partial deletions of NPL sites and is appropriate if (1) the portion of the Superfund site is marked for deletion in CERCLIS and the state concurs with the EPA's decision to delete the portion of the site; or (2) after consultation with the state and a thirty-day public comment period, the entire site is marked for deletion in CERCLIS. A site or portion of a site is deleted from the NPL when "no further response is appropriate" (see 40 C.F.R. § 300.425(e)). No further response is appropriate when responsible parties or the EPA has completed all response actions, or when a remedial investigation shows "no significant threat." Either the EPA or a petition from any person may initiate the deletion process.

Paragraph (c) of Section II addresses a property that is in the vicinity of a CERCLIS site but currently is not affected by the release of hazardous substances (e.g., a site may be known as the Jones Industrial Park but the release affects only a portion of the industrial park property). Paragraph (c) is appropriate when the EPA has sufficient information regarding the level and extent of contamination at a site to determine that the property is not part of the release. When a site is listed in CERCLIS, the EPA generally delineates the release of hazardous substances as a geographical area and defines the site by reference to that area. Thus, the actual release is not limited to that property but either may extend beyond the property due to contaminant migration or may not occupy the full extent of the property.

Section III provides language to address situations where the EPA has compiled an Administrative Record for the site. If the EPA regional office has compiled an Administrative Record for the site, Section III is added to the letter to indicate the availability of this information.

Under the situations addressed in this letter, the EPA is not in a position to provide any opinion on the appropriate use of the property or obligations associated with ownership or operation of the property under any present or future environmental law or regulation or principle of common law. The letter recommends that the interested party contact the appropriate state agency for further information regarding the state's intention toward the property.

Federal Superfund Interest Letter

When the site is found in the CERCLIS site inventory, an EPA regional office may issue a Federal Superfund Interest Letter to explain what actions have been taken by the agency toward remediation of the site (e.g., site sampling, removal action). The letter also may indicate whether the EPA anticipates further action at the site and the type of action anticipated. In addition to the opening paragraph, there are four parts to the Federal Interest Letter.

Section I of the letter provides the recipient with the status of the property—whether the property is, or may be part of, a CERCLIS/NPL site. Section II describes the EPA's planned or ongoing activities (e.g., preliminary assessment, removal, or remedial design). Federal Interest Letters may be considered for sites in the CERCLIS site inventory, including those on the NPL or eligible for the NPL, sites undergoing an EPA removal or remedial action, or where the EPA has incurred or will incur response costs.

Section III of the Federal Interest Letter provides language regarding the application of a CERCLA policy, statutory provision, or regulation to a party's particular set of circumstances. As stated in the policy, and of particular importance to Section III of the Federal Interest Letter, is the limitation on issuing comfort/status letters to situations where the requesting party provides information showing that (1) a project found to be in the public interest (e.g., an economic redevelopment project) is hindered or the value of a property is affected by the potential for Superfund liability, and (2) there is no other mechanism available to adequately address the party's concerns other than a letter from the EPA with a statement regarding the applicability of a specific Superfund policy, statutory provision, or regulation. These criteria should be met before an EPA regional office considers sending the party a Federal Interest Letter. As appropriate, a copy of the relevant policy or statutory/regulatory language should be attached to the letter.

Section IV provides language for the closing paragraph. This section of the letter also encourages the EPA regional office to include pertinent fact sheets (or any other relevant information), and refers the party to the administrative record repository.

State Action Letter

The State Action Letter is intended to provide comfort at sites where the EPA may have either no current Superfund involvement or a secondary role under the state's lead of site activities. A state may participate in such activities as lead agency through a cooperative agreement (CA) between the state and the EPA regional office. A state and EPA regional office also may develop a Memorandum of Agreement (MOA) in which the region and the state articulate the roles each will have regarding the cleanup of contaminated properties.

The State Action Letter seeks to advise parties that the EPA does not intend to take federal action under CERCLA when the state has the primary role of overseeing cleanups pursuant to either state or federal requirements and, where appropriate, the parties performing the cleanup are working cooperatively under state direction. The EPA may, however, consider taking action at a site if it receives new information about site conditions requiring federal action or the responding party and the state are unwilling or unable to ensure compliance with the negotiated agreement between the state and responding party or the state and the EPA.

EPA regional offices may respond with a State Action Letter to two different types of inquiries. The first type of inquiry may be from a state requesting that the EPA send a State Action Letter regarding a particular site. Whenever possible and appropriate, EPA regions should seek to provide a letter responsive to the state's request. The second type of inquiry may be from an outside party. The EPA regional office should prepare a State Action Letter for that party in consultation with the state, if appropriate.

The policy states that the State Action Letter is appropriate to send to parties in the following situations:

- The site is designated "state-lead" in CERCLIS;

- The site is designated "deferred to state" in CERCLIS (See "Guidance on Deferral of NPL Listing Determinations While States Oversee Response Actions," OSWER Directive No. 9375.6-11 (May 3, 1995));

- The site was designated "deferred to state" and is subsequently designated "archived" in CERCLIS; or

- The site is listed in CERCLIS and is being addressed under a state voluntary cleanup program (VCP) pursuant to an approved MOA between the region and state.

For sites not listed in CERCLIS but located in a state that has entered into a VCP MOA with an EPA regional office (and the region believes that the site is being addressed pursuant to the state's VCP), the regional office should issue a No Previous Federal Superfund Interest Letter.

Policy on CERCLA Enforcement against Lenders and Government Entities

The U.S. EPA and the Department of Justice (DOJ) have issued a joint memorandum, dated September 22, 1995, and entitled "Policy on CERCLA Enforcement Against Lenders and Government Entities That Acquire Property Involuntarily,"[14] which explains that the two agencies "intend to apply as guidance" the provisions of the EPA lender liability rule promulgated in April 1992. That rule was struck in 1994 when the U.S. Court of Appeals for the District of Columbia Circuit ruled that EPA lacked authority to issue the rule as a binding regulation.[15] However, that decision did not preclude EPA and DOJ from following the provisions of the rule as enforcement policy.

The agencies recognize in the memorandum that, due to the "unintended" effects of CERCLA, lenders may be reluctant to lend money to an owner or developer of contaminated property or may be hesitant to exercise their rights as secured creditors when debtors default on loans for such property. Further, government entities that acquire contaminated property involuntarily may be

---

[14]The memorandum was subsequently published in the Federal Register at 60 Fed. Reg. 63517 (Dec. 11, 1995). A copy is reproduced in Appendix E.

[15]*See* Kelley v. EPA, 15 F.3d 1100 (D.C. Cir. 1994), *reh. denied,* 25 F.3d 1088 (D.C. Cir. 1994), *cert. denied,* 115 S.Ct 900 (1995).

unwilling to undertake cleanup actions at these sites. CERCLA contains exemptions for government entities and lenders that acquire property involuntarily, but neither the legislative history of CERCLA, nor the case law, provided sufficient explanation of when a lender or government entity's acquisition or transfer of contaminated property is insulated from CERCLA liability. The EPA did, however, address this issue in its 1992 lender liability rule and clarified when a lender or government entity was exempted from CERCLA enforcement as an owner or operator of contaminated property. The memorandum advises lenders and government entities that EPA and DOJ policy is to apply the guidance from the 1992 Rule to such situations.

Asset Conservation, Lender Liability, and Deposit Insurance Protection Act of 1996

On September 30, 1996, President Clinton signed the Asset Conservation, Lender Liability, and Deposit Insurance Protection Act of 1996 (the Act) into law.[16] The new legislation amends CERCLA and clarifies the circumstances under which a lender can or cannot be held liable under CERCLA. Importantly, the Act reinstates the EPA's Lender Liability Rule.[17] The Act lists several "safe harbor" activities, shields fiduciaries from CERCLA liability, extends lender liability protection to underground storage tanks, and provides protection for certain involuntary acquisitions of contaminated property by government entities.

---

[16]Pub. L. No. 104-208.

[17]The Act prohibits further judicial review of that rule, but notes that it may be amended. Such amendments would be subject to judicial challenge.

Other Federal Initiatives

The EPA is not the only federal agency pursuing brownfields redevelopment initiatives. Other federal agencies are likewise seeking creative solutions to brownfields problems.

Brownfields National Partnership Action Agenda

The Interagency Working Group on Brownfields was established in July 1996 as a forum for federal agencies to exchange information on brownfields-related activities and to develop a coordinated national agenda for addressing brownfields. The Interagency Working Group is developing a brownfields strategy—the Brownfields National Partnership Action Agenda—that will more effectively link environmental protection with economic development and community revitalization programs, and guide the Brownfields Initiative into the future.

The Brownfields National Partnership Action Agenda includes more than 100 communities from more than 25 organizations including more than 15 federal agencies. These commitments represent a $300 million investment in brownfields communities by the federal government and an additional $165 million in loan guarantees. The resulting action will help cleanup and redevelopment at up to 5,000 properties, leveraging from $5 billion up to $28 billion in private investment, supporting 196,000 jobs, protecting up to 34,000 acres of greenfields, and improving the quality of life for as many as 18 million Americans who live near brownfields.

Highlights of the Action Agenda include:

- The EPA will fund $125 million for assessment, cleanup, state cleanup programs, and job training.

- The Department of Housing and Urban Development (HUD) will provide $155 million in community development and housing support and an additional $165 million in loan guarantees.

- The Economic Development Administration (EDA) will grant $17 million for brownfields redevelopment in distressed areas.

- The Department of Transportation (DOT) will fund $4.2 million for sustainable transportation addressing brownfields issues.

- The General Services Administration (GSA) will conduct $1 million of environmental surveys on federal properties to expedite brownfields development.

- The National Oceanic and Atmospheric Administration (NOAA) will provide $900,000 for waterfront and coastal revitalization.

- The Department of Health and Human Services (HHS) will commit $500,000 to support brownfields economic development and job creation and work with the Departments of Labor (DOL) and Education to link job training initiatives.

- The Department of Energy (DOE) will provide $315,000 to link DOE cleanups with brownfields communities.

- HHS will lead an Administration-wide effort to develop a public health policy for brownfields to protect community residents.

- The Treasury Department will work with Congress to pass the $2 billion brownfields tax incentive proposed by President Clinton.

- The EPA, the Department of Justice (DOJ), and the states will collaborate to establish national guidelines for state voluntary cleanup programs.

Brownfields Showcase Communities

The Brownfields National Partnership Action Agenda also calls for the selection of 10 Showcase Communities across the country to demonstrate that, through cooperation, federal, state, local, and private efforts can be concentrated around brownfields to produce environmental cleanup, stimulate economic development, and revitalize communities. This proposal will result in cleaning up contaminated properties, creating jobs, expanding local economies, and improving the quality of life in affected communities. The Brownfields Showcase Communities approach provides sustainable local solutions to local problems—solutions that can be replicated throughout the nation.

Communities involved in the Brownfields Initiative have asked for more interaction among all levels of government, the private sector, and nongovernmental organizations. To that end, the EPA and other federal agencies have joined together to strengthen and improve their collaborative efforts to clean up and reuse contaminated property. The Brownfields Showcase Communities proposal is the centerpiece of that plan and a pattern for future efforts. The Communities selected will serve as models for broad-based cooperative efforts to support locally based initiatives.

Implementation steps include:

- Screening and selecting 10 communities as Brownfields Showcase Communities (EPA, the Departments of Commerce and the Interior, DOT, GSA, HHS, and HUD have been involved in the planning process). Selection criteria include community need, current brownfields activity and other related federal activity, local commitment and state involvement, and community size and location.

- Providing resources and technical assistance to each Showcase Community to coordinate federal brownfields activities and support state and local brownfields activities.

- Working with local Brownfields task forces and advisory boards to link federal, state, local, and nongovernmental activities with community members.

- Reporting annually and evaluating progress.

For more information about the status of the Brownfields National Partnership Action Agenda, contact Linda Garczynski of EPA Headquarters at (202) 260-4039.

Empowerment Zone/Enterprise Community (EZ/EC) Program

The Department of Housing & Urban Development (HUD), the lead agency in charge of administration of the federal Empowerment Zone/Enterprise Community (EZ/EC) Program, also provides grants and incentives for revitalization of distressed communities. Many areas that have been designated as federal enterprise communities and empowerment zones have brownfields properties. The EZ/EC Program offers participating enterprise communities and empowerment zones important economic incentives that could possibly be used for cleanup and redevelopment of brownfields sites. For enterprise communities, grants and incentives include:

- Eligibility for tax-exempt bonds to finance private business start-up and operations within community boundaries;

- Three million dollars in EZ/EC Social Service Block Grant (SSBG) funds from the U.S. Department of Health and Human Services (HHS); and

- Special consideration for funding from numerous other programs, including HUD's Economic Development Initiative (EDI) and its Section 108 loan program.

The empowerment zones receive these same grants and incentives plus:

- Up to $100 million in EZ/EC SSBG funds;

- An employer wage credit for zone residents engaged in trade or business within the zone; and

- Internal Revenue Code Section 179 tax deductions for business properties within the zone.

Although the EZ/EC Program does not include any funds specifically earmarked for brownfields initiatives, communities can identify funding for brownfields as part of grants received from the EZ/EC SSBG program, and HUD's Economic Development Initiative (EDI) and Section 108 loan program.

EZ/EC SSBG Funding

U.S. Department of Health and Human Services (HHS) regulations require that SSBG funds be used to finance approved program options exercised to achieve any one of three broad goals. Goal #2 is to achieve or maintain self-sufficiency, including reduction or prevention of dependency. Program options for this goal include the funding of programs to provide training and employment for disadvantaged adults and youths in construction, rehabilitation, or improvement of affordable housing, public infrastructure, and community facilities. A community could define a brownfields redevelopment program as meeting the requirements of Goal #2 by providing training and employment opportunities for disadvantaged individuals through their direct involvement in the improvement of public infrastructure and community facilities. Alternatively, communities could use SSBG funds for other types of activities if their strategic plan explains how these activities will meet the Goals listed in the HHS regulations, as well as why an approved program option was not selected. Although a community may choose to do other than an approved program option, there are certain types of activities that the SSBG funds may not be used for, including the purchasing or improving land or facilities. However, this restriction can be waived by HHS.

Economic Development Initiative

HUD has also made available Economic Development Initiative (EDI) funds of varying amounts to empowerment zones and enterprise communities. HUD is using these grant funds to encourage communities to use its existing Section 108 Loan Guaranty Program to obtain loans for development projects at subsidized interest rates. Historically, communities have not used all of their Section 108 loan authority because HUD regulations require them to pledge their future grant funds as collateral. In the event of a loan default, the community would have to repay the loan with these future grant funds. Many communities have been reluctant to risk future entitlements with loans to high-risk projects. To provide a financial incentive to communities to accept this risk, HUD is requiring communities to use their Section 108 loan authority before they can receive an EDI grant. For example, if a community received a $22 million EDI grant, it would have to use at least $22 million of Section 108 loan authority to use the EDI grant.

EZ/EC Strategic Plans

The Enterprise Zone/Enterprise Community Task Force, an interagency group made up of HUD, HHS, the USDA, and other federal agency representatives, works with the selected communities to refine their strategic plans for implementation.

Each community participating in the federal EZ/EC program is allocated a certain amount of funds. These funds must pass through the state, which must obligate the funds in accordance with a strategic plan that the designated EZ/EC community must submit for the first two years of its program. The strategic plan must identify benchmark activities for those years, and must indicate all federal funds expended for development in the zone. When the strategic plan is approved by the EZ/EC Task Force, the community is able to expend the allocated grant funds.

EZ/EC designees are required to submit periodic reports to HUD's Office of Community Planning and Development regarding progress made on the benchmarks established by the strategic plan. These periodic reports will also reflect any modifications to the strategic plan that the designated community may have negotiated with Task Force offices over the course of implementation of the local program to take advantage of changing opportunities and circumstances.

EZ/EC Designations

The EZ/EC designations were made on December 21, 1994. Urban communities received one of four designations:

1. Urban empowerment zone;
2. Supplemental urban empowerment zone;
3. Urban enhanced enterprise community; or
4. Urban enterprise community.

In June 1995, HUD announced the selection of six urban empowerment zones. These six urban empowerment zones are:

1. Atlanta, Georgia
2. Chicago, Illinois
3. Baltimore, Maryland

4. Detroit and Wayne County, Michigan

5. New York County and Bronx County, New York

6. Philadelphia, Pennsylvania and Camden, New Jersey

Two urban supplemental empowerment zones were also selected. These zones will receive EDI grant funds, but will not be eligible for the same incentive as regular empowerment zones. The two supplemental urban empowerment zones are:

1. City of Los Angeles, and Los Angeles, Vernon, and Lynwood Counties, California

2. City of Cleveland and Cuyahoga County, Ohio

Four urban enhanced enterprise communities were also chosen. These communities will have more flexibility in the use of HUD funds than other enterprise communities and are eligible for EDI grants. The four urban enhanced enterprise communities are:

1. Oakland, San Leandro, and Alameda, California

2. Boston, Massachusetts

3. Kansas City, Missouri and Kansas City, Kansas

4. Houston, Texas

In addition, 60 enterprise communities were selected, making a total of 72 EZ/EC communities. Since their designation, each community has been working with HUD, HHS, other federal agencies, and the EZ/EC Task Force to finalize their strategic plans, and turn them into action plans for program implementation. In order to use the EZ/EC grant funds, each community must have their plans approved by the Task Force.

Baltimore, Maryland Empowerment Zone

Recognizing that the remediation of contaminated sites is critical to urban redevelopment, the city's strategic plan directly addresses brownfields. Proposals in the strategic plan indicate that site remediation will be a key focus of the city's empowerment zone.

Historically, the City of Baltimore has been a center for manufacturing and other heavy industry, including steelmaking, shipbuilding, textiles and chemicals. Over the last 25 years, however, industry has declined, resulting in unemployment, a reduced tax base, and a significant number of contaminated sites.

The Baltimore City Planning Department has been addressing contaminated sites for some time. The Department has established a working group of stakeholders, including developers, regulatory agency representatives, environmental attorneys, economic development advocates, and community groups, to address brownfields issues. This working group became a standing committee when Baltimore was awarded one of the EPA's national brownfields assessment pilot grants. In April 1997, EPA Region 3 also awarded Baltimore County, Maryland a $200,000 grant for a Regional Brownfields Assessment Pilot.

The City of Baltimore established a nonprofit organization, the Empower Baltimore Management Corporation, to execute the strategic plan for the Baltimore empowerment zone. In coordination with the City Planning Department, the Corporation is the chief agency for implementing the EZ/EC program. The Corporation is a broad-based organization consisting of businesses, community members, nonprofit institutions, and government agency representatives. The EPA, HUD, and HHS have all participated in the strategic planning for the zone. The EPA's participation in the strategic planning process has enhanced consideration of brownfields problems.

Baltimore's strategic plan included a proposal to create an Ecological Industrial Park that will serve as a magnet for environmentally sustainable economic development in the zone. Castle Capital, a company that specializes in Continuous Ablative

Regenerator (CAR) resource recovery technology, planned to locate in the Park as the anchor tenant. The Company agreed to dedicate a section of its CAR capacity to recover oils and other resources in degraded land sites and remove soil contamination. Such efforts are expected to recover the land for further development in the Park and improve community environmental standards.

Baltimore's EZ/EC program included use of a consultant to survey landowners in the area concerning land use and status of their parcels. Part of the survey included identification of vacant and potentially contaminated sites that could be made part of the industrial park. Although financing sources for the Park had not been identified, a portion of the funds will likely come from the city's share of the EZ/EC SSBG grant, or other grant funds available through HUD's EDI program.

The strategic plan also included a proposal for the establishment of the Baltimore Industrial and Commercial Redevelopment Trust. The goal of the Trust would be to recycle and rehabilitate contaminated properties. The Trust would identify contaminated sites and seek potential purchasers or users to produce substantial economic and social benefits in the empowerment zone. The Trust would initially take title to a brownfields site, perform environmental assessments, and provide for remediation of the property using one of four funding sources: potential purchaser's funds; the value of a purchaser's tax credits associated with purchasing and redeveloping the land; the Trust's own funds; or federal or state Superfund money.

The Trust would not take title to any site already listed on CERCLA's National Priority List (NPL). For other sites, Baltimore would ask the EPA or Maryland's environmental agency to provide liability assurances to protect prospective owners or operators against potential CERCLA liability.

Baltimore anticipates two outcomes from the operation of the Trust. First, by removing the threat of financial and legal liability, new entrepreneurs would be attracted to activities within the empowerment zone. Second, the Trust would be an active participant in the identification of non-NPL properties, and would work to facilitate cleanup and improvement of the environmental condition of these properties.

The Trust would initially be financed through $1 million in Community Development Block Grant funds that would be used to identify parcels and conduct Phase I and Phase II environmental site assessments. In subsequent years, $500,000 per year of federal funds would be used to conduct site assessments for selected properties. The federal funds would be matched on a 2:1 ratio by city and/or state funds.

Baltimore has been using the incentives and funds from the EZ/EC Program to address brownfields issues. The timing of the Planning Department's brownfields initiative, coinciding with the commencement of the EZ/EC Program, may have helped to ensure that site cleanups and redevelopment activities were a focus of the city's EZ/EC strategic plan. The involvement of the EPA in the strategic planning process also enabled the empowerment zone to focus on brownfields issues.

Legislative Reforms

In addition to the administrative and regulatory initiatives developed by the EPA and other federal agencies, landowners, prospective purchasers, developers, lenders, municipalities, and other participants in brownfields cleanup and redevelopment projects must keep a watchful eye on potential legislative reforms to address brownfields problems. Due, in part, to the lack of comprehensive federal legislation on brownfields, more than 30 states have already instituted voluntary cleanup and brownfields programs. These programs are discussed in detail in Chapter 2, and brownfields project sponsors should become well acquainted with these programs. Although a federal brownfields law has not yet been enacted, numerous bills have been sponsored and introduced to Congress during the past few years in an attempt to create a unified approach to brownfields cleanup and redevelopment.

For example, on April 17, 1997, Congressman Regula (R-OH) introduced a bill in the House (H.R. 1392), referred to as the Brownfields Reuse and Real Estate Development Act, designed to (1) ensure the quality of state brownfield cleanup and redevelopment efforts by establishing federal criteria for state voluntary cleanup programs and (2) provide certainty by removing the threat of federal enforcement during and after the cleanup of brownfield facilities and properties.

The proposed legislation would require the U.S. EPA to establish certification criteria for state voluntary cleanup programs. In order for a state voluntary cleanup program to be certified by the EPA, the program must provide:

- Adequate opportunities for meaningful public participation;

- Technical assistance throughout each voluntary cleanup;

- Adequate resources for cleanups and program administration;

- Adequate oversight and enforcement authority;

- Documentation to be provided by the state to the owner or prospective purchaser, upon completion of cleanup, that the cleanup of the eligible facility is complete; and

- Assurance that the cleanup undertaken under the program will protect human health and the environment.

Following certification, any "eligible facility" that is, or has been, the subject of response action undertaken pursuant to a certified state voluntary cleanup program is protected against administrative or judicial action under CERCLA or RCRA by any party other than the state with respect to any release or threatened release of hazardous substance at the facility. Subject to some qualifications, an "eligible facility" is defined as "an abandoned, idled or under used commercial or industrial facility or property for which real or perceived environmental contamination complicates expansion, redevelopment, or reuse."

The proposed legislation would also amend Section 107 of CERCLA, by adding a new subsection 107(n) regarding "innocent landowners." This new subsection would state specifically that if a party who has acquired real property establishes that an environmental site assessment was conducted within 180 days prior to the time of acquisition, the party will have made "all appropriate inquiry" within the meaning of the innocent landowner defense provided in Section 101(35)(B) of CERCLA. However, in order for an environmental site assessment to meet the requirements of this new provision, it must be an assessment conducted in accordance with the standards set forth in ASTM Standard E15270994, titled "Standard Practice for Environmental Site Assessments: Phase I Environmental Site Assessment Process," or an alternative standard issued by rule by the U.S. EPA.

The proposed legislation also would amend Section 107 of CERCLA, by adding several new provisions regarding "bona fide prospective purchaser liability." Proposed subsection 107(o) is specifically designed to shield prospective purchasers of contaminated property from ownership liability under § 107(a)(1) of CERCLA. A "bona fide prospective purchaser" is defined as a person who acquires ownership of a facility after the date of enactment of the new subsection, or a lessee of such a person, who can establish each of the following by a preponderance of the evidence:

1. All active disposal of hazardous substances at the facility occurred before that person acquired the facility.

2. The person made all appropriate inquiry into the previous ownership and uses of the facility and its real property in accordance with generally accepted commercial and customary standards and practices. Standards described in section 107(n)(2) (relating to innocent landowners) will satisfy this requirement. In the case of property for residential or other similar use, purchased by a nongovernmental or noncommercial entity, a site inspection and title search that reveal no basis for further investigation satisfy this requirement.

3. The person provided all legally required notices with respect to the discovery or release of any hazardous substances at the facility.

4. The person exercised appropriate care with respect to hazardous substances found at the facility by taking reasonable steps to stop on-going releases, prevent threatened future releases of hazardous substances, and prevent or limit human or natural resource exposure to hazardous substances previously released into the environment.

5. The person provides full cooperation, assistance, and facility access to persons authorized to conduct response actions at the facility, including the cooperation and access necessary for the installation, integrity, operation, and maintenance of any complete or partial response action at the facility.

6. The person is not affiliated with any other person liable for response costs at the facility, through any direct or indirect familial relationship, or any contractual, corporate, or financial relationship other than that created by the instruments by which title to the facility is conveyed or financed.

Still, to the extent that there are unrecovered response costs at a site for which the owner is not liable by reason of the bona fide prospective purchaser exemption, the proposed legislation contains a new subsection 107(p) to guard against a bona fide prospective purchaser's obtaining a financial windfall in the event that cleanup actions at the site increase the fair market value of the property above the fair market value that existed within six months before the response action was taken. In such situations, the United States has a lien on the property for unrecovered response costs up to an amount equaling the increase in fair market value of the property attributable to the response action at the time of a subsequent sale or other disposition of the property. However, no lien arises with respect to property for which the property owner preceding the first bona fide prospective purchaser is not a liable party or has resolved its liability under CERCLA or where an environmental site assessment gives the bona fide prospective purchaser no knowledge or reason to know of the release of hazardous substances.

Finally, the new legislation would add a new subsection 107(q) to CERCLA designed to protect from CERCLA liability the owner or operator of property contaminated by the release of hazardous substances on a contiguous parcel where the owner or operator did not cause, contribute, or consent to the release and provides full cooperation to persons authorized to conduct response activities at the site.

A similar bill (H.R. 1395) was also introduced in the House on April 17, 1997 by Congressman Rothman (D-NJ), referred to as the Brownfields and Environmental Cleanup Act of 1997. H.R. 1395 contains similar provisions relating to innocent landowners and bona fide prospective purchasers but also would set up a program to award grants to states or local governments to inventory and conduct site assessments of brownfield sites, as well as a program to award grants to be used by state and local governments to capitalize revolving loan funds for the cleanup of brownfield sites.

In addition, Congressman Gary Franks introduced a bill in March 1997 that would establish a federal brownfields cleanup loan program. Representatives Bliley and Oxley also proposed an amendment to CERCLA that would provide for $45 million annually for redevelopment grants and interest-free loans to spur brownfields development. The proposal would also eliminate the need for local governments and companies to obtain federal permits to begin brownfields cleanups.

President Clinton has also announced a tax-incentive proposal that would put $2 billion toward tax breaks for parties cleaning up and redeveloping abandoned sites. The tax plan would make cleanup expenses for both large and small businesses fully deductible the year in which a site is remediated. The incentives are targeted at areas where the poverty rate is 20 percent or higher, to existing EPA brownfield pilot areas, and to existing and upcoming Empowerment Zones and Enterprise Communities. EPA Administrator Carol Browner stated her belief that this program could facilitate redevelopment of some 30,000 sites that might otherwise be neglected.

CHAPTER 2

STATE BROWNFIELDS PROGRAMS

Introduction

Over the past several years, more than 30 states have unveiled brownfields programs to encourage productive reuse of abandoned, idle, or underutilized sites that are hampered by actual or suspected contamination. These state programs—called voluntary cleanup programs, brownfields programs, land recycling programs, and similar names—basically offer financial incentives and liability protections in exchange for voluntary investigation and cleanup of brownfield properties. Many states have created voluntary cleanup funds, grant programs, low-interest loan programs, tax breaks, and other economic incentives to assist brownfield project sponsors in their cleanup and redevelopment efforts. Importantly, under most programs, once cleanup is completed to the satisfaction of the state environmental agency, a participant in the voluntary cleanup program may be issued various liability protections and assurances, including a No Further Action letter, Certificate of Completion, or formal covenant not to sue.

Voluntary cleanup programs are particularly popular—at least with private parties—because they allow the private parties to initiate cleanups and avoid some of the costs and delays associated with other enforcement-driven programs. Most programs provide technical guidance and oversight, in some cases assisting with site assessment and cleanup. Many programs attempt to provide clearer standards on permissible levels of various types of contamination. Some programs apply special cleanup standards to participants in the program. Others incorporate land use controls that anticipate future use that usually involves less public exposure to the site (e.g., 500 employees at an industrial site as opposed to thousands of consumers at a mall). The land use controls are not meant to eliminate all risks to human health or the environment but provide assurance of an appropriate public exposure/use of a site.

Not all contaminated sites are eligible for participation in state voluntary cleanup programs. For instance, the existence of groundwater contamination may bar participation in voluntary cleanups. In addition, most programs apply only to parties not responsible for existing site contamination. It is important to note at the outset that these voluntary cleanup programs generally only apply to sites that are not listed on the CERCLA National Priorities List (NPL), the EPA's CERCLIS database, or state hazardous waste remediation priority lists. Thus, the most severely contaminated sites fall outside the scope of most brownfields redevelopment activities. Brownfields redevelopment is not driven by environmental cleanup and is not meant to be a substitute for cleanup under the Superfund program. Rather, the impetus behind federal and state brownfields initiatives is primarily an economic one, aimed at economic revitalization of blighted urban areas that are saddled with abandoned or underused industrial and commercial properties. As such, the primary focus of federal and state brownfields programs is on accelerated cleanup and redevelopment of those sites that can be cleaned up and returned to productive, sustainable use in a relatively short period of time and that pose lesser degrees of financial and environmental risk to potential developers and investors. Contrary to popular belief, most brownfield sites are not heavily contaminated properties. In fact, many brownfields sites harbor only low levels of contamination, or are merely stigmatized by suspected contamination.

Table 2-1 provides a reference list of state brownfield programs. The majority of these programs are examined in detail in this chapter.

TABLE 2-1 State Legislation on Brownfields

State	Statutory Reference
Arizona	Ariz. Rev. Stat. § 33-4-3
Arkansas	Ark. Stat. §§ 8-7-1101 through 8-7-1104
California	Cal. Health & Safety Code §§ 512; 25260 through 25268; 25395 through 26300
Colorado	Colo. Rev. Stat. Ann. § 25-16-301
Connecticut	Conn. Gen. Stat. Ann. §§ 22a-133, 22a-454, 22a-471
Delaware	Del. Code Ann. tit. 30, § 2010
Illinois	Ill. Rev. Stat. ch. 415, para. 5/4(y), 5/58 through 5/58.12; Ill. Admin. Code tit. 35, §§ 740.100 through 740.625
Indiana	Ind. Code § 13-7-8.9-18
Louisiana	La. Rev. Stat. § 30:2285
Maine	Me. Rev. Stat. Ann. tit. 38, §§ 342-343
Maryland	Md. Code Ann., Envir. §§ 4-401(1), 7-201(n-1), 7-501 through 7-516; Md. Ann. Code art. 83A, §§ 3-901 through 3-905; Md. Code Ann., Tax-Prop. §§ 9-229 and 14-902
Massachusetts	Mass. Gen. Laws ch. 21E
Michigan	Mich. Stat. Ann. §§ 299.601 through 299.618, 324.20101 through 324.20142
Minnesota	Minn. Stat. § 115B.175
Missouri	Mo. Rev. Stat. § 447.714

State	Statutory Reference
Montana	Mont. Code Ann. §§ 75-10-730 through 75-10-738
Nebraska	Neb. Rev. Stat. § 81-15.181-188
New Hampshire	N.H. Rev. Stat. Ann. § 147-F
New Jersey	N.J. Admin. Code tit. 7, § 26
New York	N.Y. Envtl. Conserv. Law §§ 3-0301.2, 56-0101, 56-0502; 6 N.Y. Comp. Codes R. & Regs. tit. 6, pt. 375-4
North Carolina	N.C. Gen. Stat. § 130A-310
Ohio	Ohio Stat. Ann. § 3746.01-.12
Oklahoma	Okla. Stat. tit. 27A, §§ 2-15-101 through 2-15-110; Okla. Reg. tit. 252, §§ 220-1-1 through 220-7-3
Oregon	Or. Rev. Stat. §§ 465.260, 465.327 Or. Admin R. §§ 340-122-010 through 340-122-140
Pennsylvania	35 Pa. Stat. §§ 6026.101 through 6026.908; 25 Pa. Code ch. 250
Tennessee	Tenn. Code Ann. § 68-212-104
Texas	Tex. Health & Safety Code Ann. §§ 361.601 through 361.613; Tex. Admin. Code tit. 30, §§ 333.1 through 333.11
Vermont	Vt. Stat. tit. 10, § 6615a
Virginia	Va. Code Ann. §§ 10.1-1429.1 through 10.1-1429.4; Va. Admin. Code §§ 20-160-10 through 20-160-130
Washington	Wash. Rev. Code ch. 70.105D; Wash. Admin. Code § 173-340-300
West Virginia	W. Va. Code § 22
Wisconsin	Wis. Stat. § 144.765

California's Brownfields Initiatives

California has developed a number of legislative and regulatory initiatives to encourage cleanup and redevelopment of brownfield properties. These programs are designed to foster successful partnerships with developers, redevelopment agencies, community groups, state and local agencies, and other stakeholders to demonstrate how revitalization of brownfields sites can support and enhance sustainable growth and development. These programs include:

- Voluntary Cleanup Program—Established in 1993, the program allows the Department of Toxic Substances Control to provide oversight to motivated parties to assess and/or cleanup lower priority sites. This program is discussed in detail below.

- Expedited Remedial Action Program (SB 923)—A pilot voluntary cleanup program that provides numerous incentives to responsible parties to accelerate environmental cleanups. The Program is limited to 30 sites that meet specified criteria. This program is discussed in detail below.

- Prospective Purchaser Policy—A DTSC policy on Prospective Purchaser Agreements (PPAs), which includes a model PPA (with a covenant not to sue), application form, and eligibility criteria. This policy is discussed in detail below.

- CalSites Validation Program—In late 1993, the DTSC initiated the CalSites Validation Program (CVP), similar in some respects to the U.S. EPA's removal of "No Further Remedial Action Planned (NFRAP)" site from CERCLIS. The CalSites database is an automated database used to track properties that may be affected by hazardous substances. DTSC created the CalSites database in 1991 and, at that time, listed approximately 26,500 entries, even though the DTSC had evidence of releases at only a small fraction. Because the lending and real estate communities often relied on CalSites to determine financing, leasing, or sale of property, the listing of a property on CalSites caused potential problems for a site owner even if the site was not contaminated. As lenders and real estate brokers subsequently "redlined" many properties, the over-inclusive list created significant impediments to brownfields development. Under the new CVP, the DTSC reevaluated the listings and updated the criteria for inclusion in the database. Reevaluation of the database was conducted in three years (completed in 1996). Over 22,500 entries were deleted, which has helped to remove the brownfields "stigma" of those properties.

- Private Site Management Program (AB 1876)—Created a new program for credentialing private site managers (PSMs) to oversee site assessments and cleanups at low-level hazardous substances sites with minimal DTSC oversight. This law will replace the established Registered Environmental Assessor (REA) program with registered Class I and Class II assessors; only Class II assessors will be eligible to act as PSMs. The program took effect on January 1, 1996 and implementation is scheduled for late 1997.

- Local Cleanup Agreements (SB 1248)—Effective on January 1, 1996, the law formally recognizes local agency cleanup programs allowing local health agencies to enter into written agreements to supervise cleanups, set cleanup goals and provide certification of cleanup completion.

- Management Memo #90-11, Responsible Party—Owner-ship of Property Over Contaminated Ground Water (December 1990)—Similar to the U.S. EPA's Guidance for Owners of Properties Containing Contaminated Aquifers, the DTSC established an enforcement policy designed to reassure owners of property onto which a groundwater contamination plume has migrated that they will not become a target of enforcement or cost recovery action solely on the basis of land ownership, provided that they do not cause or contribute to the contamination.

- Management Memo #92-4, Approval of a Partial Site Cleanup (April 1992)—Allows issuance of a "clean parcel letter" for sites where a designated portion of the property has been cleaned up, which in turn allows redevelopment, sale, or continued business operations on these parcels.

- Unified Agency Review of Hazardous Materials Release Sites (AB 2061)—Enacted in 1993, the law is designed to expedite cleanups by allowing the responsible party to petition a "Site Designation Committee" to designate a single state or local "administering agency" to oversee response actions for a site.[1] The administering agency is required to issue a certificate of completion upon satisfactory completion of remedial actions. The certificate represents a conclusive determination that the responsible party has complied with all state and local laws, ordinances, regulations, and standards, and is, in effect, a statutory release of liability, subject to certain reopeners. The release is not, however, applicable to liability under CERCLA or other federal laws.

---

[1]Cal. Health & Safety Code §§ 25260-25268.

- Hazardous Material Liability of Lenders and Fiduciaries (SB 1285)—Provides limited liability exemption for lenders and fiduciaries for releases of hazardous substances on property in which they have a legal interest, but did not "directly" cause or contribute to release or potential release of a hazardous substance.

- Polanco Legislation for Redevelopment Agencies (AB 3193 and SB 1425)—Adopted in 1990, the Polanco legislation enacted a hazardous substance release cleanup program as part of the California Community Redevelopment Law.[2] The law grants local redevelopment agencies qualified immunity from state and local laws if cleanup is conducted in accordance with a remedial action plan approved by the DTSC, Regional Water Quality Control Board or local agency. The liability immunity extends to, among others, certain persons entering into development agreements for a brownfield site, their successors in title, and capital providers.[3]

- Mello-Roos Community Facilities Act Amendments (AB 2610)—Enacted in 1990, these amendments created the first long-term financing options for hazardous substances cleanup on both public and private property. Under this law, Community Facilities Districts are authorized to operate revolving loan funds to conduct cleanups. The Community Facilities District is an entity through which a local government is empowered to levy special taxes and issue bonds for site cleanups, if authorized by two-thirds of the vote of qualified voters in the District.

---

[2] Cal. Health & Safety Code §§ 33459-33459.8.
[3] Cal. Health & Safety Code § 33459.3.

Voluntary Cleanup Program

The primary vehicle driving the state's brownfields efforts is the Voluntary Cleanup Program (VCP) established by the California Environmental Protection Agency's Department of Toxic Substances Control (DTSC) in 1993. The DTSC's Voluntary Cleanup Program was established administratively, using existing statutory authority under the California Hazardous Substances Account Act.[4] The program offers a streamlined program to protect human health, cleanup the environment, and get property back into productive use. Corporations, real estate developers, and local and state agencies entering into VCP agreements are able to restore properties quickly and efficiently, rather than having their projects compete for the DTSC's limited resources with other low priority hazardous waste sites.

Under the Program, volunteers—who may or may not be responsible parties—initiate projects to undertake site investigation or other response action under the DTSC oversight. Most sites are eligible, however, those already on the DTSC's annual workplan (also known as "state Superfund" sites), on the National Priority List (NPL), federal facilities or those not within DTSC's jurisdiction (e.g., some petroleum sites) are ineligible. Further, if another agency currently has oversight, such as county (for underground storage tanks), the Regional Water Quality Control Board (for contamination that is primarily limited to groundwater), the current oversight agency must consent to transfer the cleanup responsibilities to the DTSC before the proponent can enter into a VCP agreement. Additionally, the DTSC can enter into an agreement to work on a specified element of cleanup, such as risk assessment or public participation, if the primary oversight agency gives its consent.

---

[4]Cal. Health & Safety Code §§ 25350-25359.

If no exclusions apply, the proponent submits an application to the DTSC, providing details about site conditions, proposed land use, and potential community concerns. No fee is required to apply for the Voluntary Cleanup Program. Once DTSC accepts the application, the proponent meets with DTSC professionals to negotiate the agreement. The agreement can range from services for an initial site assessment, to oversight and certification of a full site cleanup, based on the proponent's financial and scheduling objectives. The VCP agreement specifies the estimated DTSC costs, scheduling for the project, and the DTSC services to be provided. Because every project must meet the same legal and technical cleanup requirements as state Superfund sites, and because DTSC staff provide oversight, the proponent is assured that the project will be completed in an environmentally sound manner.

In the agreement, the DTSC retains authority to take enforcement action if, during the investigation or cleanup, it determines that the site presents a serious health threat, and proper and timely action is not otherwise being taken. Project proponents do not admit legal liability for the site remediation upon entering into a VCP agreement and either side may terminate the project, for any reason, with 30-day written notice.

Under the VCP, DTSC is committed to a team approach to achieve successful project completion. Projects are subject to the same cleanup standards and DTSC approvals as sites in the Hazardous Substances Account Act base program. However, proponents may choose to conduct projects in a phased manner and establish a schedule and, most often, the length of time for project completion is compressed. Many proponents choose to complete the Preliminary Endangerment Assessment (the initial assessment with a risk analysis component) to determine if the property warrants further work. Both regulatory approval and project streamlining are critical factors in arranging financing and meeting development schedules.

The VCP emphasizes the use of presumptive remedies and innovative technologies to expedite remediation. Additionally, site-specific risk analysis and land use restrictions can be used as a basis for establishing remediation standards that are geared to the planned use of the property. Using land use controls to limit future exposure to contaminants is authorized in DTSC's base Hazardous Substances Account Act program and is outlined in DTSC's June 1990 Official Policy and Procedure on Development and Implementation of Land Use Covenants. These land use restrictions run with the land and bind future successors and assigns.[5]

When the site assessment/remediation is complete, DTSC issues either a "No Further Action" (NFA) letter or certification of completion, depending on the project circumstances. Either signifies that the DTSC has determined that the site does not pose a significant risk to public health or the environment. While neither constitutes a release or covenant not to sue, both significantly minimize future liability concerns. Additionally, because response actions conducted under the VCP are consistent with the CERCLA National Contingency Plan, project proponents may seek cost recovery from other responsible parties under CERCLA.

Expedited Remedial Action Program

The Expedited Remedial Action Program (ERAP) was established in 1994, under the authority of the California Expedited Remedial Action Reform Act of 1994.[6] The ERAP provides a

---

[5]Cal. Health & Safety Code § 25355.5.
[6]Cal. Health & Safety Code §§ 25396-25399.2.

separate track, pilot voluntary cleanup program limited to 30 sites that meet specific criteria. The DTSC is designated as the lead agency to oversee investigation and remediation of ERAP sites pursuant to Unified Agency Review of Hazardous Materials Release Sites program.[7] The ERAP is designed to encourage and expedite cleanups by offering a number of incentives, including:

- Requiring the DTSC to review and evaluate submissions within set timeframes;

- Requiring extensive potentially responsible party (PRP) search and notice by the DTSC;

- Allowing more flexibility in the remedy selection—using site-specific cleanup goals based on the proposed property use and, with the exception of "hot spots," there is no preference for treatment;

- Providing extensive rights to dispute DTSC technical decisions;

- Providing for liability allocation based on fair and equitable principles;

- Providing for state funding for up to 10 sites with "orphan shares" (to the extent funding is available), where responsible parties are found to be insolvent, or cannot be identified or located;

- Providing qualified future liability protection by a certificate of completion;

- Providing a cleanup process independent of the National Contingency Plan; and

---

[7]Cal. Health & Safety Code §§ 25260-25268.

- Requiring that the DTSC and the responsible party enter into mutual covenants not to sue under CERCLA.

One of the means by which this legislation can be used to foster brownfields redevelopment is the requirement that cleanup standards are developed based on the planned use of the property. The ERAP explicitly authorizes land use controls to limit future exposure.

Prospective Purchaser Policy

To address some of the major brownfields issues and remove or lessen the liability that prospective purchasers face, the DTSC has developed a Prospective Purchaser Policy. The policy is consistent with, yet less conservative than, the EPA's Prospective Purchaser Guidance discussed in Chapter 1. The DTSC's policy differs with the U.S. EPA's policy in some important respects. For example, the DTSC does not limit consideration to sites in which response actions have been conducted or planned. Thus, the DTSC will entertain Prospective Purchaser Agreements (PPAs) at Voluntary Cleanup Program sites. Further, the DTSC considers benefits to the public, in terms of job creation, an increased tax base, opportunities for disadvantaged groups, and the like, as a key criterion to determine Prospective Purchaser eligibility.

The policy explains how to enter into a PPA, includes a model PPA (with a covenant not to sue) and an application form, and eligibility criteria. The process has been streamlined to reduce negotiation and DTSC review time, lower transaction costs, ensure statewide consistency, and promote compliance with current settlement practices and procedures. As a matter of general policy, the DTSC will not pursue site mitigation enforcement against prospective purchasers/tenants/lessors who become site owners or operators if all of the following conditions are met:

- They do not exacerbate or contribute to the existing contamination;

- Their operation will not result in health risks to persons on the site;

- They are not a responsible party (or affiliate of a responsible party) with respect to the existing contamination;

- They allow access for, and do not interfere with, remediation activities;

- Unauthorized disposal is not occurring on the site; and

- There are other viable responsible parties who are willing to conduct any necessary remediation.

The DTSC also recommends that prospective purchasers do not engage in activities that require use of substances of concern at the site to ensure that no question would arise regarding any contribution to, or exacerbation of, the existing contamination. Generally, the DTSC does not participate in private real estate transactions. However, the DTSC will consider entering into an agreement with a bona fide prospective purchaser if it will result in substantial benefits to the state, if remediation would not otherwise be conducted without agency action, and if the prospective purchaser satisfies the eligibility criteria.

The DTSC acknowledges that a PPA with a prospective purchaser of contaminated property, given appropriate safeguards, may result in environmental benefit through commitment to perform response actions. Additionally, PPAs can benefit the affected community, or the state as a whole, by encouraging the reuse of properties where the perceived liability may pose a barrier. A critical factor for determining eligibility for a PPA is that the prospective purchaser must establish with the DTSC the project benefits to the public in terms of job creation, and increased tax base, and/or opportunities for disadvantaged groups.

The DTSC will consider all of the following criteria to determine a prospective purchaser's eligibility for a PPA:

1. The site falls under the jurisdiction of the DTSC because of an actual hazardous substance release.

2. The prospective purchaser is willing to enter into an agreement with the DTSC. The agreement provides that the prospective purchaser is willing to pay DTSC oversight costs and the response action will completely remediate the site or will make significant progress toward complete remedy.

3. Unauthorized disposal of hazardous waste is not currently occurring at the site.

4. The prospective purchaser is not a responsible party or affiliate of a responsible party with respect to the hazardous substance release(s) existing at the time the PPA is executed.

5. A Preliminary Endangerment Assessment (PEA) or equivalent assessment has been performed and provided to the DTSC, identifying the hazardous substance release(s) at the site.

6. The hazardous substance release site is not the subject of an active enforcement action or agreement with another agency with jurisdiction to address the remediation at the site unless that agency transfers oversight to the DTSC.

7. A substantial benefit will be received by the public as a result of the PPA, which would not otherwise be available (e.g., potential environmental benefits, significant progress towards site remediation, value to the community in terms

of additional jobs, an increased tax base, or opportunities for disadvantaged groups).

8. The continued operation at the site or new site development, with the exercise of due care, will not exacerbate or contribute to the existing contamination or interfere with the investigation of the extent, source, and nature of the hazardous substance release(s), and/or implementation of remedial or removal actions.

9. The effect of continued operation or new development on the site will not result in health risks to those persons likely to be present at the site.

10. The prospective purchaser is financially viable ad willing to provide instruments of financial assurance. Financial assurance is needed to ensure that the prospective purchaser has sufficient funds to complete the agreed-upon investigation and remedial action; any existing site condition is not exacerbated due to lack of action; and the DTSC is reimbursed for its oversight costs.

11. The prospective purchaser is a "bona fide prospective purchaser" (i.e., a person or entity that is purchasing all or part interest in real property, but is not affiliated with any person potentially liable for response costs at the site). The bona fide prospective purchaser must provide evidence of these conditions to the DTSC.

Since not all brownfields properties are eligible for a PPA, the policy also outlines several other options that prospective purchasers may pursue to limit their potential risk of liability. The DTSC's objective is to strike a balance between providing sufficient assurance to prospective purchasers to foster redevelopment and treating responsible parties in an equitable manner. The DTSC only has authority to negotiate a PPA on its own behalf and no other state agency. The State Water Resources Control Board has also issued a similar guidance memo on PPAs. The Prospective Purchaser Policy is available for review on the DTSC's Internet homepage at http://www.calepa.cahwnet.gov/dtsc.htm.

In July 1995, the DTSC completed its first PPA in the form of a Buyer/Seller Agreement for the former Golden Eagle Refinery in Carson, California. Under this three-party agreement between the buyer, seller, and the DTSC, the seller (the responsible party) agreed to conduct all remaining site cleanup. The buyers (who are not responsible parties) received a covenant not to sue, and agreed to provide access and not contribute to, or exacerbate, the contamination. The agreement, which runs with the land, extends the covenant not to sue to future owners and occupants of the site, as long as they abide by the provisions of the agreement. Groundbreaking activities began in August 1995 and 40 acres of the site will be developed into a 500,000 square-foot open-air shopping mall. The mall is expected to be completed in late 1997. An additional 35 acres will be available for retail, high tech research and development, and industrial uses. The project will generate approximately 2,000 jobs and tax revenues in excess of $12 million annually.

Colorado's Voluntary Cleanup and Redevelopment Act

The State of Colorado's authority for its Voluntary Cleanup Program, referred to as "VCUP," is derived from the Colorado Voluntary Cleanup and Redevelopment Act (Act), which was passed in 1994. The Act was designed to facilitate the cleanup of property previously contaminated with hazardous substances or petroleum and return it to productive use.[8] The Act permits and encourages voluntary cleanups by providing a method to determine cleanup responsibilities in planning reuse of a property. The VCUP is tasked to operate quickly and with a minimum of administrative processes and cost. Accordingly, no regulations have been promulgated to implement the Act.

A property owner may obtain approval of a voluntary cleanup plan by submitting an application to the Colorado Department of Public Health and Environment (CDPHE). The applicant can obtain an advisory opinion from CDPHE regarding the adequacy of its proposal. If the property owner has already conducted cleanup efforts, the owner can seek a finding by CDPHE that the existing cleanup is satisfactory (i.e., that the contamination is at a level requiring that no further action be taken to clean up the site). A property owner may also submit the application for approval of a proposed voluntary cleanup plan or to secure a no further action determination from DPHE in order to satisfy a prospective buyer or lender, or to develop the property. Because the advisory opinion gives the applicant immunity from state law liability, it can provide some comfort to prospective purchasers or lenders.

Memorandum of Agreement with U.S. EPA

Although the Comprehensive Environmental Response, Compensation and Liability Act (CERCLA or Superfund) establishes a federal program for the cleanup of sites that are contaminated with hazardous substances, the law also envisions and provides for state involvement at sites handled under the Superfund program. A state and an EPA regional office may develop a Memorandum of Agreement (MOA) in which the EPA and the state articulate the roles each will have regarding the

---

[8]Colo. Rev. Stat. Ann. § 25-16-301.

cleanup of contaminated properties. The CDPHE and EPA Region VIII have such an MOA in place to define the roles and responsibilities of the each agency with respect to activities conducted under the authority of the Colorado Voluntary Cleanup and Redevelopment Act. Under the MOA, the CDPHE and the EPA seek to facilitate the productive reuse of brownfield properties by working with the private sector to eliminate impediments to financing, transfer, and redevelopment. Under the MOA, CDPHE is in charge of implementing the VCUP to allow owners of contaminated properties to voluntarily propose cleanup actions or petition for no further action determinations for eligible sites.

The MOA states that once an application to clean up a site in accordance with the VCUP has been submitted to CDPHE, the EPA "will not plan and does not anticipate undertaking any federal action" under CERCLA, at such a site unless: "(1) the site is an 'NPL Caliber' site or the site poses an imminent and substantial endangerment to public health, welfare or the environment and exceptional circumstances warrant EPA action; (2) CDPHE's approval of the cleanup plan becomes void; or (3) the applicant fails to complete or materially comply with the cleanup plan as approved by CDPHE."

Site Screening and Communication

After receiving an application under the VCUP, the state conducts a site screening. Site screening is two-fold. First, sites are screened for eligibility. Section 25-16-303(3)(b) of the Act excludes:

- Sites listed or proposed for listing on the National Priorities List (NPL) of Superfund sites;

- Sites subject to a RCRA corrective action;

- Sites subject to an order or agreement issued by the Colorado Water Quality Control Division;

- Sites that have or should have a RCRA permit or interim status for the treatment, storage, or disposal of hazardous waste; and

- Sites regulated under the state's underground storage tank program.

After an initial review of the site history, the lead reviewer at CDPHE discusses the site with officials who administer each of the above programs to determine whether or not the site is excluded under one of the listed criteria.

If the site qualifies for the VCUP, a second screening is performed to determine existing actions proposed by the U.S. EPA and the EPA's level of potential interest in the site. The purpose of this communication is to avoid duplication of effort between the federal and state agencies. First, the state reviewer will determine whether the site is found on the CERCLA information system database, known as the Comprehensive Environmental Response, Compensation, and Liability Information System or "CERCLIS." If the site is listed on the EPA's CERCLIS database, the state reviewer will contact appropriate EPA staff to discuss the site status and proposed EPA actions. Second, the state reviewer will determine whether the site is subject to an EPA CERCLA Administrative Order. If it is, the state reviewer will review the application as required by the Act, but the EPA's agreement to forbear planning or undertaking any action under CERCLA, as described in the MOA, becomes void.

Sites Listed on CERCLIS

If all or a portion of the site is listed on CERCLIS, the state will request that the EPA suspend activities to allow the cleanup to proceed under the VCUP. Should the EPA decide to proceed with its planned actions, the state may choose to deny the application, or may process the application and coordinate approval of the application with the EPA.

For a CERCLIS site for which the EPA has planned but will agree to suspend investigatory or response actions in lieu of the owner's compliance with the Act and VCUP, CDPHE will keep the EPA informed of the owner's progress toward completion of the remedial action. CDPHE will also notify the EPA of the owner's completion or failure to complete the remedial action. In the event the owner implements the cleanup plan completely and to the satisfaction of CDPHE, under the MOA, the EPA is required to remove the site from its CERCLIS database.

Sites Not Listed on CERCLIS

If the site is not listed on CERCLIS, the state will evaluate the information submitted by the applicant to determine whether the site might be considered "NPL Caliber." The EPA has generally defined "NPL Caliber" to mean sites where significant human exposure to hazardous substances has been documented or where sensitive environments have become contaminated. Examples of what the EPA considers "NPL Caliber" site characteristics are sources of contamination that may have contributed to the following:

- Public drinking water supplies or private wells are contaminated with a hazardous substance above the concentration listed in the Risk-Based Concentration Table for tap water.

- Soils on school, day care center, or residential properties are contaminated by a hazardous substance significantly above background levels and are above concentrations for soil ingestion (residential) listed in the Risk-Based Concentration Table.

- Soils on school, day care center, or residential properties are contaminated by lead concentrations significantly above background levels and the lead soil concentration is above 400 parts per million.

- A hazardous substance is detected in an off-site air release in a populated area and the release is above the concentration listed in the Risk-Based Concentration Table for ambient air.

- A highly toxic substance known to persist and bioaccumulate in the environment (e.g., PCBs, mercury, dioxin, polynuclear aromatic hydrocarbons) is discharged into surface waters.

- A highly toxic hazardous waste known to be mobile in the subsurface (e.g., vinyl chloride, trichloroethylene, acetone, phenol, cadmium, mercury) is discharged to significant useable aquifers.

- Sensitive environments are contaminated with a hazardous substance significantly above background levels and water quality standards, where appropriate.

Even though the application for VCUP may not address off-site problems, if the releases from the applicant's property have contributed to off-site exposure to hazardous substances, the EPA considers the sources of hazardous substance contamination, as well as the areas where contamination has migrated to be an "NPL Caliber" site.

If the CDPHE determines a site to be of "NPL Caliber," it will notify the applicant of its determination as early on the 45-day review period as possible. CDPHE and the applicant will then jointly decide whether to inform the EPA of CDPHE's determination and to request the EPA's review of and concurrence with the cleanup plan and application. If the CDPHE and the applicant jointly decide to seek the EPA's review and approval, the EPA will provide its comments on the application as quickly as possible. If the CDPHE and the applicant jointly decide not to solicit the EPA's review and approval of the application, CDPHE may either approve or deny the application. In the event CDPHE approves the application for the "NPL Caliber" site without the EPA's review and concurrence, the applicant may still implement the cleanup plan, but the EPA's forbearance not to plan or undertake any action under CERCLA, as described in the MOA, becomes void.

Resources and Capabilities

CDPHE utilizes trained environmental professionals to review voluntary cleanup applications. The specialty of these individuals may vary, but includes: geology, hydrology, engineering, risk analysis, and chemistry. These environmental professionals have applied this expertise to underground storage tank remediation, RCRA corrective action, solid waste facility permitting, and Superfund remedial action. On an as needed basis, the appropriate expertise can be utilized to assist the state's lead reviewer. The maximum number of applications that can be reviewed per month is eight, in order to ensure that authorized staff have sufficient time to review applications in sufficient detail.

Standards and Risk Analysis

CDPHE will implement a risk-based cleanup approach based on the proposed land use and will utilize applicable standards and remediation objectives in cleanup decisions. CDPHE will take under consideration site-specific cleanup standards if they are based on risk and utilize appropriate land use assumptions. Although a site-specific risk assessment prepared using the EPA's RAGS document can be submitted by the applicant at his/her option, the 45-day time period available for review of an application containing such a risk assessment may be insufficient and need to be extended.

Therefore, CDPHE will use relevant standards derived from applicable statutes, regulations, guidance, and the application of the risk-derived numbers developed by the EPA, CDPHE or other governmental authorities. In all cases, an analysis of the risk entails an evaluation of targets and receptors and the potential for pathways of exposure to be realized. In all application evaluations, the CDPHE reviewers will examine the proposed cleanup standards, the proposed remedial method, and the proposed land use in concert to ensure that protection of health and the environment is achieved by the implementation of the plan.

Public Participation

The Act has no requirements for public participation or review of applications. However, all files are public documents and available for public review upon request. In addition, CDPHE routinely contacts the local health department to see if there is any knowledge of, or interest in, the site, and will make a copy of the application available for local review if requested. Local governments may have additional public participation requirements related to the redevelopment of property (e.g., zoning regulations) which are applicable to these sites.

Notwithstanding any local government public participation procedures or requirements for redevelopment of these sites, in order to obtain the EPA's forbearance not to plan or undertake any action under CERCLA, as contained in the MOA, within 30 days of approval of its VCUP application, the applicant will provide adequate public notice of its cleanup plan. "Adequate public notice" will be determined on a site-specific basis and should include publication of the availability of the cleanup plan in a local newspaper or posting of any public notice required by building permit or zoning ordinance procedures. For large sites or sites where public interest is likely due to publicity or proximity to Superfund sites, CDPHE may request that the applicant hold a public meeting to explain its cleanup plan.

Cleanup Verification

In accordance with the Act, verification of the completion of a cleanup plan under the VCUP is left to the applicant. Verification that the cleanup has been performed in accordance with the CDPHE-approved cleanup plan is provided by the property owner submitting a certification from a qualified environmental professional that the plan has been fully implemented. Should this certification be falsified, the Act renders void the CDPHE's approval and the EPA's forbearance not to plan or undertake any action under CERCLA.

Since conditions encountered in the field during the plan implementation may be different than those represented in the approved cleanup plan, the applicant may not be able to certify that it has substantially complied with the cleanup plan as approved by CDPHE. CDPHE is available to discuss changing field conditions and the impact of such changes on the cleanup plan. Thus, CDPHE should be informed of these deviations from the plan as they occur, determine if the plan should be modified and may require the applicant to submit a revised application based on this new information.

No Further Action Petition

In order to obtain the EPA's forbearance not to plan or undertake any action under CERCLA as provided in the MOA, the applicant must submit a written petition requesting a "No Further Action" determination on the subject property following completion of the cleanup plan. This petition must include a completion report that describes how the applicant has complied with the initial or modified cleanup plan as approved by CDPHE. CDPHE will review the report to ensure compliance with the approved cleanup plan and may conduct an inspection of the subject property to obtain readily available information concerning the property's current condition.

Within 45 days of the submission of the petition, CDPHE will notify the EPA and the applicant whether the petition for a "No Further Action" determination has been approved or disapproved. If the CDPHE approves the petition for "No Further Action," the EPA must forbear planning or undertaking any action under CERCLA, as required by the MOA. The EPA, however, reserves the right to take all appropriate response and enforcement actions under CERCLA in the event a "No Further Action" determination is deemed "approved" as a result of a failure of CDPHE to review and approve or deny an application prior to the expiration of the 45-day time limit provided in the Act.

Connecticut's Brownfields Redevelopment Programs

During the 1995 legislative session, the Connecticut General Assembly adopted several important amendments to the Connecticut Property Transfer Law,[9] which provide incentives for voluntary cleanup and redevelopment of brownfield sites.[10] These amendments include adoption of two separate and distinct voluntary cleanup schemes.

Voluntary Cleanup Program #1: Public Act 95-183

Under the first voluntary remediation scheme, adopted with enactment of Public Act 95-183, the Connecticut Transfer Act was amended to enable the owner of certain eligible property to remediate any contamination prior to transfer, thereby allowing the transferor to file a negative declaration with the Connecticut Department of Environmental Protection (DEP) at the time of transfer. Eligible properties are sites listed on the state inventory of hazardous waste sites or any real property or business operation at which more than 100 kilograms of hazardous waste is generated in any single month since November 19, 1980. The Connecticut Transfer Act requires that the transferor deliver to the transferee a notarized certification that there has been no discharge of hazardous waste on the site or that any such discharge has been cleaned up in accordance with state law. Failure to comply renders the transferor strictly liable for all cleanup and removal costs. A copy of the certification must be filed with the Connecticut DEP within 15 days after the transfer. If the transferor cannot give the required certification, one of the parties to the transaction must

---

[9]Conn. Gen. Stat. Ann. §§ 22a-134 to 22-134e.
[10]Pub. Act 95-183 and 95-190.

certify to the state that it will remediate the contamination under the supervision of the state.

The first voluntary remediation scheme gives the Connecticut DEP the option of reviewing and approving voluntary cleanup or allowing a licensed environmental professional (LEP) to verify the cleanup. If the DEP proceeds with review and approval, the property owner must submit various technical plans and reports and a proposed schedule for investigation and remediation. If the DEP declines to conduct review and approval, the property owner may hire LEPs to oversee site cleanup. In such case, within 90 days, the owner must submit a statement of proposed action for investigating and remediating the site and a schedule for implementing the plans. The use of LEPs may eliminate many of the costly delays inherent in state-supervised cleanups. LEPs certify that a property has been cleaned to applicable standards, thereby making properties more attractive to future investors and eliminating the need for lengthy negotiations to obtain a sign-off letter from the DEP. Written approval from the DEP, or verification from a LEP, that a remediation is complete may serve as the basis for a Form II negative declaration when the property is transferred, provided no spills occur following the cleanup.

Voluntary Cleanup Program #2: Public Act 95-190

A second voluntary remediation scheme, adopted with enactment of Public Act 95-190, supplements the state's Urban Sites Initiative (discussed below). This scheme encourages voluntary cleanup in areas already suffering environmental contamination. Only sites with groundwater classified as GB or GC and not already the subject of an order, consent order, or stipulated judgment may take advantage of this voluntary remediation program.

An owner seeking to voluntarily clean up a site must first conduct a Phase II environmental site assessment or Phase III investigation at the site. A Phase II assessment determines whether the site has been impacted, while a Phase III investigation determines the extent of the impact.

After the investigation is performed, a Phase III remedial action plan must be prepared by a LEP and submitted to DEP. In addition, notice must be given in two of three ways: (1) publication; (2) erecting and maintaining for at least 30 days a sign at least 6 by 4 feet, visible from the road, that reads: "Environmental cleanup in progress at this site. For further information contact:" with a telephone contact number; or (3) mail notice to each owner of record of property that abuts the affected property. DEP may review the plan and judge its adequacy at any time in the process. Remedial action must then be supervised by a LEP.

Upon completion of the cleanup, a final action report must be prepared by the LEP and submitted to the DEP. The LEP must verify that the remediation was conducted in accordance with the applicable remediation standards. Unless DEP decides to audit the report, it is approved. Audits must be announced within 60 days and conducted within six months.

Owners must then execute and record an environmental use restriction, unless the LEP presents evidence and the DEP issues a written finding that a restriction is not necessary. The type of evidence submitted by the LEP may include proof that the remediation meets applicable residential or GA/GAA standards. Environmental use restrictions help to limit potential health risks resulting from exposure to hazardous substances remaining on nonresidential brownfield properties. Use restrictions, as implemented in several states, may prohibit uses such as residential development or activities that could create exposure risks or interfere with remedial measures.

If an owner engages in this voluntary remediation and executes an environmental use restriction, which is recorded on the land records, the DEP may, in consultation with the attorney general, enter into a covenant not to sue with the owner or lessor.[11] It requires payment of a fee of three percent of the value of the property as appraised after the cleanup. Such a covenant prevents the state from pursuing the owner or mortgagor for any spill prior to the date of the covenant. The covenant runs with the land. The covenant not to sue does not, however, protect the owner from third-party actions.

Comparison of Voluntary Cleanup Programs

Public Act 95-183 voluntary remediation is only available to owners of listed hazardous waste sites and facilities at which more than 100 kilograms of hazardous waste is generated in single month. Public Act 95-190 voluntary remediation is only available to sites located in areas where the groundwater is classified as GB or GC. Some sites may fall into both categories. In such case, owners can choose to perform voluntary cleanup under either or both programs. Completion of cleanup under both schemes allows an owner to file a Form II negative declaration.

Public Act 95-183 voluntary remediation costs $2,000 in up-front fees to the DEP. in addition to the actual costs of investigation and cleanup. It may also require owners to notify the DEP earlier in the process, since only the actual remediation plan is submitted under Public Act 95-190.

---

[11]See Conn. Gen. Stat. §§ 22a-133aa, 22a-133bb, 22a-133cc.

Public Act 95-190 contains provisions some owners may find disagreeable. For example, it requires public notice, while Public Act 95-183 does not. More importantly, it requires that owners record an environmental use restriction unless waived by the DEP. However, one potential advantage of Public Law 95-190 is the availability of the covenant not to sue.

Urban Sites Remediation Program

In addition to the voluntary cleanup initiatives implemented with the 1995 amendments to the Connecticut Transfer Act, the state has several other programs in place to encourage redevelopment of brownfield sites. In 1993, the Connecticut legislature enacted Public Act 93-428, which established the Urban Sites Remediation (USR) program. This program authorizes the state to own a brownfield and take responsibility for remediating the site. The state Department of Economic and Community Development (DECD) establishes a list of priority sites based on cost, time, complexity, economic development potential and other factors. DECD may accept liability for up to $15 million of cleanup costs provided it accepts no liability under federal law. The Connecticut Department of Environmental Protection (DEP) assumes responsibility for cleaning up the site before sale and the state recaptures a portion of the costs under the purchase and sale agreement. The USR program limits the scope of cleanup to levels necessary for the predetermined reuse of the property, thereby reducing costs below a precontamination level. The program sets up a fund for assessment and remediation costs and helps to convey a sense of closure to developers, as the state takes on the burden of complying with its own laws. The most significant deficiency of the USR program us the small number of sites it encompasses and its inability to shield against federal liability.

Neighborhood Revitalization Zones

Neighborhood Revitalization Zones help local communities become more actively involved in revitalizing foreclosed or abandoned properties that have become victimized by crime, environmental risk, and "brown-lining" policies that result in the lack of development capital. The process requires residents, businesses, and municipal officials to submit a strategic plan to the Office of Policy and Management, which will coordinate a multi-agency state review by the Governor's Urban Advisory Council. The council identifies impediments to redevelopment and requests waivers of modifications of regulations. It also assists in requesting corresponding federal waivers or variances. Finally, the council works with local entities in coordinating other public and private resources to address issues of public safety, education, needs of youth and the elderly, and job training.

Community Redevelopment Laws

Numerous municipal and economic redevelopment programs under Connecticut law, particularly the Manufacturing Assistance Act, permit combinations of taxable and tax-exempt bond financing general obligation debt and municipal acquisition of sites pending rehabilitation. A community, acting through its redevelopment agency, can purchase a subject property and select a developer who agrees to certain terms and conditions of redevelopment. The municipality may even contract for assumption of all legal liability for preexisting contamination. Results may include income from sale or long-term lease, enhanced property taxes and job creation.

In addition, at the federal level, the Empowerment Zone/Enterprise Communities Program designates certain urban and rural areas to qualify for tax-exempt bond financing of "qualified enterprise zone businesses," a new category of exempt facility private activity bonds. In many cases, such businesses are also eligible for enhanced expense deductions. The State Enterprise Zone Program and Enterprise Corridor Zone Program provide tax incentives to eligible businesses within a designated community or area.

DECD can access Urban Act Grant Program funds to address urgent economic development needs and leverage other public and private funding sources.

The Urban Jobs Program also provides discretionary tax incentives to qualifying businesses located within a Targeted Investment Community.

Finally, Community Development Incentive Programs administered by the DECD are available to assist large-scale development projects by packaging financial assistance programs and offering tax abatements and credits under the Urban Jobs and Development Act.

Tax Increment Financing

Tax Increment Financing (TIF) downgrades subject property value based upon discovery of contamination so the site can enjoy a corresponding upgrade after remediation, thereby establishing the tax differential and creating a fund to finance a portion of the costs. Because TIF relies on the anticipated growth in property tax revenues a development project will generate, it does not lower the revenues collected or impose special assessments.

Delaware's Voluntary Cleanup Program

Under the authority of the state's Hazardous Substance Cleanup Act of 1990 (HSCA),[12] the Delaware Department of Natural Resources and Environmental Control (DNREC) established the Voluntary Cleanup Program (VCP).[13] The VCP is designed to assist property owners, developers, lenders, and other participants in the investigation, cleanup and redevelopment of contaminated sites. The key functions of the VCP are to set standards for site investigation, to provide review of the adequacy and completeness of site investigations, and to approve cleanup plans for identified contamination. By obtaining VCP approval of the investigation and cleanup plans, landowners, lenders, and potential developers can be reasonably confident of the extent of environmental problems on the property, can determine the most appropriate cleanup action, and calculate the cost of cleanup measures needed to satisfy VCP requirements. The voluntary investigation and cleanup process provides the information needed to make sensible financial decisions about developing or transferring contaminated or potentially contaminated property.

Implicit in the voluntary nature of the VCP is the recognition that voluntary parties have a choice to participate or not participate in the program. Thus, a voluntary party can terminate their participation at any point by written notification to the DNREC. If a voluntary party decides to terminate participation in the VCP and the voluntary party is not otherwise a responsible party, as defined by the HSCA, the DNREC would not take further administrative action to mandate future investigation or cleanup by the voluntary party. However, if the voluntary party is the owner of the property,

---

[12]Del. Code Ann. tit. 7, ch. 91.
[13]*See* Delaware Voluntary Cleanup Program Guidance, Delaware Department of Natural Resources and Environmental Control, February 1995.

it will be required to cooperate with the DNREC at a future date to investigate and, if necessary, clean up the property.

Parties seeking assistance under the VCP are expected to adhere to certain standards in the investigation of contamination on a property, the evaluation and recommendation of response actions, and the level of cleanup attained. Parties entering into the VCP may choose to conduct the investigation and evaluation of response alternatives on their own, before seeking the DNREC's assistance in oversight of the cleanup activities. All of the information gathered and evaluation performed must be submitted along with the workplan under a VCP Agreement between the volunteer and the DNREC.

VCP Site Eligibility

For a site to be eligible for cleanup under the VCP, it may have to meet certain criteria. DNREC, at its sole discretion, may decide that a site is not eligible for cleanup if:

- A property has contamination detected in the soil or groundwater at a risk value greater than a cancer risk of 10^{-4} or a hazard index of 10 or greater;

- A public/domestic water supply well on the property contaminated at or above either the Maximum Contaminant Level (MCL); a cancer risk of 1×10^{-5} or a hazard index = 1;

- A property has either groundwater or soil contamination located near a public/domestic well (i.e., 300 feet to a public well; 150 feet to a domestic well) which the VCP determines has the potential to contaminate the well;

- The contamination from the property impacts the surface water which is used as a drinking water source and the MCLs are exceeded;

- The contamination from the property impacts surface water quality and an exceedance of at least one order of magnitude of the State of Delaware Surface Water Quality Standards is determined;

- A property is subject to RCRA corrective action; or

- For any other reason documented in writing to the applicant.

Properties that do not meet the VCP site eligibility criteria may be referred to the enforcement program under the HSCA. Referral of a site to the enforcement program may also take place if the voluntary party chooses to discontinue participation in the VCP and the property is the site of a release or a potential release of a hazardous substance. Referral could also take place if it becomes evident that the voluntary party is unable to continue, or demonstrates a lack of cooperation in dealing with the VCP staff, or if not completing the necessary investigation activities and response actions in a timely manner. Parties will generally only be given one opportunity to demonstrate their cooperation by volunteering to conduct the necessary investigation and response actions at a site.

VCP Application and Agreement

Parties that wish to perform an environmental investigation and cleanup of a property must fill out a VCP Application Form. The VCP Application is used to assist parties in determining whether remedial action is warranted at their sites and whether to request a VCP Agreement. Once an applicant has completed the VCP

Application process and has been approved to enter the VCP, the applicant may elect to enter into a VCP Agreement with the DNREC. DNREC has developed a legal agreement for persons who request its assistance and oversight during site investigations and cleanups. The VCP Agreement has been structured to reflect the voluntary nature of a person's involvement in the program. Key provisions of the VCP Agreement include the following requirements:

- Performance of property cleanups in accordance with HSCA regulations;

- Adherence to all applicable federal, state, and local laws ad regulations;

- DNREC staff access and oversight;

- Reimbursement of DNREC staff oversight costs;

- A hold harmless clause;

- An agreement termination clause for both the DNREC and the voluntary party; and

- A provision to indemnify the state.

VCP agreements will not include:

- Provisions for stipulated penalties for noncompliance;

- Provisions for public notice of the agreement; or

- A dispute resolution clause during the Remedial Investigation/Feasibility Study (RI/FS).

A modified VCP agreement is available during the Remedial Design/Remedial Action (RD/RA) phase, if the voluntary party requests the inclusion of dispute resolution procedures in the agreement.

VCP Site Investigation Process

After signing the VCP Agreement and the payment of a deposit (up to $5,000) for oversight cost to the DNREC, the voluntary party will submit the name of the consultant and the laboratory for the DNREC's approval. The approved consultant and the laboratory will be provided with copies of the HSCA regulations, and other applicable guidance documents and policies.

After approval of the consultant, based on the DNREC's policy on "Minimum Qualifications Requirements for Consultants/ Contractors under the HSCA" and the laboratory, based in HSCA "Standard Operating Procedure for Chemical Analytical Program," the voluntary party will submit a workplan for the investigation and study for the DNREC's approval. Along with this workplan, the voluntary party must submit information on all previous investigation and study conducted by the party for the DNREC's approval and acceptance. The DNREC will take into account and give credit for all previous investigation and study by the voluntary party if these meet the standards under the existing guidelines, policies, and procedures of the DNREC. The workplan must identify all the data and information available, data gaps that need to be filled, and additional studies required for the preparation of a proposed plan for remedy. Following completion of the workplan, the investigation and cleanup of the property will proceed according to the schedule agreed upon by the DNREC and the applicant.

Soil and Groundwater Screening Levels

In an effort to streamline the investigation and cleanup process, the DNREC has developed screening levels for soil and groundwater contamination. Screening Levels have been developed for both residential and industrial/commercial land use settings. The screening levels are derived from the Interim Guidance on Reporting Levels of Hazardous Substances Discovered during Site Assessments under the Delaware Hazardous Substances Cleanup Act (revised March 1996). These levels have been developed for 107 chemicals. For chemicals not included in the DNREC guidance, screening levels may be obtained from the U.S. EPA Region 3 Risk-Based Concentration Tables. These tables contain an additional 500 chemicals.

Screening levels are used as guidance to screen out properties from further investigation and/or to initiate investigations. Properties that have contaminant concentration values above the trigger levels will be required to perform an environmental investigation consistent with the HSCA regulations and guidance. Properties with limited contamination, which have a completed environmental investigation under DNREC oversight and discovered that contaminant levels are below screening levels in both the soil and groundwater media may receive a "No Further Action" letter from the DNREC.

DNREC, at its sole discretion, may allow voluntary parties to clean up properties to screening levels in lieu of performing a health-based risk assessment in accordance with HSCA regulations. Cleanup of the soil to an industrial/commercial screening level is determined by the DNREC on a case-by-case basis. Screening levels for soil can be modified, if necessary, to account for potential groundwater contamination.

Written Assurances

Parties that undertake a VCP investigation and cleanup of a property can obtain a written assurance from the DNREC. DNREC will issue a Certificate of Completion of Remedy to the voluntary party once the cleanup of the property has been completed to the

DNREC's satisfaction. The VCP also provides a prospective purchaser of a site with contribution protection from liability under the HSCA, if the purchaser signs a Consent Decree with the DNREC and provides assurances on the cleanup of the site.

Illinois Site Remediation Program

Under authority of the Illinois Environmental Protection Act,[14] the Illinois Environmental Protection Agency administers the Site Remediation Program which provides oversight, technical assistance, and no further remediation determinations to parties seeking to perform voluntary investigation and cleanup of contaminated sites.[15] The Illinois EPA intends for the program to be flexible and responsive to the needs of Remediation Applicants (RAs), to project constraints, and to variable remediation site conditions. The Illinois EPA provides the necessary degree of oversight to ensure that a RA completes an adequate cleanup.

Site Eligibility

A remediation site is eligible for the program unless it is on the National Priorities List or the investigation or remedial activities for which Illinois EPA review, evaluation, and approval are sought, are required under:

- a current state or federal solid or hazardous waste permit or hazardous waste treatment, storage, or disposal site pursuant to applicable federal laws and regulations;

---

[14]Ill. Rev. Stat. ch. 415, para. 5/4(y), 5/58 through 5/58.12.
[15]Ill. Admin. Code tit. 35, §§ 740.100 through 740.625 (implementing regulations for Site Remediation Program).

- state or federal underground storage tank laws and regulations; or

- a federal court order issued by the U.S. EPA, and compliance with the Program would be contrary to the terms of that order.

Program Application and Service Agreement

Completion of the Site Remediation Program Application and Service Agreement Form (DRM-1) is required of parties requesting enrollment in the Program. The application form requires information on the remediation site, the RA, the property owner, and project objectives. In addition, the RA is required to either: (1) make an advance partial payment of $500 when submitting the application, or (2) request that the Illinois EPA estimate the total costs to the Illinois EPA of providing the requested services and assess an advance partial payment not to exceed $5,000 or one-half of the total anticipated costs of the Illinois EPA, whichever is less. Advance partial payments are nonrefundable. Within 30 days of receipt of the Application and Service Agreement and any initial project documents, the Illinois EPA will approve or deny the application based on completeness and eligibility. If the Application and Service Agreement and attached documents are in good order and the advance partial payment has been paid, the Illinois EPA will issue an enrollment letter identifying the Illinois EPA project manager assigned to the project.

Successful participation in the Program requires that a RA adhere to six stipulations contained in the Application and Service Agreement form. These conditions are:

1. Conformance with the procedures of the Illinois Environmental Protection Act and implementing regulations;

2. Agreement to allow or otherwise arrange remediation site visits or other remediation site evaluation by the Illinois EPA when requested;

3. Agreement to perform the remedial action plan as approved under the Program;

4. Agreement to pay any reasonable costs incurred and documented by the Illinois EPA in providing such services under the Program;

5. Advance partial payment to the Illinois EPA for such anticipated services; and

6. Demonstration, if necessary, of authority to act on behalf or in lieu of the owner or operator.

Review and evaluation services agreements may be modified as agreed upon by the Illinois EPA and a RA, in which case other stipulations may apply.

Site Investigation and Remediation by Licensed Engineer

All remediation site activities must be conducted by, or under the supervision of, an Illinois-licensed professional engineer (LPE). Remediation site investigations must define environmental conditions existing at the remediation site, the related contaminants of concern, and associated factors that will aid in the identification of risks to human health and the environment, the determination of remediation objectives, and the remedial design. Site investigations must satisfy data quality objectives for field and laboratory operations to ensure that all data are scientifically valid and of known precision. All plans and reports submitted for review and evaluation must be prepared by, or under the supervision of, an Illinois LPE. Any plan or report submitted to the Illinois EPA must be accompanied by a Site Remediation Program Form (DRM-2). The four plans and reports required for most corrective action projects are: (1) Site Investigation Report (Comprehensive or Focused); (2) Remediation Objectives Report; (3) Remedial Action Plan; and (4) Remedial Completion Report.

The Illinois EPA has 60 days from the receipt of any plan or report to conduct a review and either approve or disapprove the plan or report, or approve the plan or report with conditions. If any plans or reports are submitted concurrently, the Illinois EPA's timeline for review shall increase to a total of 90 days for all plans or reports so submitted. Upon completion of the review, the Illinois EPA must notify the RA and its consultant in writing of its final determination on the plan or report.

No Further Remediation Letter

Successful participation in the program results in the issuance of "clean-site" No Further Remediation (NFR) letter by the Illinois EPA. The NFR letter is a certification that the RA has demonstrated—through proper investigation and, where warranted, remediation—that the site does not pose a threat to human health or the environment. The NFR letter is filed with the Recorder or Registrar of Titles of the county in which the remediation site is located so that it forms a permanent part of the chain of title, thereby notifying future owners of the terms of the NFR letter. In addition to the "clean-site" NFR letter, the Illinois EPA is authorized to issue a "chemical-specific" NFR letter to those RAs that have successfully demonstrated proper remedial actions for a release of a specific contaminant of concern. This limited remediation may appeal to those RAs that are trying to satisfy either a contractual relationship or a regulatory concern for a specific release of hazardous substances, pesticides, or petroleum. The Illinois EPA and U.S. EPA have entered into a Superfund Memorandum of Agreement under which the U.S. EPA concurs that further response actions will not be required by the U.S. EPA at sites covered by a NFR letter. The U.S. EPA will not plan or anticipate federal action under CERCLA at a site enrolled in the Site Remediation Program.

Maryland's Brownfields Program

In February 1997, Governor Glendening signed emergency legislation that created a Voluntary Cleanup Program within the Maryland Department of the Environment (MDE), created a Brownfields Revitalization Incentive Program within the Department of Business and Economic Development, and expanded protection for lenders involved with contaminated properties.[16] The Voluntary Cleanup Program reforms the process used to clean up eligible properties that are, or are perceived to be, contaminated by hazardous waste. In addition to providing a streamlined remediation approval process, the legislation changes the liability scheme for certain prospective owners of eligible properties in the Voluntary Cleanup Program to encourage the transfer of properties and clarifies liability to the state for all program participants. These changes are intended to provide more certainty regarding environmental requirements to both responsible parties and future owners of a property. This certainty allows a

---

[16]Md. Code Ann., Envir. §§ 4-401(1), 7-201(n-1), 7-501 through 7-516 (Voluntary Cleanup Program); Md. Ann. Code art. 83A, §§ 3-901 through 3-905 (Brownfields Revitalization Incentive Program).

party to more accurately predict costs and time lines associated with a cleanup and increase the likelihood of cleanup and redevelopment.

Voluntary Cleanup Program

Key components of the Voluntary Cleanup Program include eligibility requirements, application requirements, the streamlined cleanup process, and liability limitations. Eligible applicants may be either responsible parties or prospective owners who do not and have not previously owned the property and did not cause or contribute to the contamination at the property. Parties who knowingly or willfully violated a law or regulation concerning hazardous waste are not eligible. Eligible properties are those properties that are contaminated, or perceived to be contaminated, by hazardous substances. Ineligible sites include those sites on the National Priorities List, under active enforcement activities by the MDE, subject to a state-issued controlled hazardous substances permit, or contaminated after October 1, 1997 and owned or operated by a responsible party.

An eligible party applies for participation in the Voluntary Cleanup Program by submitting a completed application, a Phase I and Phase II environmental site assessment, all known environmental data and reports, a description of a proposed voluntary cleanup project, and an application fee of $6,000. Applicants and participants are required to pay for MDE oversight costs. Should the cost of application review and oversight exceed $6,000, a participant will be billed by the MDE for additional costs. Unused fees are returned. MDE determines, within 60 days, whether the party is eligible, whether the party is admitted into the Program as an "inculpable person (the prospective owner)" or "responsible person" and whether any cleanup is necessary. If no cleanup is required, MDE, at that time, will issue a "no further requirements" determination, stating that there are no further requirements related to the investigation of hazardous waste at the property.

If cleanup is required and a response action plan is submitted to MDE for approval, MDE must review the proposed plan within 120 days. If the plan is approved, MDE will issue a "response action plan approval letter" which states that no further action will be required to accomplish the plan objectives other than those included. After the plan is implemented to the satisfaction of MDE and achieves the cleanup criteria, the MDE will issue a "Certificate of Completion" within 30 days following the completion of the cleanup. The Certificate is transferable with the property to anyone who did not cause or contribute to contamination at the site.

The Certificate of Completion states that the requirements of the response action plan have been completed, that implementation of the plan achieved the cleanup criteria, and that MDE may not bring an enforcement action against the participant regarding the property. The participant is released from further liability to the state for the remediation of the property for contamination identified in the environmental site assessment and is not subject to a contribution action. MDE and the U.S. EPA have signed a Memorandum of Understanding that will also provide participants with certain protections from federal enforcement action after a site has been cleaned up to state standards.

The Certificate of Completion will not prevent the MDE from taking further action under certain circumstances, including:

- Fraud or material misrepresentation is used to obtain the Certificate of Completion;

- Previously undiscovered, exacerbated, or new contamination is found;

- A person fails to comply with requirements for property use, monitoring, or maintenance;

- The site poses an imminent and substantial threat to public health or the environment.

In addition, there are "reopeners" for each of the liability limitations—the "no further action requirements" determination, response action plan approval letter, and the Certificate of Completion—which apply to specific situations where the participant may be required to take further action. These reopeners are broader for participants designated as responsible parties than for those who are designated inculpable persons.

Brownfields Revitalization Incentive Program

The Brownfields Revitalization Incentive Program will provide financial incentives for the redevelopment of brownfields. This Program is expected to target loans, grants and property tax credits toward properties contaminated by hazardous waste or oil, thereby stimulating the redevelopment process where cleanup will have significant environmental, economic development and urban revitalization benefits.

The Brownfields Revitalization Incentive Program is administered by the Department of Business and Economic Development. Only persons not responsible for contamination are eligible of these incentives. To qualify for financial incentives, a site must be:

- Addressed in the Voluntary Cleanup Program;

- Contaminated by hazardous substances or oil;

- A former industrial or commercial site located in a densely populated urban area and substantially underutilized; or

- An existing or former commercial or industrial site that poses a threat to public health or the environment; and

- Located in a jurisdiction that has enacted a local ordinance granting a brownfields property tax credit.

Lender Liability Relief

As part of Maryland's Brownfields Program, lenders have been given certain exemptions from liability to assist property owners and prospective purchasers in obtaining needed financing for brownfields redevelopment. Lenders are exempt from liability where they:

- Undertake efforts to complete an approved response action plan;

- Secure loans that they make for cleanup costs;

- Take action to secure and stabilize a site to protect the value of their security interest so that the asset may eventually be transferred and redeveloped.

This lender liability relief creates an element of certainty that should enable borrowers to use their property as acceptable collateral.

Minnesota's Voluntary Investigation and Cleanup Program

Minnesota was the first state to implement a voluntary cleanup program. Minnesota's Voluntary Investigation and Cleanup (VIC) Program addresses the liability and technical issues associated with buying, selling, and developing property contaminated with hazardous substances. Because of the potential for liability as an owner of contaminated property, property owners, buyers, developers, financial institutions, and other participants in property transactions frequently need to determine the nature and extent of possible contamination on the subject property.

In response to a growing need for agency review and oversight of voluntary investigations and response actions, primarily involving property transactions, a Property Transfer Program was established in 1988 under the Minnesota Environmental Response and Liability Act (MERLA).[17] The Property Transfer Program consists of two distinct components. Under the first component, referred to as File Evaluation Program, parties interested in information about potentially contaminated property can request information assistance from the Minnesota Pollution Control Agency (MPCA). The MCPA provides MPCA file and database information that might be used to determine whether the property of interest, or surrounding properties within a one-mile radius, have been the site of a release or threatened release of hazardous substances. The second component, originally referred to as the Property Transfer/Technical Assistance Program, is the Voluntary Investigation and Cleanup (VIC) Program. The key functions of the VIC Program are to set standards for a site investigation, to provide MPCA review of the adequacy and completeness of such investigation, and to approve cleanup plans (response action plans) to address identified contamination. By obtaining MPCA approval of investigation and response action plans, landowners, lenders, and potential developers can determine the extent of environmental contamination on the property, can devise the most appropriate cleanup action, and can calculate the cost of cleanup measures needed to satisfy statutory requirements.

---

[17]Minn. Stat. § 115B.17, subd. 14.

The VIC program is designed to provide information needed to make sensible financial decisions about developing or transferring contaminated or potentially contaminated property. Implicit in the voluntary nature of the program is the recognition that voluntary parties have a choice to participate or not participate in the VIC Program. A voluntary party can terminate participation in the program at any point by written notification to appropriate VIC Program staff. If a voluntary party decides to terminate participation in the VIC Program and the voluntary party is not otherwise a responsible party, as defined by the MERLA, the MCPA staff would not take further administrative action to mandate future investigation or cleanup by the voluntary party. However, if the voluntary party is the owner of the property, it will be required to cooperate with the MCPA or the responsible party(ies) so that the MPCA or responsible party(ies) can complete additional investigation and response actions.

Program Improvements

Various improvements have been made to the VIC Program since it was originally established in 1988. Most significantly, the Minnesota legislature amended MERLA with enactment of the Land Recycling Act of 1992,[18] which clarifies the application of cleanup liability to specific parties and provides statutory mechanisms to obtain liability protections. The Land Recycling Act offers incentives to promote voluntary investigation and cleanup activities under oversight and approval of the VIC Program. Future liability protection is available to eligible parties when MCPA-approved response actions are conducted and completed by VIC Program participants. Liability protection applies to the party who undertakes and completes response

---

[18]Minn. Stat. § 115B.175 (Land Recycling Act).

actions and to the owner of the identified property (if those parties are not responsible for the release or threatened release), as well as financing parties, and successors and assigns of the person to whom liability protection applies.[19]

The Land Recycling Act allows the MPCA to approve partial response action plans—plans that do not address all identified releases or threatened releases—but additional conditions and requirements must be met.[20] Voluntary response actions may also be undertaken by responsible parties; however, the response action of a responsible party must address all releases and threatened releases. A partial cleanup is not allowed and a responsible party is not eligible for statutory liability protection.[21] VIC Program participants can obtain written assurances from the MCPA in the form of a technical approval letter, a "no action" letter, an "off-site source determination" letter, a "no association determination" letter, or a Certificate of Completion.

Michigan's Brownfields Initiatives

Brownfields redevelopment is a priority for the Michigan Department of Environmental Quality (DEQ). The Environmental Response Division (ERD) is responding to this commitment with improved program coordination, focused efforts on the redevelopment of brownfields sites, and a number of initiatives that offer regulatory and financial assistance to encourage brownfield cleanup and reuse. The following legislative and regulatory initiatives have been developed to stimulate brownfields redevelopment:

---

[19]Minn. Stat. § 115B.175, subd. 6.
[20]Minn. Stat. § 115B.175, subd. 2.
[21]Minn. Stat. § 115B.175, subd. 6(a).

- Environmental Remediation Law—In 1995, the Natural Resources and Environmental Protection Act of 1994 was amended with new provisions designed, in large part, to encourage and assist developers who want to return brownfields properties to productive use more quickly and at a lower cost than before, while still protecting human health and the environment. The 1995 amendments are examined in detail below.

- Redevelopment of Urban Sites (REUS) Action Team—A task force of City of Detroit and DEQ specialist are working together on the REUS Action Team to speed cleanups on contaminated sites in Detroit that have economic development potential. Seven sites have been identified where lack of funding for cleanup actions was the critical impediment, and that met the funding criteria for Michigan's Environmental Protection Bond program. Large-scale cleanups are nearing completion at three of these sites using Bond funds—Revere Cooper & Brass, Lear-Siegler, and Ananconda Brass. Fifty additional sites have been targeted for cooperative accelerated efforts. The REUS Action Team works with developers and the people they depend on, such as attorneys, consultants, and bankers, to gain an understanding of the liability protections, flexible cleanup standards, and funding possibilities in Michigan's cleanup program that were designed to facilitate reuse of property.

- Brownfields Redevelopment Grants and Loans—Michigan has implemented a number of legislative and regulatory initiatives that offer sources of funding for Michigan's cleanup program and place an increased emphasis on the use of state cleanup funds to promote brownfields redevelopment, including:

- Brownfield Redevelopment Financing Act—In July 1996, Governor John Engler signed the Brownfield Redevelopment Financing Act which empowers municipalities to create authorities that are able to develop and implement brownfields redevelopment financing plans (i.e., tax increment financing plans) to capture state and local property taxes from a site of environmental contamination. The taxes that can be recaptured are all state and local property taxes, including taxes levied for school operating purposes, that come form the increased value of an eligible property over a base year (the year the property was added to the brownfield redevelopment financing plan). These captured property taxes can be used to cover the costs of a variety of response activities, including Baseline Environmental Assessments and due care activities required under Michigan's Environmental Remediation Law.

- Cleanup and Redevelopment Fund (CRF)—This fund was established in July 1996, along with several dedicated sources of revenue. The DEQ is authorized to seek an annual appropriation from the CRF in order to conduct cleanup projects at sites of environmental contamination. Addressing sites with serious public health and/or environmental problems is the first priority for use of the CRF. However, after these needs are met, at least 50 percent of the remaining CRF money appropriated each fiscal year will be dedicated to cleanup projects that will promote site redevelopment in urbanized areas.

- Revitalization Revolving Loan Fund and Program— Under this program, also established in July 1996, ERD will provide loans to local governments for site assessments, demolition, and limited response activities to prepare sites for redevelopment. Both known and suspected sites of contamination are eligible for loan-funded activities. The first revolving loans were made available in Summer 1997.

- Site Reclamation Grants—ERD is providing funding to local units of government to investigate and remediate known sites of environmental contamination that will be used for identified economic development. As of Spring 1997, 28 grants totaling over $19 million have been made to 23 Michigan communities.

- Site Assessment Grants—ERD is providing funding to local units of government for environmental investigation of property with redevelopment potential, to make it easier to sell these sites. In 1993, $10 million was made available to eligible Michigan communities. As of Spring 1997, 82 grants totaling nearly $9.6 million had been made to 38 Michigan communities.

Amendments to Michigan's Environmental Cleanup Law

Michigan's primary environmental cleanup law is contained in Part 201 of the Natural Resources and Environmental Protection Act of 1994. Part 201, formerly known as the Michigan Environmental Response Act (MERA), was amended in June 1995 and retitled "Environmental Remediation."[22] The principal objectives of the amendments are to (1) put fairness in the liability scheme by only holding persons who caused the contamination

---

[22]Mich. Stat. Ann. §§ 324.20101 through 324.20142.

responsible for the cleanup;[23] (2) create more flexible cleanup standards; and (3) assist in returning brownfields to productive reuse.

Performance of Baseline Environmental Assessment

Under the new amendments, new purchasers of property, new operators, and lenders who foreclose, have the ability to obtain an exemption from liability for existing contamination through performance and submittal of a Baseline Environmental Assessment (BEA).[24] The purpose of the BEA is to distinguish existing contamination from any releases that might occur after the new owner or operator takes over the property. This "new owner" exemption supplements covenants not to sue (CNTS) for redevelopment.[25] The exemption applies by operation of law; however, persons who want an extra degree of certainty can request that the Michigan Department of Environmental Quality (DEQ) review the BEA and, at the option of the person seeking DEQ review, a plan for property use.[26]

In order to make the BEA process as simple and inexpensive as possible, the DEQ has tied the amount of data required for a BEA to the nature and extent of future hazardous substance use by the new owner. In cases where the new owner will not use hazardous substances, or the use will be different from that which previously occurred at the property, BEAs are easy to perform.[27] A lender that is foreclosing on the property that is idle may do a limited BEA. If operations are to continue on the property after foreclosure, the lender should expand the scope of the BEA as appropriate to the

---

[23]Mich. Stat. Ann. § 324.20126.
[24]Mich. Stat. Ann. § 324.20126(1)(c).
[25]Mich. Stat. Ann. § 324.20133.
[26]Mich. Stat. Ann. § 324.20129a.

hazardous substance use that will occur during its ownership. The party to whom the lender transfers the property can conduct a BEA at the time of transfer.[28] This BEA can have a different scope than the BEA conducted by the lender. The new owner remains liable for contamination caused by its activities[29] and for the exacerbation of existing contamination.[30]

Liability Protections

The new amendments also provide a number of different liability protections. Owners and operators of residential property are exempt from liability for contamination that occurred before their purchase or occupancy provided that hazardous substance use at the property is consistent with residential use.[31] Liability for de minimis contamination is eliminated (i.e., where contaminant concentrations are below residential cleanup standards) by eliminating such property from the definition of "facility."[32] State and local units of government are not liable for contamination caused by a person who leases property from that unit of government, provided that the unit of government is otherwise not liable.[33] Lessees who use property for retail, office, or commercial purposes are not liable, unless they are responsible for an activity causing a release or threat of a release.[34] The amendments also retain liability protection available under the former MERA for a person who acquires contaminated property, but did not know and had no reason to know that the property was contaminated at the

---

[27]Mich. Stat. Ann. § 324.20101(1)(d).
[28]Mich. Stat. Ann. § 324.20126(1)(c).
[29]Mich. Stat. Ann. § 324.20126(2).
[30]Mich. Stat. Ann. § 324.20107a(2).
[31]Mich. Stat. Ann. § 324.20126(3)(f).
[32]Mich. Stat. Ann. § 324.20101(1)(l).
[33]Mich. Stat. Ann. § 324.20126(3)(e).
[34]Mich. Stat. Ann. § 324.20126(3)(j).

time of acquisition.[35] The amended law also retains the liability protection afforded governmental units that acquire contaminated property involuntarily,[36] lenders who do not participate in the management of a facility,[37] and fiduciaries.[38] The protections afforded commercial lending institutions under the former MERA are expanded to all persons who loan money for the purchase or improvement of real property, or who hold a reversionary or security interest.[39]

Land Use-Based Cleanup Standards

New, flexible, and clear cleanup standards, based on reasonable risk assumptions, give developers and other performing remediation the option to propose solutions to contamination based on future use of the property and affected resources. Exposure assumptions used to calculate cleanup criteria account for the differences in potential exposure to contamination that results from difference in land use.[40] The categories for cleanup criteria are residential, commercial, industrial, and recreational.[41] In addition, under the new amendments, new owners do not need to completely remediate all on-site contamination before they can put brownfield properties back into productive use. They now only need to perform "due care" activities—response actions necessary to ensure that their employees and customers can use the property

---

[35]Mich. Stat. Ann. § 324.20126(3)(h).
[36]Mich. Stat. Ann. § 324.20126(3)(a).
[37]Mich. Stat. Ann. § 324.20101(1)(a).
[38]Mich. Stat. Ann. § 324.20101(1)(b).
[39]Mich. Stat. Ann. § 324.20101(1)(s).
[40]Mich. Stat. Ann. § 324.20120a.
[41]Mich. Stat. Ann. § 324.20120a(1)(a)-(e).

safely, ensure that their activities do not make the contamination worse, and protect against foreseeable actions of third parties.[42]

Montana's Voluntary Cleanup Program

In 1995, the Montana legislature amended its Comprehensive Environmental Cleanup and Responsibility Act (CECRA)[43] with enactment of the Voluntary Cleanup and Redevelopment Act (VCRA),[44] which creates a program to encourage parties to voluntarily perform cleanup of contaminated properties. The Voluntary Cleanup Program specifies application requirements, voluntary cleanup plan requirements, agency review criteria and time frames, and conditions and contents of no further action letters.

Any party, including a site owner, operator, or prospective purchaser, may apply for participation in the Voluntary Cleanup Program by submitting a voluntary cleanup program to the Montana Department of Environmental Quality (DEQ). The plan must include: (1) an environmental assessment of the property; (2) a remediation proposal; and (3) the written consent of current owners of the property to both implementation of the voluntary cleanup plan and access to the property by the applicant and its agents and the DEQ. The applicant is also required to reimburse DEQ for any cost that the state incurs during the review and oversight of the voluntary cleanup effort.

Various incentives are provided to parties who voluntarily perform cleanup. Liability protection is provided to entities that would otherwise not be responsible for the site cleanup. Cleanup

---

[42]Mich. Stat. Ann. § 324.20107a.
[43]Mont. Code Ann. §§ 75-10-701 through 75-10-725.
[44]Mont. Code Ann. §§ 75-10-730 through 75-10-738.

can occur on an entire site or a portion of the site. DEQ cannot take enforcement action against any party conducting an approved voluntary cleanup. The DEQ review process is streamlined; DEQ has 30 days to determine if a voluntary cleanup plan is complete. When the DEQ determines that an application is complete, it must decide within 60 days whether to approve or disapprove of the application; this 60 days includes a 30-day public comment period. DEQ's decision is based on the proposed uses of the property identified by the applicant and a risk assessment conducted by the applicant, if necessary. Once a plan has been successfully implemented and DEQ costs have been paid, the applicant can petition the DEQ for closure. DEQ must determine whether closure conditions are met within 60 days of the petition and, if so, the DEQ will issue a no further action letter for the property or portion of the property addressed by the voluntary cleanup.

As of December 1996, the DEQ had approved eight voluntary cleanup plans for mining, manufactured gas, wood treatment, dry cleaning, salvage, and automotive repair facilities. Applicants had also expressed interest in voluntary cleanups at 13 other facilities.

New Hampshire's Brownfields Program

In July 1996, New Hampshire joined a host of other states by enacting brownfields legislation designed to encourage voluntary cleanup and redevelopment of contaminated properties.[45] New Hampshire's Brownfields Program is designed to provide incentives for both environmental cleanup and redevelopment of contaminated properties by parties who did not cause the contamination. This is accomplished under a process by which eligible parties can obtain a "Covenant Not to Sue" from the New

---

[45]N.H. Rev. Stat. Ann. § 147-F, effective July 1, 1996.

Hampshire Department of Justice (DOJ) and a "Certificate of Completion" from the New Hampshire Department of Environmental Services (DES) when investigation and cleanups are performed in accordance with DES cleanup requirements.

Eligibility Criteria

Essentially, any person who did not cause the existing contamination of the property is eligible for participation in the program. This may include:

1. Prospective purchasers;

2. Current property owners if they did not cause or contribute to the contamination;

3. Secured creditors or mortgage holders; or

4. Municipalities owed real estate taxes on the property.

Any property contaminated with hazardous waste, hazardous materials, or oil is eligible for the program, *unless:*

1. There is non-compliance with an environmental or corrective action order and DES determines that the property will not be brought into substantial compliance as a result of participation in the Brownfields Program; or

2. The property is eligible for substantial reimbursement from one of the state petroleum discharge reimbursement funds (the Oil Discharge and Disposal Cleanup Fund, the Fuel Oil Discharge Cleanup Fund, or the Motor Oil Discharge Cleanup Fund) toward the total costs of cleanup. If, however, cleanup costs for a petroleum-contaminated site exceed petroleum reimbursement fund coverage limits, the site may then be eligible for participation in the Brownfields Program.

Eligibility Determination

To apply for an eligibility determination, the applicant must submit the following information:

- A signed, complete application form (provided on request by DES).

- All supporting information required as part of the application package.

- An environmental site assessment report. This may also include submittal of an initial characterization report or site investigation and/or remedial action plan for sites that are further along on the investigation and cleanup process.

- A non-refundable application fee of $500.00.

After receipt of an application package, DES will provide a completeness determination within ten days and, if the application package is complete, a written notice of eligibility determination within 30 days.

Liability Protection

The New Hampshire program contains the following specific liability protections of benefit to eligible parties:

- An eligible person is not liable for the remediation of additional contamination or increased environmental harm caused by preremedial or site investigation activities, unless attributable to negligence or reckless conduct by the eligible person.

- If the eligible person cannot complete the site cleanup, the "Covenant Not to Sue" provides protection from liability as long as the site is stabilized to the satisfaction of DES and the site is not left in worse condition than it was before the cleanup was started.

- The "Covenant Not to Sue" is transferable to other eligible parties. The conditions for transfer to new persons may vary depending on the status of site cleanup at the time of transfer.

- Both the "Covenant Not to Sue" and the "Certificate of Completion" are recorded in the county registry of deeds to permanently document the extent of these protections.

It is important to note that these liability protections extend only to actual or potential liabilities arising under state law. The New Hampshire Brownfields Program does not relieve parties from compliance with other applicable state, federal, and local laws and regulations. Still, the EPA has recently implemented several policies which provide liability relief under certain circumstances and guidelines under which the EPA will issue "comfort letters" for EPA-listed sites.[46] If federal liability issues are a concern for a brownfield site, DES will provide guidance and assistance upon request.

Remedial Action and Certificate of Completion

The eligible party may submit a workplan for additional site investigation with an initial non-refundable program participation fee of $3,000. The total fees paid to the State will vary depending on the complexity of the site and the amount of DES time required to review and approve reports; however, in most cases, the fees are not expected to exceed the initial program participation fee.

---

[46]*See* Chapter 1 for discussion of EPA comfort/status letters. Copies of sample comfort/status letters are reproduced in Appendix D.

After DES approves a work plan, the eligible person will perform the necessary investigations and data analysis. After review of the investigation reports or at any other stage in this process, if DES concludes that cleanup goals have been fully attained, DES will issue a "Certificate of No Further Action" and close the site. If the reports confirm site contamination, the eligible person must develop a remedial action plan (RAP), which describes the proposed actions to clean up the site and submit the RAP to DES for approval. Upon RAP approval, DES will issue a "Notice of Approved Remedial Action Plan" and the DOJ will issue a "Covenant Not to Sue" to the eligible person, each of which may contain conditions relative to the required actions at the site. The "Notice of Approved RAP" must be recorded in the registry of deeds by the eligible party. Upon completion of active site cleanup and DES approval of a completion report prepared by the eligible party, DES will issue a "Certificate if Completion." Depending on the site, the "Certificate of Completion" may include conditions such as use restrictions, environmental monitoring requirements, and routine site maintenance requirements. When received by the eligible party, the "Certificate of Completion" and the related "Covenant Not to Sue" will also be recorded in the county registry of deeds.

New Jersey's Voluntary Cleanup Program

The New Jersey Department of Environmental Protection (DEP) has developed a Voluntary Cleanup Program to help private parties cleanup and reuse brownfields sites. Under the program, a party conducting the cleanup enters into a nonbinding Memorandum of Agreement (MOA) with the DEP to establish the scope and schedule of remedial activities. These actions range from a basic preliminary assessment and site investigation to determine if contamination exists at a site to remedial actions necessary to clean up the site. Under the MOA, the party conducting the cleanup agrees to pay the DEP's oversight costs for the opportunity to have a DEP Case Manager review site assessment and cleanup results quickly and to provide written opinions and recommendations with regard to the findings presented. Oversight costs may be between $1,500 and $10,000 depending upon the amount of material that has to be reviewed and the number of site visits that have to be made. Once the cleanup of identified areas is completed to the satisfaction of the DEP, a No Further Action letter is issued. Unlike other state Voluntary Cleanup Programs, New Jersey's program does not offer a covenant not to sue in addition to a No Further Action letter.

This program provides flexibility to private parties to conduct site remediation at their own schedule. Previously, remedial work was performed under Administrative Consent Orders that included timelines and stipulated penalties if work was not completed on schedule. The DEP has been using MOAs since 1992, except for cases of immediate environmental concern, to facilitate brownfields reuse. Because this is a "voluntary" program, the participant can terminate the MOA at its convenience even if areas of environmental concern are not remediated, as long as they do not pose an immediate health risk. Consequently, should a deal fall through, a participant can terminate the MOA without having to complete the cleanup.

Liability Protection

Local government entities that acquire property through foreclosure, condemnation or similar means are not liable for past contamination under New Jersey's primary hazardous waste cleanup law, the New Jersey Spill Compensation and Control

Act.[47] This recent provision to the Spill Act encourages local governments to take title to abandoned brownfields sites and then conduct preliminary assessments (PAs), site investigations (SIs), and remedial investigations (RIs). With this information, municipal or county governments are better able to market such properties for reuse. Lending institutions also have been freed of liability for contamination when providing financial support to brownfields redevelopment projects. Developers of property in qualified municipalities are also offered liability protection for third party costs if they did not cause the past contamination and they have cleaned up the site to DEP standards. The DEP has also requested that the U.S. EPA recognize that a state-approved cleanup meets federal cleanup standards, thus eliminating the fear of future enforcement action by the EPA.

Remediation Loans and Grants

Municipalities may apply for grants and loans up to $2 million per year for investigations and cleanup activities from the state's Hazardous Site Discharge Remediation Fund. The New Jersey Economic Development Authority (EDA) plays a key role in financing these grants and loans, working with the DEP to cover eligible costs and provide loan servicing. Grants are specifically provided to municipalities for a preliminary assessment (PA), site investigation (SI), and remedial investigation (RI) when a municipality holds a tax sale certificate on a property or has acquired a property through foreclosure or similar means. Loans can be used for remedial cleanup action and the loans are provided at a reduced interest rate. Municipalities may also obtain loans for a PA, SI, and RI when they are responsible parties. Using data obtained from these activities, local officials can develop accurate

---

[47]N.J. Stat. Ann. § 58:10-23.11.

cost estimates of any cleanup work required at a site, thereby improving the marketability of the property.

Private parties required to perform remedial activities and individuals who want to conduct such actions voluntarily may qualify for loans of up to $1 million per year if they are unable to obtain private funding. As of June 1996, the DEP and EDA had approved $17 million in loans and $11 million in grants. These monies come from a $55 million fund created when the state legislature supported this effort by dedicating an unused portion of a state Hazardous Waste Bond issue and a portion of New Jersey's Economic Recovery Fund. These monies have funded 82 grants and loans to municipalities and 54 grants and loans to businesses since the program began.

Tax Abatement

In 1996, the New Jersey legislature passed the Environmental Opportunity Zone Act,[48] which authorizes municipalities to offer up to ten years of property tax savings. Tax increases may not exceed 10 percent annually, and the value attributable to the improvements is not taxed at all during the first year. By the tenth year, the property is assessed at its true market value.

New York's Brownfields Programs

New York has two programs designed to facilitate redevelopment of brownfields. The first program, called the Voluntary Cleanup Program was designed for volunteers to step forward to investigate and cleanup sites. The second program, the Environmental Restoration Projects (Brownfields) Program was

---

[48]N.J. Rev. Stat. § 54:4-3.150 *et seq.*

created with New York's Clean Water/Clean Air Bond Act of 1996. This program was designed to provide financial assistance to municipalities to clean up brownfield sites.

Voluntary Cleanup Program

New York State's Voluntary Cleanup Program covers any contaminated property located in the state for which the federal government does not have lead responsibility for the remediation. Any person, other than a potentially responsible party, may participate in the program and voluntarily clean up eligible properties. The volunteer executes a commitment document with the DEC which, at the volunteer's choice, may be either a consent order or an agreement. The volunteer and the DEC execute the agreement, which will include a workplan for the site. In the commitment document, the volunteer commits to perform investigation only, remediation only, or a combination of investigation and remediation. The volunteer also commits to reimburse the DEC's oversight costs. On-site cleanup must render the property safe for human health and the environment given the contemplated use. If there is any off-site migration of contamination, the volunteer is only obligated to remove the on-site source of the contamination. In addition, the DEC will impose institutional controls, if necessary, and the volunteer cannot challenge them or their enforcement.

Once approved cleanup standards have been met, the DEC issues a letter declaring that the DEC agrees that the volunteer has cleaned the site to the agreed-upon cleanup level and that, barring an event triggering a reopener, the DEC does not contemplate the need for further action at the site. The DEC will also release the volunteer from liability for further remediation of past contamination, also subject to certain reopeners.

Environmental Restoration Projects Program

The New York Clean Water/Clean Air Bond Act of 1996 was passed by the state legislature in July 1996. The $1.75 billion Bond Act provides funding for a variety of programs, including clean water projects, safe drinking water projects, solid waste initiatives, air quality projects, and brownfields restoration projects. Passage of the Bond Act established a $200 million fund for brownfields restoration projects. Known as the Brownfield Program, the fund will provide grants to municipalities for the investigation and/or cleanup if municipally owned contaminated properties. These properties may then be marketed for redevelopment by the municipality or used by the municipality for a variety uses, including industrial, commercial, or public use. The program is administered by the New York Department of Environmental Conservation (DEC). The Brownfield Program will provide reimbursement of up to 75 percent of the eligible costs for the investigation of a brownfield property. The DEC issued a *Brownfield Program Procedures Handbook* in July 1997 to assist municipalities in applying for grant funding under the program to investigate properties that are either contaminated or suspected of being contaminated. A municipality is eligible for financial assistance under the Brownfield Program provided the following criteria are met:

1. The municipality will own the subject property prior to approval of state assistance. The municipality does not have to own the property at the time of application, nor at the time of DEC approval of the application. However, the municipality must have ownership before execution of the State Assistance Contract.

2. The project's purpose is to investigate hazardous substances located on the property.

3. The municipality has not generated, transported, or disposed of, nor arranged for disposal of hazardous substances on the property; and has not undertaken any indemnification obligation respecting a party responsible under law for the remediation of the property.

4. The property is not a Class 1 or Class 2 site listed on the New York State Registry of Inactive Hazardous Waste Disposal Sites at the time of application.

5. The applicant must demonstrate, at a minimum, that the project is intended to result in a benefit to the environment and in either an economic benefit to the state or a public recreational use of the property.

The municipality must enter into a State Assistance Contract with the state, in which, among other things, the municipality agrees to initiate field work within 12 months of the DEC's written approval of its application and that it will complete the project in accordance with DEC-approved plans and schedules. A municipality that receives an investigation grant receives liability protection regarding the contamination at the site.

Ohio's Voluntary Action Program

In June 1994, Ohio enacted the Ohio Real Estate Reuse and Cleanup Law.[49] This legislation sets up a Voluntary Action Program (VCP) to allow cleanups to proceed without intense government oversight and, if done correctly, would release the owner from further liability. Sites that are covered under RCRA's underground storage tank regulations, are on the CERCLA National Priorities List, or are under enforcement action by the

---

[49]Ohio Rev. Code. § 3746.26.

state are not eligible for the program. The major provisions of this legislation include:

- *Established cleanup standards.* Ohio EPA will develop protective standards designed to suit the intended use of the industrial property. Cleanups for residential use would have tougher standards than for industrial use.

- *Liability immunity for lenders, trustees, local governments, and contractors.* Lenders and trustees holding a security interest in contaminated property are released from environmental liability. Liability is also limited for local governments and contractors involved in voluntary cleanups. This protection is expected to free up necessary funding and encourage contractors and local governments to take part in cleanup projects.

- *Covenant not to sue for volunteers.* A volunteer who complies with all program requirements and certifies that the property has been cleaned to acceptable standards will be released from liability. The Ohio EPA will issue a covenant not to sue that protects the volunteer from state civil liability associated with the cleanup. Ohio EPA may deny a covenant if incomplete information is submitted. Covenants must be filed with county deed recorders, and deed restrictions will ensure that properties cleaned up to an industrial or commercial level will not be used for a residential purpose unless additional cleanup work is performed. Covenants may be revoked if applicable standards are not met and the volunteer does not adhere to a compliance schedule.

- *Certification and auditing.* Ohio EPA will certify consultants and laboratories that want to do business with property owners who are performing voluntary cleanups.

Anyone participating in a voluntary cleanup would have to use the services of Ohio EPA-certified professionals. The agency is also given the right and responsibility to audit laboratories, records of certified professionals, and cleanup sites to make sure that they are conforming to specific standards.

- *Property Revitalization Board.* The law establishes a Property Revitalization Board made up of directors from various state agencies to serve as a clearinghouse for information on economic and financial incentives available to persons undertaking voluntary cleanup actions. The board also reviews cleanup proposals from property owners who cannot remediate the property to cleanup standards due to extreme financial or technological hardship.

- *Cost Recovery.* The law allows property owners to recover cleanup costs from other parties that contributed to the contamination at the site.

- *Consolidated permitting.* The law streamlines the permitting process by requiring only one permit that encompasses all environmental protection requirements, thus simplifying and speeding up cleanup efforts.

- *Tax Abatement.* Upon issuance of a covenant not to sue from the Ohio EPA, the Department of Taxation will grant VAP participants a tax exemption for cleanup of the contaminated property. The exemption, which is issued by an order of the tax commissioner, gives the participant a tax abatement for 10 years on the increase in the assessed value of property after cleanup and the increase in the assessed value of improvements, buildings, fixtures, and structures that exist at the time the tax abatement order is granted.[50]

Financial Assistance for VAP Remediations

In an effort to further promote participation in the VAP, the Ohio EPA, Ohio Water Development Authority, Ohio Department of Development, and the Ohio Department of Taxation offer a number of financial assistance programs to facilitate financing of brownfields redevelopment projects.

Water Pollution Control Loan Fund (WPCLF)

In order to encourage participation in the VAP and to assist participants in improving Ohio's water resources, the Ohio Water Pollution Control Loan Fund (WPCLF) can provide low interest financing for some activities associated with voluntary cleanups. Any activity performed under the VAP rules and guidelines that will result in water quality benefits to surface and/or groundwater is eligible for WPCLF financing. This can include Phase I and Phase II activities, such as literature searches, evaluation studies, sampling, monitoring, laboratory tests, as well as the actual cleanup itself. The WPCLF will provide up to a total of $3 million to a project for these eligible activities.

Anyone taking responsibility for the cleanup of an eligible property under the VAP may apply for WPCLF assistance. This can include individuals, businesses, and political subdivisions. Long-term loans can be repaid over a period of 20 years, with principal payments reduced for up to three years. The interest rate is indexed at 175 basis points below the 20-year Bond Buyer

---

[50]Ohio Rev. Code. § 5709.87.

General Obligation Bond Index and is adjusted every April 1 and October 1. A 3.2 percent rate is available for short-term loans of up to five years. Other terms and conditions can be negotiated based on the specific project and needs of the recipient. Loans are awarded based on a review of the proposed project, including the water quality benefits and environmental impacts. The Ohio EPA also reviews the source of repayment, including the nature and amount of collateral as applicable.

Pollution Prevention Loan Program

The Ohio Office of Pollution Prevention (OPP) works with companies and other Ohio EPA divisions on a voluntary, nonregulatory basis to help companies modify operating processes to generate less pollution in a cost-effective and technically feasible manner. The OPP, working in conjunction with the Ohio Department of Development (ODOD), offers low-interest loans (two-thirds of the current prime rate as quoted in the Wall Street Journal) from $25,000 to $350,000 to businesses and facilities with less than 500 on-site employees to incorporate pollution prevention techniques. The technical review is performed by the OPP with the subsequent financial review performed by the ODOD.

Ohio Water Development Authority Loan Program

Financial assistance is available from the Ohio Water Development Authority (OWDA) for the remediation of property owned either publicly or privately, and the eligible borrowers may be either local governments or private businesses. For loans to local governments that are undertaking brownfield remediation projects for land that ultimately will be used for a public purpose, the OWDA offers planning and construction loans at a market rate of interest. Local governments interested in obtaining such a loan should identify potential revenue sources that will be used to repay the loans.

Private entities (i.e., individual proprietors or private partnerships or corporations) seeking financial assistance for brownfield remediation projects may be eligible for loans from the OWDA. The provision of direct financial assistance to a private entity for a brownfield remediation project will require, among other things, documentation that a VAP-certified engineer is directing the remediation effort, an analysis of the financial strength of the borrower, a real estate appraisal, an evaluation of the potential effectiveness of the remediation project and a tailoring of terms and conditions for each loan.

The OWDA does not possess all of the necessary resources or expertise to evaluate private borrowers and their respective projects for financial assistance. Recognizing that private financial institutions tend to have these resources and this expertise, the OWDA's goal is to play a more effective role by utilizing its financial resources to attract and facilitate involvement by private lenders. Towards this end, OWDA seeks to stimulate and encourage the commercial and real estate banking community and public finance bankers to take the lead in providing financial assistance to private entities that undertake brownfields remediation projects. OWDA intends to offer various forms of credit enhancement or financial assistance to help induce private financial institutions to provide the financing that private businesses may require for brownfields remediation projects.

Brownfield Site Cleanup Tax Credit Program

The Brownfield Site Cleanup Tax Credit Program may provide a taxpayer with a state franchise or income tax credit for the voluntary remediation of a contaminated site in Ohio. The Director of the Ohio Department of Development (ODOD) will determine whether a Brownfield Site Cleanup Tax Credit is appropriate. The nonrefundable credit will be based on a percentage of the eligible cost of remediation, including the costs of Phase I and Phase II property assessments incurred during the period July 1, 1996 through June 30, 1999. The level of tax credit is 10 percent of eligible costs or $500,000, whichever is less. In designated eligible areas of the state, the level of the tax credit is 15 percent of the eligible costs or $750,000, whichever is less. This tax credit is only available to those companies who have participated in the VAP and have received a covenant not to sue from the Ohio EPA. Many types of taxpayers, including Corporations, S-Corporations, Limited Liability Companies, Partnerships, and Sole Proprietorships are eligible for the tax credit.

Brownfield Grant Assistance Program

The Brownfield Grant Assistance Program assists nonprofit development organizations located within a "distressed community." This program is administered by the ODOD, Office of Business Development. Eligibility for the program requires that participants have first obtained a covenant not to sue from the Ohio EPA. The maximum level of grant funding is $500,000 and there must be a local match of at least 25 percent. All grant recipients must file annual progress reports over a five-year monitoring period. Use of funds include land acquisition, infrastructure improvements, and the renovation of existing buildings.

Competitive Economic Development Program

The Economic Development Program in the Office of Housing and Community Partnerships (OHCP) offers grants to nonentitlement counties and cities to assist in the expansion and retention of business and industry in Ohio, which create and retain permanent private sector job opportunities, principally for low- and moderate-income persons. The funds may be used by a business in the form of a loan for brownfield remediation if full-time permanent jobs will be created and/or retained. The terms of the loans vary from project to project with a maximum loan of $500,000. The economic development program receives its funds from the U.S. Department of Housing and Urban Development Community Block Grant program.

Oklahoma's Brownfields Program

Effective June 14, 1996, the Oklahoma legislature enacted the Oklahoma Brownfields Voluntary Redevelopment Act[51] to: (1) provide for the establishment of a voluntary cleanup program by the Oklahoma Department of Environmental Quality (DEQ), (2) foster voluntary redevelopment and reuse of brownfields by limiting the liability of property owners, lenders, and lessees, and (3) to provide a risk-based system for all brownfield sites based on the proposed use of the site. In January 1997, the DEQ adopted regulations for implementation of the brownfields program.[52] The DEQ regulations establish standardized procedures for applicants who desire to voluntarily remediate abandoned, idled, or underused contaminated industrial and commercial properties and receive

---

[51]Okla. Stat. tit. 27A, §§ 2-15-101 through 2-15-110 (Brownfields Voluntary Redevelopment Act).
[52]Okla. Reg. tit. 252, §§ 220-1-1 through 220-7-3 (Department of Environmental Quality's Brownfield Rules).

liability protection by entering into an agreement with the DEQ and completing an approved workplan. The DEQ's brownfields program also provides standardized procedures for applicants who desire to obtain "no action necessary" determinations for properties where contamination does not pose an unreasonable risk to human health or the environment, given the proposed use of the property.

In order to participate in the DEQ's brownfields program, the applicant must submit an application to the DEQ for a consent order for risk-based remediation of a brownfield site or for a no action necessary determination. The application must set forth sufficient information for the DEQ to assess whether the applicant is eligible to apply for liability protection under the brownfields program, including the following:

1. A description of the brownfields site, including concentrations of contaminants in the soils, surface water, or groundwater; air releases that may occur during remediation; and any monitoring that is to occur after issuance of the Certificate of Completion or Certificate of No Action Necessary.

2. A remediation plan or a proposal that no action is necessary to remediate the brownfield considering the presented levels of regulated substances at the site and the proposes future use of the property.

3. The current and proposed use of groundwater on or near the site.

4. The operational history of the site and the current use of areas contiguous to the site.

5. The present and proposed uses of the site.

6. Information concerning the nature and extent of any contamination at the site and any possible impacts on areas contiguous to the site.

7. Analytical results from a laboratory certified by the DEQ or other data that characterizes the soil, groundwater or surface water on the site.

8. An analysis of the human and environmental pathways to exposure from contamination at the site based on the property's proposed future use.

If the DEQ determines, based on the information in the application, that the applicant is eligible for the program, the applicant and the DEQ enter into a Memorandum of Agreement (MOA). Under the MOA, the applicant agrees to develop a site characterization plan and pay for the DEQ's oversight costs. The applicant must submit a workplan, a quality assurance plan, a sampling and analysis plan, and a health and safety plan for site characterization. The DEQ may make a no further action determination if the application indicates that the existence of contamination, given the proposed use of the property, does not pose an unreasonable risk to human health or the environment. If no remediation is deemed necessary, the DEQ must issue a Certificate of No Action Necessary. If a site cleanup plan is necessary, the applicant and the DEQ must execute a Consent Order for the site remediation, including site-specific risk-based cleanup levels. If the DEQ determines that the applicant has successfully completed the requirements of the consent order, it must certify the completion by issuing a Certificate of Completion. Both the Certificate or No Action Necessary and the Certificate of Completion provide liability assurance that the DEQ will not pursue any administrative or civil action against the applicant, lenders, lessees, and successors and assigns associated with the contamination at the site.

Oregon's Voluntary Cleanup Program

Oregon developed its Voluntary Cleanup Program (VCP) in 1991 to provide an avenue for owners and operators of contaminated property to investigate and clean up their sites with oversight by the Oregon Department of Environmental Quality (DEQ). Through environmental cleanup, the VCP facilitates the use, sale, financing, and development of contaminated properties and brownfields. The VCP is flexible, enabling cleanups to be completed in a manner that meets the needs of a site owner, operator, prospective purchaser, or developer. The VCP provides a framework for participants to obtain technical and regulatory assistance and DEQ approval of investigation and cleanup activities.

Any site is eligible; however, sites that are subject to federal action, such as CERCLA National Priority List sites and sites covered by RCRA, are usually excluded from the program. Sites can be divided into separate manageable units to allow development to occur on a portion of a site or to keep larger projects focused and cost-effective. If the site only needs soil cleanup, Oregon's numeric soil cleanup standards may be used to set cleanup levels.

The first step in the VCP is for the participant and the DEQ to sign a letter of agreement that covers liability issues and indemnification, and obligates the participant to pay DEQ's oversight costs. Either party can terminate the agreement upon 15 days written notice. For complex sites that require more extensive remedial action, a more formal agreement is executed, which includes a negotiated scope of work plan for the project. Upon final approval of the remedial action, a Record of Decision (ROD) is prepared. If the cleanup follows the ROD and the approved action is successful, the DEQ issues a No Further Action letter. The No Further Action letter documents that the DEQ will take no further action against the participant if the remedy is successful and all information received by the DEQ is correct.

Prospective Purchaser Agreements

The VCP can also work with potential purchasers of contaminated property through Prospective Purchaser Agreements (PPAs) to provide for site cleanup while offering liability protection. A prospective purchaser can be an individual, business, government agency, or any other entity with the interest and ability to purchase contaminated property, where the contamination was neither caused nor aggravated by the prospective purchaser. PPAs must be negotiated and finalized before the property is purchased. The basic requirements for eligibility for PPAs are:

1. The prospective purchaser is not responsible for cleanup of the contamination of the property;

2. The law requires that the contamination be cleaned up;

3. The prospective purchaser's proposed use for the property will not make the contamination worse or interfere with necessary cleanup; and

4. A substantial public benefit will result from the agreement.

Of the four criteria, determining whether a prospective purchaser proposal will result in "substantial" public benefit is a key consideration in the DEQ's decision to approve or deny an application for a PPA. Substantial public benefits include:

- Generation of substantial funding or other resources facilitating remedial measures at the property.

- Commitment to perform substantial remedial measures at the property.

- Productive reuse of a vacant or abandoned industrial or commercial facility.

- Development of the property by a government entity or nonprofit organization to address important public purpose.

Substantial public benefit is determined on a case-by-case basis. Other substantial public benefits may be proposed by the prospective purchaser and the DEQ encourages creative and innovative approaches.

The prospective purchaser completes the Prospective Purchaser Application form and submits a $2,500 deposit to the DEQ to begin formal negotiation of the PPA.[53] During negotiations with DEQ staff, the prospective purchaser shares technical information about the contamination of the property and strives to reach an agreement that meets the needs of the prospective purchaser and the state. If the prospective purchaser agrees to conduct cleanup actions at the property, the cleanup must be undertaken through the VCP. When the PPA is completed, or the negotiations cease, any balance remaining from the $2,500 deposit is refunded.

A PPA may be an administrative consent order or other administrative agreement or a judicial consent decree. Agreements must be recorded in the real property records of the county where the property is located. Following satisfactory performance of its obligations under the PPA, the prospective purchaser is released from liability for any release of hazardous substances at the site

---

[53]To obtain a program package, call the Prospective Purchaser Program Coordinator at (800) 452-4011.

existing on the property as of the date of acquisition of the property.

Pennsylvania's Land Recycling Program

On May 19, 1995, the Pennsylvania legislature enacted the Land Recycling and Environmental Remediation Standards Act,[54] which provides for the recycling of existing industrial and commercial sites, further defines the cleanup liability of new industries and tenants, establishes a framework for setting environmental remediations standards, sets up the Voluntary Cleanup Loan Fund, the Industrial Land Recycling Fund, and the Industrial Sites Cleanup Fund to aid industrial site cleanups. The Land Recycling Program promotes voluntary participation among local businesses, government, financial institutions, and Pennsylvania Department of Environmental Protection (DEP) to effectively restore contaminated properties to safe and productive uses. While making these sites safe for communities and workers, the Land Recycling Program also promotes the addition of jobs and economic stimulus to distressed communities and the preservation of farmland and greenspace. The four cornerstones of the Land Recycling Program are uniform cleanup based on health and environmental risks, standardized review procedures, releases from liability, and financial assistance.

Uniform Cleanup Standards

The Land Recycling Program establishes environmental remediation standards to provide a uniform framework for cleanups. Land Recyclers have a choice of three types of cleanup standards: background standards, statewide standards, and site-

---

[54]35 Pa. Stat. §§ 6026.101 through 6026.908.

specific standards. Special industrial area standards are also available for certain sites and certain program participants.

- Background standards—restores a site to its condition before contamination occurred.

- Statewide health standards—regulations establish statewide health standards for contaminants for each environmental medium.

- Site-Specific standards—involves a detailed process for developing a risk assessment based on the conditions and exposures at the site.

Standardized Review Procedures

The Land Recycling and Environmental Remediation Standards Act describes the submission and review procedures to be used at sites using each of the three types of cleanup standards, thus providing a uniform process for all sites statewide. Uniformity will make it easier for companies and consultants to prepare submissions and follow through the steps necessary to complete remediation of a site.

Releases from Liability

Owners and developers of a site that has been remediated according to required standards and procedures receive a release from liability. The Economic Development Agency, Fiduciary and Lender Environmental Liability Protection Act further extends liability protection to financiers, such as economic development agencies, lenders, and fiduciaries. These provisions are intended to reduce the liability concerns that may inhibit involvement with contaminated and abandoned sites.

Financial Assistance

The Land Recycling and Environmental Remediation Standards Act also established the Industrial Sites Cleanup Fund to help innocent parties conduct voluntary cleanups. Grants or low-interest loans can cover up to 75 percent of the cost of completing an environmental study and implementing a cleanup plan. Eligible applicants for grants include political subdivisions, and local economic development agencies that have ownership of the site and are overseeing the cleanup. Eligible applicants for loans include local economic development agencies, political subdivisions, and others determined to be eligible by the state Department of Commerce. In addition, the Industrial Sites Environmental Assessment Act established the Industrial Sites Environmental Assessment Fund, which authorizes the Department of Commerce to make grants to municipalities, nonprofit economic development agencies, and other public agencies. The grants are to finance environmental assessments of industrial sites located in municipalities that have been designated as distressed communities by the Department of Commerce. Up to $2 million will be transferred annually to this fund from the state's Hazardous Sites Cleanup Fund.

Texas Voluntary Cleanup Program

In 1995, the Texas legislature enacted the Texas Voluntary Cleanup Law[55] to provide incentives for cleanup of thousands of contaminated properties necessary to complete real estate transactions by removing liability of future landowners and lenders and by providing a process to facilitate completion of voluntary response actions in a timely and efficient manner. Pursuant to the

---

[55]Tex. Health & Safety Code Ann. §§ 361.601 through 361.613.

new law, the Voluntary Cleanup Program (VCP) was established as part of the Pollution Cleanup Division of the Texas Natural Resource Conservation Commission (TNRCC). The TNRCC adopted final rules for implementation of the VCP on March 27, 1996.[56]

The VCP addresses sites that represent a real or perceived threat to public health and the environment through contaminated soil, groundwater or surface water, and air. By entering into the VCP and successfully cleaning up the property, landowners, lenders, and potential developers can be reasonably confident that they know the nature and extent of any environmental problems on the property. Once the property is successfully remediated, as necessary, the TNRCC issues a Certificate of Completion which is recorded in the county deed registry where the property is located.

The Certificate of Completion releases lenders and future landowners from liability to the state with regard to existing contamination at the site, allowing the sale or transfer of the property where the previous contamination might have otherwise posed a barrier to the sale or transfer of the property. They are also protected in the event that more stringent regulations are passed, which, without the Certificate of Completion, might have required additional cleanup. Also, the TNRCC will not initiate enforcement action against persons fulfilling the terms of the VCP agreement regarding performance of response actions. By becoming an applicant, any person (not just owners and lenders) who is not already a responsible party, may obtain a release of liability upon issuance of the Certificate of Completion.

Virtually any site is eligible for the VCP, provided that it is not subject to a TNRCC order or permit, or under the jurisdiction of the Texas railroad Commission. Additionally, a site may be

---

[56]Tex. Admin. Code tit. 30, §§ 333.1 through 333.11 (Voluntary Cleanup Rules).

rejected from participation in the VCP if the site is subject to any other administrative, state, or federal enforcement action, or where a federal grant requires an enforcement action be taken.

The first step toward participation in the VCP is to obtain and complete the VCP application package. A complete application includes an application form, an environmental site assessment, and an application fee of $1,000. Once the application is received and the site is accepted into the program, the voluntary party then enters into a VCP Agreement with the TNRCC.

The VCP Agreement is a nonbinding agreement between the applicant and the TNRCC that sets forth the terms and conditions of evaluation of the workplans and reports, and commits the applicant to pay the TNRCC's costs. After acceptance into the VCP, a TNRCC project manager contacts the applicant and the agreement negotiations begin. To ensure a complete agreement, the applicant should designate applicable rules and regulations and provide a schedule of activities that will be necessary to achieve a Certificate of Completion for the site. Once all of the terms of the agreement are agreed upon, both the applicant and the TNRCC project manager sign it. Once the agreement is signed, the assigned VCP project manager may begin reviewing and commenting on any work plan and report submittals. Either party may terminate the agreement at any time by giving 15 days written notice. However, without a Certificate of Completion, there is no release of liability.

Vermont's Redevelopment of Contaminated Properties Program

In 1995, Vermont passed legislation to create the Redevelopment of Contaminated Properties (RCP) Program within the Department of Environmental Conservation (DEC).[57] Participation in the program allows a potential purchaser to acquire and clean up property in exchange for liability protection.

Both the applicant and the site to be redeveloped must meet certain eligibility criteria. The applicant cannot be liable under Vermont's hazardous waste liability statute[58] for any release of a hazardous substance at the property and cannot have been previously involved in any way with hazardous waste activities at the property. Applicants that acquire an ownership interest in the property during the period between submittal of an application, acceptance into the program assume the risk of denial. The property must meet at least one of several criteria: (1) vacant; (2) abandoned; (3) substantially underutilized, or (4) to be acquired by a municipality. Ineligible properties are (1) those at which only the release of petroleum has occurred that is subject to the Petroleum Cleanup Fund; (2) any property listed on the National Priorities List of Superfund sites; and (3) facilities undergoing RCRA corrective action.

In order to enter the RCP program, the applicant must pay a $5,000 deposit toward DEC oversight costs and submit an application containing the following information:

- A preliminary environmental assessment

- A certification, under oath and notarized, from each person who would benefit from any protection from liability under the program that:

  - Each person has accurately disclosed all information currently known to the person, or in the person's possession or control, which relates to releases or

---

[57]Vt. Stat. tit. 10, § 6615a.
[58]Vt. Stat. tit. 10, § 6615.

threatened releases of hazardous substances at the property;

- Neither that person nor any of its principals, owners, directors, or affiliates or subsidiaries:

  -- currently holds or ever held, an ownership interest in the property, or in any related fixtures or appurtenances, excluding a secured lender's holding indicia of ownership in the property primarily to assure the repayment of a financial obligation;

  -- directly or indirectly caused or contributed to any releases of hazardous substances at the property;

  -- currently operates, or ever operated or controlled the operation, at the property, of a facility for the storage, treatment, or disposal of hazardous substances from which there was a release;

  -- disposed of, or arranged for disposal of, hazardous substances at the property; or

  -- generated hazardous substances that were disposed of at the property.

- Any information requested by the Secretary of the Agency of Natural Resources regarding the property.

Upon approval of the application, the participant develops a site investigation and corrective action workplan. Upon satisfactory completion of the cleanup, the participant receives a Certificate of Completion from the DEC, which provides protection from state environmental liability. If an participant withdraws from the program after commencement of the site investigation, but prior to receipt of a Certificate of Completion, the participant cannot leave the property in a condition that presents a greater threat to human health and the environment than existed before commencement of the site investigation activities.

Virginia's Voluntary Remediation Program

The Virginia Voluntary Remediation Program (VRP) provides a mechanism for eligible participants to voluntarily enter into a relationship with the Virginia Department of Environmental Quality (DEQ) to clean up properties not clearly mandated for remediation under existing environmental laws. The VRP is intended to encourage cleanup of contamination that might not otherwise take place, and to reduce future liability for owners and lenders. The VRP also serves as a convenient and appropriate vehicle for cleanup of brownfields sites—those sites that have economic redevelopment potential but which currently lie idle because of environmental liability concerns.

The VRP was formally initiated through enactment of Virginia's Voluntary Remediation Act[59] in 1995. The statute required DEQ to develop and administer the VCP on a case-by-case basis until promulgation of regulations scheduled for July 1997. The DEQ published its VCP regulations in the Virginia Register on May 26, 1997.[60] The VCP basically consists of a five-step process to bring a site from entry to completion in the program:

1. First, the DEQ will determine eligibility for the program based on an evaluation of information submitted by the applicant.

---

[59]Va. Code Ann. §§ 10.1-1429.1 through 10.1-1429.3.
[60]13 Va. Regs. Reg. 2234-2244 (May 26, 1997), *to be codified at* Va. Admin. Code §§ 20-160-10 through 20-160-130.

2. Second, the applicant submits a registration fee assessed as one percent of the total cost of remediation at the site, with a maximum fee of $5,000.

3. Third, the participant submits a Voluntary Remediation Report.

4. Fourth, the DEQ must concur with the Voluntary Remediation Report.

5. Fifth, if a participant satisfactorily completes the cleanup, the DEQ will issue a Certification of Satisfactory Completion of Remediation. This certificate provides a release from future DEQ enforcement action regarding the contamination addressed under the VRP.

Any person who owns, operates, has a security interest in, or enters into a contract to purchase or use an eligible site and who wishes to voluntarily remediate the site may participant in the program. Eligible sites are those sites where remediation has not been clearly mandated by the U.S. EPA, the DEQ, or a court pursuant to CERCLA, RCRA, the Virginia Waste Management Act, the Virginia State Waste Control Law, or other applicable statutory or common law; or jurisdiction under any of these statutes has been waived. Sites where an eligible party has completed remediation of a release are potentially eligible for the program if the actions can be documented in a way that are equivalent to the requirements for prospective remediation, and provided they can meet applicable remediation standards. The cleanup goals established for VRP sites are risk-based and include consideration of current and future site use, potential ecological receptors, and institutional and engineering controls.

Remediated Property Fresh Start Program

In 1996, the Virginia legislature amended its Voluntary Remediation Act by adding a new Article entitled "Remediated Property Fresh Start Program" to limit the liability of those who acquire certain remediated properties located in the state.[61] Under this program, any person not otherwise liable under state law or regulation that acquires any title, security interest, or any other interest in property located in the state, following listing on CERCLA's National Priorities List and remediation to the EPA's satisfaction, will not be subject to civil enforcement or remediation action under state law, or to private civil suit, "related to contamination that was the subject of the satisfactory remediation, existing at or immediately contiguous to the property prior to the person acquiring title, security interest, or any other interest in such property." This limitation on liability also extends to subsequent transferees of those who acquire title, security interest, or other interest in the remediated property. However, a holder of title, security interest, or any other interest in remediated property prior to satisfactory remediation are not relieved of liability by reacquisition. Further, there is no limitation on the liability of a person who acquires the property after satisfactory remediation for damage caused by contaminants not included in the remediation.

Washington's Independent Remedial Action Program

Pursuant to the authority of the Washington Model Toxics Control Act,[62] the Washington Department of Ecology has a program that permits private parties to clean up certain

---

[61]Va. Code Ann. § 10.1-1429.4.
[62]Wash. Rev. Code ch. 70.105D.

contaminated sites without government oversight. Independent cleanup actions may not be allowed at sites being negotiated or formally discussed with the Department of Ecology, or if cleanup is currently being addressed under an order or decree.[63]

Under the Independent Remedial Action Program (IRAP),[64] property owners proceed with independent cleanups and then submit an Independent Remedial Action Report to the Department of Ecology within 90 days of the completion of cleanup.[65] The Department then reviews the Report to determine whether the site meets Model Toxics Control Act cleanup standards or requires additional remedial action. If the cleanup is satisfactory, the Department issues a "No Further Action" designation for the site on the state's hazardous waste site tracking system. By designating a site "No Further Action," the Department states that it has no intention of pursuing additional cleanup at the site, but could require more work if contamination at the site threatens human health or the environment at a future date.

Wisconsin's Land Recycling Law

Recognizing that incentives were needed to encourage local governments and private parties to make productive use of contaminated properties, in 1994, the Wisconsin legislature enacted the Land Recycling Law.[66] Under the Contaminated Lands Recycling Program, participants clean up contaminated sites and obtain releases from liability for contamination that occurred prior

---

[63]Wash. Admin. Code § 173-340-510(5).
[64]Wash. Admin. Code § 173-340-300.
[65]*See* Guidance on Preparing Independent Remedial Action Reports Under the Model Toxics Control Act, Chapter70.105D RCW, Pub. No. 94-18 (Wash. Dept. of Ecology, March 1994).
[66]Wis. Stat. § 144.765.

to their acquisition of the property. The Land Recycling Law created the following liability protections:

- Exempts certain purchasers from future liability when the entire property is cleaned up by the purchaser.

- Exempts municipalities from responsibility for remedial action if the property is acquired by the municipality through tax delinquency proceedings or bankruptcy court order if the release of hazardous substances was not caused by some action or failure to take action by the municipality.

- Limits cleanup costs if the purchaser acquired tax delinquent or bankrupt property from the municipality and enters into an agreement with the Wisconsin Department of Natural Resources (DNR).

- Exempts lenders from responsibility to clean up contaminated property that they acquire through foreclosure, provided certain conditions are met.

- Exempts fiduciaries from responsibility to clean up contaminated property that they acquire, if certain conditions are met.

Prospective Purchaser Protections

In order to provide an incentive to a purchaser to acquire, remediate, and return contaminated property to productive use, the Land Recycling Law provides that a purchaser of contaminated land is not responsible for further remedial action on the property and the Department of Justice may not pursue an action under CERCLA against the purchaser, if the property meets designated conditions. These conditions include: (1) conducting a thorough environmental investigation of the property that is approved by the

DNR; (2) remediating the property in accordance with DNR rules and any contract entered into with the DNR pursuant to those rules; (3) obtaining certification from the DNR that the property has been satisfactorily remediated; and (4) maintaining and monitoring the property as required by the DNR. A purchaser may be a governmental body, a corporation, a partnership, association, or an individual. The purchaser's exemption from responsibility for further remedial action continues notwithstanding the occurrence of any of the following:

- future statutes, rules, or regulations that impose greater responsibilities on property owners;

- the purchaser's remediation is not completely successful; or

- the contamination from the hazardous substances that is the subject of the remediation is discovered to be more extensive than anticipated by the purchaser and the DNR.

If the purchaser later decides to sell or transfer the property, the purchaser's successor receives the benefit of the liability protection if the successor maintains the property and, if the purchaser obtained the DNR certification by various fraudulent means, the successor was unaware of the fraud.

The purchaser is not exempted from the requirement to report to the DNR the presence of a hazardous substance on the property. Also, a purchaser is not eligible for the exemption if the purchase is not an arms-length, good faith transaction; the purchaser participated in the management of or owned the business or entity that caused the contamination; the purchaser owned the property when the hazardous substances was released or the purchaser caused the original release of the hazardous substance.

The Land Recycling Law also provides a method by which a purchaser may cease remediation, without further responsibility for remedial action, when the cost of remediation equals 125 percent of the anticipated expense of the remediation. The monetary limit may be used only if an agreement to do so has been entered into by the purchaser and the DNR. This provision only applies to the purchase of property from a municipality that acquired the property through tax delinquency proceedings or a bankruptcy court order. A purchaser that ceases remediation must properly maintain the property and use reasonable efforts to sell the property.

CHAPTER 3

BROWNFIELDS REDEVELOPMENT STRATEGIES

Introduction

Despite the potential environmental risks, the development of brownfields has certain advantages over other properties. For example, an important advantage of brownfields redevelopment is that most of these sites have a useful infrastructure already in place, including access to markets for labor, materials, and final output; access to transportation facilities; access to existing roads, water, sewer, and electric power; and the presence of existing structures. Further, site preparation costs of a brownfields redevelopment project are significantly lower than costs associated with developing raw land.

Redevelopment of a brownfield can be an expensive proposition. However, the potential profits realized from the recycling of a brownfield site may be greater than those available from the development of a "greenfield" (i.e., virgin land or other non-brownfield property). This profit potential is directly attributable to the market stigma attached to brownfields, many of which are in prime locations and may be available at steep discounts from their potential economic values. In addition, many financing strategies are currently being used by state and local governments to encourage developers, lenders, and investors to participate in the redevelopment and revitalization of brownfield properties.

Brownfields Redevelopment Process

The redevelopment of a brownfield should be approached as a step-by-step process. This process can be broken down into several basic stages: site identification, initial site assessment, economic assessment, a detailed site assessment, project development and financing, cleanup planning and execution, and redevelopment of the property. A general overview of each of these stages is presented here.

Site Identification

The first step in the brownfields redevelopment process requires identification of available sites. Private parties or municipalities that own contaminated sites in need of cleanup and reuse should market those properties to potential developers, businesses, and nonprofit organizations. Developers or businesses in need of a site should conduct a search of available properties. State and local governments can assist with site identification by developing and maintaining an inventory of sites, helping developers to identify sites with desirable characteristics, and undertaking marketing activities to promote the site assessment, cleanup, and redevelopment. In the private sector, developers can search for potential sites by using and evaluating these public resources. Initial site identification generally requires a low initial capital cost and low level financing.

Initial Site Assessment or Phase I Investigation

Once a potential site has been identified that suits the location and infrastructure needs of the planned project, an initial site assessment must be conducted to determine whether contamination is present. A number of sources can be reviewed to identify suspected contamination, including existing public records and historical data regarding the site. A full discussion of Phase I environmental site assessments is provided later in this chapter. The initial screening of sites typically involves:

- Examining historical data on past uses of the property and federal and state reports of hazardous substances on the property.

- Researching the chain of title to identify the former owners of the property.

- Researching the zoning history of the property to determine uses that were previously permitted, including records of zoning variances, special use permits, and nonconforming uses.

- Examining similar characteristics of surrounding properties.

- Checking previous environmental site assessments and/or environmental compliance audits for the property.

- Reviewing insurance policies to determine whether coverage was provided for any activities involving hazardous substances.

- Checking the local revenue department to determine whether any hazardous waste fees or taxes were paid.

Initial site assessment activities can usually be performed at moderate cost. It may be advantageous to the project sponsors to seek oversight from the state environmental agency at this stage under the state's voluntary cleanup or brownfields program—which are now in place in most states—and apply for eligibility for financial assistance through available state environmental loan or grant programs.

Economic Assessment

A key distinction must be drawn between sites that are in desirable locations—with the potential for attracting buyers and developers—and sites that have no interested buyers and few potential uses. If there is no potential economic return to outweigh the cost of restoring the site to productive use, no financing strategy will support its redevelopment until conditions have changed. To determine the development potential of a site, an economic assessment should be performed.

As with any investment, the expected return on the brownfields redevelopment project must be commensurate with the risk involved. Thus, it is essential to determine, as accurately as possible, the relationship between the project and the associated risk. Brownfields sites fall across a broad spectrum of economic development, ranging from viable sites, where the expected return on investment is high and the risk of liability is low, to nonviable sites, where the expected return on investment is low and the potential risk of liability is high. Brownfield properties may be categorized along this spectrum of economic development potential as viable sites, threshold sites, and nonviable sites.

- *Viable Sites* are sites that are already economically viable and the private market is already taking steps to redevelop. These sites either have very low potential environmental liability or such high potential rates of return that the advantages clearly outweigh the financial risks. Viable sites should require less or no direct investment of public capital. However, private developers and investors may still need assistance in dealing with the regulatory and liability issues associated with brownfields assessment, cleanup, and redevelopment. Strategies that can enhance private party interest and assist in the redevelopment process include:
  - Timely review by regulators of assessment and cleanup plans and proposals;

- Land use-based cleanup standards that reflect the intended use of the property;

- Liability clarification so that environmental risks can be quantified, and then managed or apportioned; and

- Liability releases following completion of satisfactory cleanup, such as a covenant-not-to-sue or a no-further-action letter.

These strategies can stimulate private sector investment in brownfields assessment, cleanup, and redevelopment while conserving public resources for sites that would not be otherwise commercially viable.

- *Threshold Sites* are sites that are only marginally viable and will not be redeveloped without some type of public assistance. These sites may have fewer economic advantages than viable sites, or may have a higher risk of environmental liability. Threshold sites may have significant potential for assessment, cleanup, and redevelopment, but need some form of public assistance to increase the rate of investment return or to limit liability to a level that will encourage private sector participation. Financing strategies, such as tax abatement and low-interest loans, may be used to enhance private sector interest in cleanup and redevelopment of targeted sites. Further, liability assurances may be given in exchange for private party cleanup, including a covenant-not-to-sue or no-further-action letter.

- *Nonviable Sites* are sites that have a strong potential for environmental liability and/or have minimal economic advantages. These sites either require a substantial amount of public assistance to make redevelopment feasible or, from the standpoint of developers and investors, should be avoided altogether. Nonviable sites often require a significant investment of public capital to attract private brownfields investors and developers. These sites generally involve significant environment risks and must, therefore, be restored to a state that reduces the risk to a level that is low enough to spark interest by private investors. These sites may first be suitable candidates for existing state and federal environmental programs, such as Superfund, that are targeted at sites with significant levels of contamination. Because the risk to human health and the environment—and associated liability—is often severe, brownfields redevelopment efforts are usually not targeted at nonviable sites. Presently, brownfields assessment, cleanup, and redevelopment ordinarily is directed at threshold and viable sites with less serious levels of contamination.

Detailed Site Assessment or Phase II Investigation

If the initial site assessment uncovers potential contamination, a more detailed site investigation is generally undertaken that involves environmental engineering, sampling, and chemical analysis. If the Phase II assessment discloses significant contamination problems, brownfields redevelopment may be stymied. The project sponsors may decide that the potential benefits of redevelopment are outweighed by the cost of cleanup. Even where the project sponsors are willing to go forward with the redevelopment, additional financing tools may be required at this point.

Project Development and Financing

At this stage, financial feasibility studies should be completed and financing for cleanup and redevelopment of the property will need to be arranged. This stage may also include meetings with lenders, insurers, project partners, and affected neighborhood communities.

Cleanup Planning and Execution

At this stage, project sponsors will need to select and implement a cleanup plan. This stage can involve high capital costs for site remediation, public notice requirements, and preparation of reports for regulators.

Redevelopment of the Site

Following site remediation, the final stage in the brownfields redevelopment process involves the construction or alteration of the property to render it suitable for its new use.

Practical Considerations for Brownfields Projects

In formulating a successful brownfields redevelopment plan, the project sponsors must follow each of the basic steps outlined above and evaluate financing needs for each stage of the project. In addition, a number of other considerations play a key role in the process, including performance of environmental site assessments, determination of acceptable risk-based cleanup levels that are consistent with the planned use of the property, community involvement in the cleanup and redevelopment plan, and negotiation of effective liability protections.

Performance of Environmental Site Assessments

The potential risk of liability under federal and state hazardous substance cleanup and other environmental laws makes it essential to conduct some type of environmental investigation of the brownfields property at issue. A Phase I environmental site assessment is generally undertaken to determine the presence of potential contamination. If actual or potential contamination is discovered, a more extensive Phase II environmental site assessment, possibly including groundwater and soil sampling, may be required to verify and determine the extent of any contamination.

Phase I environmental site assessments have been in use for quite some time. Beginning in the early 1980s, the original requestors of environmental site assessments were lenders in commercial property transactions that required site investigations for hazardous substances prior to providing real estate financing. In addition, some purchasers of property began conducting their own environmental investigations of property prior to purchase to minimize and manage potential environmental risks.

Phase I environmental site assessments took a variety of forms because there were no established guidelines concerning how extensive an investigation needed to be. In 1989, the Office of Thrift Supervision (OTS) issued guidelines for developing protective policies for environmental risk and liability. In 1991, Fannie Mae followed with comprehensive requirements for completion of Phase I and Phase II environmental site assessments in conjunction with Fannie Mae mortgage loan commitments. And in 1993, the Federal Deposit Insurance Corporation (FDIC) issued guidelines for federally insured banks to implement environmental risk management programs.

Other federal agencies also issued environmental site assessment standards, including the Resolution Trust Corporation (RTC) and Small Business Administration (SBA). In addition, many private organizations came out with standardized methodologies for performing environmental site assessments, including the American Society for Testing and Materials (ASTM), the National Ground Water Association, the Association of Engineering Firms Practicing in the Geosciences, the Environmental Assessment Association, and numerous banks, real estate companies, and law firms. Most notable of these is the environmental site assessment standards for commercial real estate formally adopted by the ASTM in 1993.

The ASTM environmental site assessment standards for commercial real estate have provided the legal community, the real estate industry, environmental consultants, the insurance industry, and lending institutions with widely accepted, comprehensive standards to follow when evaluating potential environmental liabilities in commercial real estate transactions. Because the ASTM site assessments standards have become the most widely accepted and adopted industry standard for evaluating commercial real estate, a brief summary of the ASTM standards is provided here. Brownfields developers are advised to consult one of the many books on the subject if additional guidance is needed.

ASTM Standard E 1528: Transaction Screen Process

The ASTM site assessment standards for commercial real estate consist of two standard practices: (1) ASTM Standard E 1528, "Transaction Screen Process" and (2) ASTM Standard E 1527, "Phase I Environmental Site Assessment." The transaction screen process (ASTM Standard E 1528) establishes the absolute minimum level of inquiry to be used in a commercial transaction. It is intended to constitute appropriate inquiry for the purposes of the innocent landowner defense under CERCLA; and, for many transactions involving low risk properties, the screen would be sufficient.

The transaction screen report consists primarily of a four-page pre-printed form with boxes where "yes," "no," or "unknown" responses to twenty-three predetermined, standardized questions concerning environmental conditions are to be indicated. Unlike the Phase I environmental site assessment (ASTM Standard E

1527), completing the transaction screen requires no technical expertise or training. The transaction screen allows a nonenvironmental professional to screen commercial real estate for potential liabilities under CERCLA. The screen does not require judgment on the part of the person completing the screen. Therefore, it may be conducted by anyone, including the purchaser or lender. The pre-printed transaction screen questionnaire is followed while conducting telephone or personal interviews, a site visit, or a government records review that is more limited than that required under the Phase I standard.

The transaction screen process is intended to aid the user in identifying whether or not a full Phase I assessment is needed. This is accomplished by the following process:

- The completion of a questionnaire regarding current and past uses of the property;

- An inquiry and review of governmental records and historical sources pertaining to hazardous waste activity on or near the property; and

- A site visit and visual inspection to complete the observation checklist.

An affirmative response to any question in the screening questionnaire creates a presumption for further inquiry. At least three parties are expected to contribute to the screen process: the owner, the occupant (if not the owner), and the person conducting the transaction screen (the user or authorized party). After the checklist is completed, it is suggested that the user revisit any "yes" answers for clarification. After this clarification, if any "yes" answers or outstanding questions on any items remain, some kind of further inquiry must be conducted, although this inquiry need not necessarily be a full phase I environmental assessment (ASTM Standard E 1527).

Use of the transaction screen is, however, not advised for industrial properties. Industrial sites will almost assuredly result in one or more affirmative answers that will trigger further inquiry. Additionally, any property that leaves any question as to the correctness of any of the answers in the checklist would indicate further inquiry. Given that the transaction screen process, by definition, does not have to be conducted or interpreted by an "environmental professional", it is quite possible that a very large percentage of properties, at first thought to be candidates for a transaction screen only, will require further inquiry because of questionable or missing information obtained during the screening process.

The lack of assessment experience of nonenvironmental professionals conducting the screening also may result in inaccurate findings. Thus, many purchasers and lenders are uncomfortable with nonenvironmental professionals performing the transaction screen and hire consultants to perform the screen. However, the purchaser or lender should also request a letter from the consultant providing a professional opinion in the form of a summary of the findings and recommendations for further action.

Transaction screens are an alternative to a Phase I site assessment when there is no reason to suspect environmental contamination and the site is not known to have been used for an industrial purpose in the past. Because transaction screens take less time and are less expensive than Phase I site assessments, they are an attractive option when a large number of properties must be evaluated. An example would be acquisition of a commercial real estate company acquisition where the acquiring company would want to assess the potential liabilities of the property prior to purchase.

The proper use of the transaction screen can eliminate the need for a costly and time-consuming Phase I site assessment in some cases. If the transaction screen indicates that no further inquiry is required, a borrower or lender can save two to four weeks' time and anywhere from $1,600 to $4,800. When a transaction screen does indicate that further inquiry is required, a complete Phase I may not be necessary. The transaction screen results may enable the environmental consultant to target a particular problem area for further investigation rather than investigating the entire property for any number of environmental conditions. Once again, a more targeted investigation could save time and money and still meet the due diligence requirements.

ASTM Standard E 1527: Phase I Environmental Site Assessment

When the screening process indicates that a Phase I site assessment is needed, or the user opts to go directly to the Phase I process, then the ASTM Standard E 1527 for performance of a full Phase I site assessment applies. A Phase I environmental site assessment is defined by the ASTM as a study designed to assess the likelihood that hazardous substances may be present on a property, resulting in liability at some point in the future. The primary focus of a Phase I environmental site assessment is on the environmental condition of real property including land, waterways, and buildings. A Phase I is specifically designed to evaluate environmental conditions in light of potential CERCLA liability.

The environmental assessment determines whether a particular parcel of real property is subject to recognized environmental conditions. ASTM Standard E 1527-97 defines recognized environmental conditions as:

"the presence or likely presence of any hazardous substances or petroleum products on a property under conditions that indicate an existing release, a past release, or a material threat of a release of any hazardous substances or petroleum products into structures on the property or in the ground, groundwater, or surface water of the property."

An environmental assessment is performed to identify these recognized environmental conditions. This does not include de minimis conditions that generally do not present a material risk of harm to public health or the environment and that generally would not be the subject of regulatory agency enforcement action.

The standard requires the use of an "environmental professional" to conduct the Phase I assessment. The definition of such a person is very vague, and basically states that the individual must have sufficient training and experience to conduct the assessment and be able to develop conclusions. Aside from being conducted by an environmental professional, the following are the main components of the Phase I site assessment:

1. Records Review
2. Site Reconnaissance
3. Interviews
4. Report

An accurate and detailed legal description of the property, including a street address and zip code, is required for the records review, and a plot map or other drawing indicating property boundaries will be required for the site reconnaissance. Names, work and home addresses, and phone numbers for owners and occupants of the property must be obtained in order to conduct the interviews. For the site assessment process to work efficiently, it is critical that this information be provided to the environmental consultant when the assessment is requested and that the information is accurate. Delays or inaccuracies in the information provided will result in delays, potential errors, and additional expense.

- *Records Review.* The ASTM standard provides that only reasonably ascertainable, standard sources must be reviewed. A reasonably ascertainable, standard source is defined as one that is publicly available, can be obtained

within reasonable time and cost restraints, and is practically
reviewable, which means it does not require extraordinary
analysis.

- Federal and state records

- Historical use information, including aerial photos,
  Sanborn fire insurance maps, property tax files,
  recorded land title records, United States Geological
  Survey topographical maps, local street directories,
  building department records, zoning records.

- *Site Reconnaissance.* A site visit that includes a walk-over
  of the entire property by an environmental professional is
  necessary to visually and physically observe the site and
  any structures in order to obtain information indicating the
  likelihood of identifying recognized environmental
  conditions.

  - Site property—identify specific current and past uses
    and conditions of the property in question.

  - Adjoining property—identify current and past uses of
    adjoining property.

  - General conditions, including geologic, hydrogeologic,
    hydrologic and topographic conditions.

  - Exterior and interior observations, including storage
    tanks, odors, pools of liquid, storage drums, hazardous
    substance and petroleum products containers, and
    unidentified substance containers.

  - Building interior observations, including heating and
    cooling systems, drains and sumps.

  - Exterior observations, including pits, ponds, or lagoons;
    stained soil or pavement; stressed vegetation; solid
    waste; wastewater; wells; and septic systems.

- *Interviews.* Interviews are necessary for obtaining information concerning uses of the site as well as information concerning the recognized environmental conditions and observations found during the site reconnaissance. The format for the interviews can be in person, by telephone, or in writing and can be conducted before or after the site visit. Individuals to be interviewed include owners and major occupants of the site and local government officials.

- *The Report.* The ASTM has developed a recommended table of contents and report format to increase the uniformity of site assessment reports and increase the efficient organization of materials and data.

Limitations on Use of ASTM Phase I Environmental Site Assessment

There is always some risk of liability involved in the purchase of a commercial property; the Phase I report simply provides an assessment of environmental conditions that must be evaluated in light of other factors influencing the transaction. Demanding a site assessment that results in a clean site guarantee or a certification that no contamination exists is unrealistic and can unnecessarily interfere with a transaction that could be lucrative for both the borrower and the lender. Environmental conditions affecting a commercial property can be identified, and the potential environmental liabilities can be managed, but the risk can never be totally eliminated.

The ASTM standards provide a systematic framework for evaluating potential environmental conditions, but do not eliminate the need for professional legal, scientific, and business judgment. When environmental risks associated with a commercial real estate transaction must be evaluated, it is important to:

- Select a qualified environmental consultant;
- Use the ASTM standards for their intended purpose;
- Design the scope of work to address site-specific considerations;
- Carefully evaluate the finished report; and
- Make a well-informed decision based on the acceptable level of risk.

If an assessment reveals potential contamination, that does not necessarily mean that the property should not be purchased or that the property is not suitable for loan collateral. An assessment, indicating that some contamination or liability may exist, can be used by the buyer or the lender in a number of ways, including the following:

- To negotiate a lower selling price;
- To negotiate more favorable contractual terms that can provide some protection against future liabilities;
- To require the borrower to purchase environmental impairment liability insurance, environmental site assessment insurance, to establish a trust to cover future response costs; or
- To require the seller to clean up the property prior to the transfer of title.

ASTM Standard E 1527 is designed to address liability arising under CERCLA and does not address every potential environmental consideration associated with a real estate transaction, such as asbestos, lead, radon, and wetland concerns. However, just because some potential liabilities are not addressed by the ASTM standard does not mean that the scope of work cannot be drafted to include these elements. The standard was designed to be flexible, and the scope of work should be drafted with enough detail so that site-specific concerns are addressed.

Phase II Environmental Site Assessments

The findings of the Phase I environmental site assessment may recommend that sampling and analysis of materials or various environmental media is needed to assess the suspected presence of contamination. This recommendation will form the basis for the scope of a Phase II environmental site assessment. Although numerous organizations have issued standards for performance of Phase I environmental site assessments, most notably the ASTM standard practices, there have been few attempts to introduce standards for performance of Phase II environmental sites assessments, and a widely recognized standard is yet to emerge. The ASTM has been working on a proposed Phase II site assessment standard, which is expected to be released in the near future.

Due to the limited scope of the Phase I environmental site assessment, and the resulting uncertainties regarding the magnitude of any known or suspected environmental problem, Phase II environmental site assessments generally consist of a phased approach of study involving multiple rounds of sampling and analysis. In practice, this phased approach is often referred to as an Initial Phase II environmental site assessment and Expanded Phase II environmental site assessment.

A more aggressive Phase II investigation provides more complete decisionmaking data early in the transaction. Phase II sampling plans should be designed to provide cost allocation information and data for possible remedial action. Prior to closing on property, the parties to a real estate transaction will need a full understanding of the risks associated with the property, such as the following:

- Cost for cleanups;
- Cleanup objectives and effects on land use;
- Timeline for implementing cleanup; and

- Estimate of the net worth of the property, given potential cleanup response actions.

Sampling techniques include electromagnetic induction surveys to detect contamination plumes, soil gas surveys to detect presence of hazardous gases in the subsurface (i.e., gasoline contamination), magnetometers to locate buried tanks and drums, sampling for PCBs and asbestos (older properties) and analysis of discolored soil, potential spills or dumping areas for soil and/or groundwater contamination. Costs of any cleanup activities are used to determine whether the property is worth buying, and to allocate cleanup costs between buyers and sellers.

Environmental Risk Assessments

If a brownfields property requires environmental cleanup, the project sponsors should consider performance of an environmental risk assessment. An environmental risk assessment provides a scientific methodology for defining acceptable risk-based cleanup levels by weighing the costs and feasibility of various cleanup options against the health and environmental risks posed by different cleanup levels at a given site. Instead of liabilities often exceeding a million dollars on a property, contaminated properties may now be addressed and remediated for substantially less.

The EPA and state regulators are now endorsing risk-based cleanup levels as an acceptable means for managing environmental risks through implementation of less costly cleanup options. At least 25 states have established, with EPA encouragement, formal risk-based cleanup programs. Many states have published conservative, risk-based criteria that apply statewide. Other states, such as California and Texas, have established ranking systems to indicate when remedial cleanups may be necessary.

In 1995, the American Society for Testing and Materials (ASTM) developed a new standard practice, referred to as the

Risk-Based Corrective Action Standard (ASTM RBCA E1739, pronounced Rebecca) to provide a standardized approach for partial, risk-based cleanups. Although the standard focuses on petroleum release sites, the RBCA methodology is valid and applicable to any chemical of known toxicity and fate and transport properties. Consequently, many states have implemented risk-based corrective action (RBCA) programs. Such programs have paved the way for broader use of risk assessments to define acceptable cleanup levels that are less stringent than cleanup to background levels.

Risk assessments have now become well-established mechanisms for deriving less stringent, site-specific cleanup criteria. When these criteria have been met, environmental regulatory agencies in some states will grant a limited waiver of liability, freeing the property owner, prospective purchaser, lender, or a third party from further enforcement action and waiving administrative penalties for property owners or operators.

While these limited waivers do not eliminate liability under federal law (in particular, CERCLA) and do not preclude third-party tort claims, they are expected to discourage the EPA or third-party plaintiffs from taking further action when the sites are being addressed under state programs. Where a Memorandum of Agreement has been signed between the EPA and a state, the EPA will accept the state's finding without EPA review. The EPA may even issue a "comfort letter" reflecting the EPA's intent to take no action against a party as long as site conditions remain unchanged.

A technically sound risk assessment can prove critical in brownfields projects because agreement must be reached among the community, the developer, and the regulatory agency regarding minimum appropriate cleanup levels. Future site use is a key factor in determining appropriate site cleanup levels. For example, if a site will be used for industrial purposes, then the clean-up levels should be based upon such future use. Where residential communities are adjacent to a site, exposure pathways and site access have increasing importance in determining acceptable cleanup levels.

Public Participation

Public participation is an important component of a successful brownfields redevelopment plan. Community involvement can avoid legal challenges and political debates that result in the needless expenditure of time, money, and resources. The support of the local community is essential to brownfields projects, particularly because affected residents and government regulators are often endorsing the redevelopment in exchange for less stringent cleanup levels. As such, the project's success depends in large part on an understanding of community needs. Many communities prefer redevelopment that provides valuable public services, creates jobs, generates tax revenues, and attracts new residents and businesses.

Liability Protections

A final key component of any brownfields redevelopment project is the successful management of potential environmental liabilities. When negotiating the cleanup and development plan for the property, the project sponsors should include provisions to limit environmental liability associated with the property. In addition, an indemnification, release, or other contractual limitation on liability should be obtained from the seller of the property. Further, it is generally prudent to purchase environmental liability insurance that is available and appropriate to the risks involved with the brownfields cleanup and redevelopment. The following checklist outlines the primary liability protections available for brownfields developers.

- *Covenant Not To Sue.* Under most state voluntary cleanup programs, the developer of a brownfields property can obtain a covenant not to sue from the state environmental agency in exchange for the cleanup of the property to acceptable levels. This covenant prevents the state from taking any civil or administrative action against the brownfields developer/owner for any liability regarding existing contamination. Covenants not to sue, or other written assurances, must be recorded into the chain of title and run with the land to put owners and purchasers on notice of the status of brownfields sites. This could create some measure of certainty in transactions involving brownfields sites.

- *Comfort Letter.* These letters appear to be a promising and flexible tool. The EPA can send a letter stating the status of the site under consideration. While not as effective as a covenant not to sue, these letters can at least provide some level of assurance to potential investors.

- *Lease With Option to Purchase.* Another tactic recommended by the EPA is to forgo an immediate purchase in favor of entering into a lease with an option to purchase. The prospective purchaser would remain a tenant while the site is being cleaned up by the responsible parties and the owner, and then exercise the option to purchase only after the cleanup is completed.

- *Indemnification.* This traditional method should not be overlooked. The seller can often indemnify the purchaser for all costs that may be incurred as a result of contamination.

- *Insurance.* Experience with environmental assessment techniques and familiarity with the costs of a variety of cleanups have grown to the point where financial outcomes can be predicted with enough reliability to set premiums. As a result, several insurance companies are now getting into the business of providing coverage for the development of contaminated land.

- *Site Cleanup Consent Decree.* When there are ongoing enforcement actions at a Superfund site, it may be possible to protect prospective purchasers by having them sign, along with responsible parties, a remedial action consent decree entered into federal court. The prospective purchaser could pay some cash towards the work and receive a covenant not to sue for as long as the remedy is underway.

CHAPTER 4

BROWNFIELDS FINANCING TOOLS

Introduction

Each stage in the redevelopment process creates different financing needs. There are two basic forms of financing strategies available to brownfields project sponsors: (1) direct strategies, which provide funding directly for assessment, cleanup, and redevelopment, and (2) indirect strategies, which enable or facilitate financing. Direct strategies include equity participation, fees, taxes, debts, and grants. Indirect strategies include legislative reforms, financial assurances, information/advisory services, and liability assurances.

Many brownfields project sponsors use a combination of these financing tools. Selection of suitable financing strategies generally depends on a particular financial barrier to development. This chapter examines financing strategies and provides brief examples of how some of them may be applied in actual practice.

Direct Financing Strategies

Direct financing strategies provide resources for assessment, cleanup, and redevelopment of brownfields properties to project sponsors, which may include communities, states, private developers, nonprofit groups, or a combination thereof. These strategies are typically used to increase the rate of return on the project by reducing capital costs or providing equity participation.

Equity Participation

Many communities consider equity participation to be an excellent financing tool to stimulate brownfields redevelopment. Equity participation can take the form of lease arrangements, reclamation banks, or municipal ownership and development of property on its own behalf. The important aspect of equity participation is that the public sponsor assumes part of the risk of the project. For many communities, this is a worthwhile risk because the assessed, cleaned up, and redeveloped property will provide a valuable source of tax revenue. In addition, although state and local governments only enjoy a CERCLA liability exemption when acquiring contaminated property involuntarily, federal regulators have historically been more reluctant to pursue legal action against public agencies than against private landowners, thus lowering the effective risk.

Some communities have found that brownfields projects can be stimulated by using a public agency to purchase or take title to abandoned sites, assess and cleanup contamination, and lease the property to private developers and businesses. The lease shields the developer or business from environmental liability as the current tenant (although not as a generator of hazardous waste) and gives the community a source of employment and revenue. The local government may decide to find a lessor before starting the project or identify tenants after the redevelopment project is underway. For example, the Commerce, California redevelopment agency purchased the 35-acre Uniroyal Tire Factory for $14 million in 1984. The agency spent $3 million on investigation and cleanup of contaminated soils—some of which was recovered in a settlement agreement with the company responsible for the contamination— and sought a private developer to lease the redeveloped land. Ultimately, a factory outlet mall, offices, and a hotel were constructed at the site and the project is expected to generate approximately $592 million in lease income over 65 years, plus $7.5 million in property taxes.

Other municipalities have opted to purchase or take title to abandoned sites, assess and cleanup contamination, and then sell the property to private developers and businesses. For example, in 1990, the Chrysler Corporation sought a site for a new manufacturing plant. One location considered by the company was a 283-acre tract owned by the City of Detroit with a mix of land uses, including industrial facilities, scrap yards, old gas stations, and abandoned parcels. The site had access to rail transportation, was centrally located, and was close to a well-trained workforce. The City of Detroit strongly supported the project, which would create 3,000 jobs, and worked with state regulators and Chrysler to negotiate a $25 million cleanup plan to contain and stabilize the contamination. Chrysler purchased the site from the city upon conclusion of the cleanup and opened the plant in January 1992.

Some communities have used land reclamation banks to stimulate brownfields redevelopment. Land reclamation banks take title to potentially contaminated sites by property tax foreclosure, eminent domain, or purchase. Then, the land reclamation bank assesses, cleans up, redevelops, and sells or leases the property to prospective purchasers or tenants. Some communities use the proceeds from the lease or sale to finance other redevelopment activities. For example, the City of Minneapolis, Minnesota has a Light Industry Land Acquisition Program that expends about $5 million each year to acquire, assess, cleanup, and redevelop brownfields sites. The funds are generated by a tax increment financing plan and used for purchase and site remediation. The city assumes all liability for cleanup and resells the land to private purchasers after redevelopment.

Land Registration and Site Assessment Fees

Fees establish direct links between the demand for services and the cost of providing them. A fee is generally charged for services rendered. In the case of brownfields, however, property owners may not be able or willing to pay fees to cover the substantial costs of cleanup. Further, the fee mechanism is not usually appropriate for cleanup activities because they require large capital investments. Brownfields developers may, however, be able to pay for land registration and inspection fees that could finance a central land registry and assessment of sites. Developers could pay fees to use a city land registry that would maintain listings of brownfields and other sites available for development with descriptions of the property and information about contamination levels. Developers might also pay for assistance with assessment and remediation of potential brownfields sites.

In some cases, voluntary cleanup programs already run on a fee-for-service basis, with state environmental agencies assisting property owners and prospective purchasers with site investigations, selection of remediation options, and coordination with federal regulatory agencies. In such instances, the private party usually reimburses the state for its costs of reviewing the proposed action against statutory and administrative requirements and providing guidance on those requirements.

For example, the Minnesota Voluntary Investigation and Cleanup Program is run on a fee-for-service basis. By obtaining approval from the Minnesota Pollution Control Agency (MPCA) for site investigations and response action plans, potential brownfields developers can determine the most appropriate cleanup option and can calculate the cost of cleanup measures needed to satisfy statutory requirements. Property owners can request assistance from the MCPA in anticipation of future property transactions, to obtain financing for current redevelopment plans, or simply to minimize the high transaction costs associated with Superfund cleanups.

Taxes

Brownfields are typically located in areas where the traditional source of local tax revenue—property taxes—is depressed. In fact, in some recent cases, courts have shown a modern trend to attribute little or no value to contaminated property. For example, in Westling v. County of Mille Lacs, 543 N.W.2d 91 (Minn. 1996), landowners successfully challenged property tax assessments of contaminated property. The Minnesota Supreme Court found that the stigma discount for environmental contamination and the estimated cost of cleaning up a landowner's property resulted in a zero value for tax purposes, even though the 13-acre industrial site generated annual rents of $114,000 and had an uncontaminated value of more than $1 million. As a result, local governments have been forced to employ more innovative revenue-raising strategies based on nontraditional taxes and real estate-based taxes that do not depend on current property values.

Tax Increment Financing

Special assessments are a charge levied against the beneficiaries of a service or improvement. In the case of a brownfield property, an entire business district or neighborhood could be considered the beneficiary of assessment, cleanup, and redevelopment. In some cases, special assessments are charged differentially, with those receiving the greatest benefits paying a larger portion of the cost. For example, property owners that were closest to a brownfields site might pay a larger share of the cleanup costs because they would experience the greatest increase in their property values after the cleanup. Alternatively, special assessments can be charged at a flat rate per individual or business.

Tax increment financing is a particular kind of special assessment that generates revenue from the incremental change in property values caused by the improvement being financed. For example, a number of local governments have issued bonds backed by an anticipated increase in property values after a brownfields cleanup has been completed. This type of financing tool is generally used for a specifically defined geographic area and often for a well-defined period of time, such as ten years. However, the local government runs the risk that bonds will have to be repaid by other means if improvements do not yield the expected benefits.

For example, in 1990, a serious contamination problem was discovered in downtown Wichita, Kansas, which threatened more than 500 companies with liability, and preventing economic development in the area. The city accepted liability for the contamination and negotiated a cleanup plan with the EPA, which the city planned to finance with an innovative tax increment financing plan. The city reduced the property values in the affected area to reflect the decrease in values due to contamination. Then, the city issued bonds backed by the anticipated increase in property values following the cleanup. This mechanism effectively dedicated revenue from future property taxes from the area to the cleanup effort.

Real Estate Transfer Taxes

Real estate transfer taxes are charged to a buyer or seller of real property at the time of transfer based on a percentage of the assessed value of the property transferred, a flat deed registration fee, or a combination of both. This financing tool is used by both state and local governments to fund land-related initiatives, including natural lands acquisition. In the case of brownfields, state and local governments might consider imposing such a transfer tax in conjunction with new property transfer laws that require sellers to report the environmental status of the property to new owners.

Property Tax Abatement

It may be possible for brownfields developers to secure property tax adjustments to enhance the cash flow of contaminated properties. Property tax abatement can be used as a financing tool to offset the expense, liability, and regulatory compliance costs associated with the redevelopment of the property. Local governments can use property tax abatements to stimulate private party interest in redevelopment of brownfields sites. In some areas, tax abatements can be approved on a project-by-project basis; in others, they can only be approved by the state legislature or local governing body.

Although a property tax abatement can free up funds for the developer of brownfields property, the tax abatement usually only reflects the reduced value of the property before redevelopment. The fair market value of the property can increase substantially even before the cleanup is finished. When this occurs, the property taxes might be adjusted upwards to reflect this increase. Higher property taxes can strain cash flow on the heels of the expenditures for the cleanup. This problem may discourage the cleanup of contaminated properties.

Although greater property tax revenues is a major benefit to local communities, states also recognize that property owners need time to recapture their investments and generate a profit. Accordingly, some states have enacted legislation that permits owners to redevelop brownfields without an immediate tax assessment on the increase in the property's value. The laws of New Jersey, Ohio, and Pennsylvania offer representative examples of tax schemes whereby taxpayers may obtain prospective tax abatements.

In 1996, the New Jersey legislature passed the Environmental Opportunity Zone Act, N.J. Rev. Stat. § 54:4-3.150 et seq., which authorizes municipalities to offer up to ten years of property tax savings. Tax increases may not exceed 10 percent annually, and the value attributable to the improvements is not taxed at all during the first year. By the tenth year, the property is assessed at its true market value.

The Ohio Real Estate Reuse and Cleanup Law, Ohio Rev. Code ch. 3746, includes a plan for abating taxes on the redevelopment of brownfield sites. The program provides two types of PTAs. Property owners may obtain a ten-year tax abatement that applies to increases in market value attributable to a cleanup. In addition, taxpayers undertaking voluntary cleanups may secure a ten-year tax abatement for development projects.

The Pennsylvania Local Economic Revitalization Tax Assistance Act, 72 Pa. Stat. § 4722 et seq., provides an abatement on "additional assessment valuation attributable to the actual costs of improvement to deteriorated property," which includes "industrial, commercial and other business property." Pennsylvania also offers PTA-type benefits on properties that suffer from nonenvironmental problems. The benefits may be available for properties in specific localities that the government is seeking to revitalize. The period of exemption may not exceed ten years, and "the schedule of taxes exempted must stipulate the portion of improvements to be exempted each year."

Tax Treatment of Brownfields Cleanup Expenses

Brownfield developers should be aware that some costs of cleanup may be deductible expenses for federal tax purposes. In 1994, the Internal Revenue Service (IRS) issued Revenue Ruling 94-38, (1994-25 I.R.B. 4 (June 2, 1994)), stating that certain soil and groundwater remediation and monitoring costs are deductible while costs to install a groundwater treatment facility must be capitalized. This ruling was the result of an internal study conducted by the IRS in 1993. The study was done because taxpayers were complaining that three prior IRS decisions created uncertainty with regard to whether environmental cleanup costs can be deducted in the year incurred or whether they must be capitalized and written off over a period of years. While Rev. Rul. 94-38 is limited to its facts, it provides taxpayers with more guidance than they previously had.

The deductibility or capitalization of environmental cleanup costs is analyzed under the traditional principles of sections 162 and 263 of the IRS Code. Section 162 allows a deduction for ordinary and necessary business expenses paid or incurred in carrying on a trade or business, such as repair costs. Section 263 disallows a deduction for capital replacements, alterations or improvements if they (i) materially increase the value of the property; (ii) substantial prolong the useful life of the property; or (iii) are incurred to adapt the property to a new or different use. Such improvements must be capitalized over a period of years.

According to Rev. Rul. 94-38, groundwater treatment facility costs must be capitalized as improvements. This may include costs for pump and treat equipment and groundwater monitoring wells. Yearly discharge permit fees may also have to be capitalized.

Rev. Rul. 94-38 does, however, allow a deduction for on-going groundwater treatment costs. These are considered repair costs. This is a departure from earlier IRS Technical Advice Memoranda: TAM 9240004 (June 29, 1992) (requiring capitalization of costs for asbestos removal) and TAM 9315004 (December 17, 1992) (requiring capitalization of costs for contaminated soil removal). The influence of these TAMs may be negligible in light of Rev. Rul. 94-38. Repair costs may include costs for an equipment contract or to install pump and treat equipment and groundwater monitoring wells, an environmental consultant to oversee this work, charcoal and other groundwater treatment materials and chemicals, groundwater sampling and laboratory fees and a licensed treatment plant operator.

The IRS uses the "matching principal" to analyze deductibility. In other words, the IRS tries to match expenses with the revenues of the taxable period to which the expense is properly attributable. The repair costs that benefit a taxpayer are deductible because they do not increase the value of the property and are expended for the current year only. Costs that do increase value, such as pump and treat equipment and groundwater monitoring wells, are capitalized.

Rev. Rul. 94-38 capitalizes environmental costs in accordance with the value test developed in Plainfield - Union Water Co. v. Commission, 39 T.C. 333 (1962), non-acq., 1964-2 C.B.8. This test compares the value of the property after the expenditure is made with the value of the property before the condition arose. If the expenditure merely brings the property to its original condition and value, then the expenditure is a deductible repair. If the expenditure increases value, then it is capitalized. The pump and treat equipment and wells are capitalized because they increase the value of the taxpayer's property.

Debt Financing

A loan is money that must be repaid in a set amount of time at a negotiated interest rate. Brownfields project sponsors may be able to identify state and federal debt finance programs that will provide capital at subsidized rates for projects that meet their eligibility criteria. Some debt finance programs are revolving, meaning that the program is at least partially financed by repayment of earlier debt.

Subsidized Low Interest Loans

Subsidized low interest loans reduce the capital costs of brownfields project sponsors. They also provide full or partial financing for projects that might otherwise be unable to obtain financing on the private capital markets, or that would be expected to pay a higher interest rate to compensate for the potential additional risk involved in a brownfields project. Many projects have made use of existing state and local loan programs for redevelopment. Others have made use of loan programs specifically targeted at brownfields assessment, cleanup, and redevelopment. For example, in Ambridge, Pennsylvania, the Commonwealth of Pennsylvania is providing subsidized loans to redevelop a 100-acre brownfields site. The site, which was previously owned by the U.S. Steel group, had been vacant for 10 years. In 1991, WorldClass Steel took ownership of the site and redeveloped 16.5 acres. In 1994, WorldClass Steel and the city made plans for a $375 million expansion that would redevelop the remaining acres. The Commonwealth is expected to finance 10 to 15 percent of the entire package at a subsidized interest rate of approximately 4 percent.

Revolving Loan Funds

In some cases, state and local loan programs operate revolving loan funds, meaning that future loans are financed by current repayments. In September 1997, the U.S. EPA also commenced a revolving loan program in conjunction with its brownfields assessment pilot program. This mechanism may be particularly appropriate for brownfields assessment, cleanup, and redevelopment, since repayment terms tend to be more flexible than commercial loans.

Bonds

Bonds can extend payment for new projects over a period of 15 to 30 years—allowing time to generate sufficient income to repay the capital invested. Typically, states and localities repay bonds with taxes, fees, or other sources of government revenue. For brownfields projects, bonds backed by tax increment financing can be particularly popular because they rely on future tax revenues anticipated from the redevelopment project. For example, in 1988, voters in the State of Michigan approved issuance of $425 million in bonds to fund cleanup actions, with $45 million dedicated to a site reclamation program that provides grants to local governments to investigate and clean up contaminated sites for economic development.

Grants

Grants for different purposes are awarded by a wide range of entities, including federal, state, and local governments, nonprofit organizations, and corporations. Brownfields assessment, cleanup, and redevelopment projects may be eligible for many existing grant programs, and the EPA has a national and regional brownfields assessment pilot grant program.

EPA Brownfields Assessment Pilot Grants

The EPA's Brownfields Initiative seeks to empower states, communities, and other stakeholders in economic redevelopment to work together in a timely manner to prevent, assess, safely clean up, and sustainably develop brownfields. The EPA funded more than 100 brownfields pilots, up to $200,000 each, through April 1997. Each of these pilots is summarized in Chapter 7.

State Grant Programs

Many states have grant programs that provide funding to localities and agencies undertaking brownfields assessment, cleanup, and redevelopment. In seeking grants, project sponsors should know that grant assistance can be found at a variety of agencies, not necessarily the primary state environmental agency.

For example, communities may be able to finance brownfields projects via a state economic development agency. Alternatively, localities can seek grants not traditionally used for site cleanup, such as groundwater protection grants, which could be awarded for protecting groundwater supplies from contamination from a brownfield. Since grant programs vary widely from state to state, localities should seek catalogs or other information directly from their state governments.

The Commonwealth of Pennsylvania has adopted an Industrial Communities Action Program (ICAP) that provides grants to communities for redeveloping contaminated sites. Project sponsors, including local governments, development agencies, and redevelopment authorities, can apply for grants for the purchase of land and buildings, site demolition and clearance, construction and renovation of infrastructure, cleanup, and other activities that assist in preparing the site for redevelopment. ICAP supported 53 projects in its first year and another 117 projects in its second year.

Private/Nonprofit Grants

Private nonprofit organizations and corporations can also be a source of grant funds for brownfields projects. Publications such as the Grants Register and the Foundation Directory can direct states and localities to organizations and corporations likely to provide grants, as well as information on criteria, amounts available, and application procedures. For example, in July 1995, the Great Lakes Commission received a $26,000 planning grant from the Great Lakes Protection Fund to identify ways to spur brownfields projects in the Great Lakes Basin. The Commission will use the funds for three tasks: reviewing the impacts of brownfields on Great Lakes basin ecosystem health; planning and conducting a regional workshop to assess the potential for cooperative arrangements on brownfields redevelopment and greenfields protection; and preparation of a more detailed report and project proposal.

Indirect Strategies

Some financing strategies available to state and local governments do not directly increase the funds available for investment in brownfields projects. Rather these indirect strategies facilitate or enable site assessment, cleanup, and redevelopment by overcoming barriers impeding the project's financing. Indirect strategies can help overcome three kinds of barriers:

- *Knowledge Gaps.* A developer or investor may be interested in, or willing to consider, financing a brownfields project but may be unaware of suitable sites or regulatory options, Informational/advisory services provided by state and local governments can overcome these knowledge gaps.

- *Perceived Liability.* Many lenders may be aware of brownfields-related issues but fear potential liability associated with a particular site, which may or may not equate to the site's actual liability risk. In addition, lenders may fear the public's perception of environmental contamination and the associated stigma, which can adversely impact the financial stability of the project. Informational/advisory services, and more importantly, financial assurances provided by states and localities can overcome problems with perceived liability.

- *Actual Liability.* Some indirect financing strategies shield property owners and redevelopers from environmental liability risk by providing liability assurances.

Informational/Advisory Services

Part of the barrier to brownfields redevelopment is that developers and capital providers often lack information about sites, the site assessment process, and liability. By educating developers and capital providers about available sites, the site assessment process, and environmental regulation, communities can help to overcome reluctance by developers and capital providers to participate in brownfields redevelopment. For example, changes in environmental regulations can affect lending decisions by capital providers. In addition, developers and capital providers should be aware of land use controls, cleanup options, and potential reuses of the property.

Land Registry

A number of communities have set up land registries that collect information about potential redevelopment sites. These registries inform developers about the potential advantages and disadvantages of sites, and allow projects to occur on sites that might otherwise be overlooked. Some communities operate land registries in conjunction with programs that fund site investigation and assessments for the parcels. Subsequently, the registry will contain detailed information about the sites and anticipated cleanup costs. For example, the City of Bridgeport, Connecticut is using EPA brownfields assessment pilot grant funds to develop an inventory of contaminated sites. The inventory will classify properties by the level of cleanup required, the method and cost of the cleanup, and the anticipated time required.

Brokering

An agency or local government can broker or facilitate agreements between federal, state, and local agencies and developers. In this case, the public sector can provide proactive services to bring the buyer and seller together, and to help negotiate brownfields redevelopment deals, and assist in arranging project financing.

Regulatory Compliance Assistance

A public environmental agency can advise developers on regulatory options and assist in obtaining cooperation from other agencies. Navigating the environmental permit process can be difficult. Assistance with the process encourages developers to continue projects that might otherwise be held up. To expedite the process, some communities have formed task forces with membership from all agencies responsible for regulating a particular brownfields site.

For example, in Elizabeth, New Jersey, the Regional Plan Association—a nonprofit organization that studies land use issues in New Jersey, New York, and Connecticut—assisted a developer in acquiring environmental permits to turn a 166-acre site in Elizabeth, once a municipal landfill, into a 1.5 million square-foot commercial hub, including a 1.2 million square-foot factory outlet center. The association worked with the developer and regulatory agencies to ensure that cleanup plans were approved and deadlines were met.

Liability Assurances

Liability assurances help to finance assessment, cleanup, and redevelopment of brownfields by giving needed certainty to lenders and other capital providers. Tools used by states and localities include No-Further-Action letters, covenants not to sue, certificates of completion, and liability releases. Each tool addresses a particular kind of uncertainty that can impede access to capital. These assurances promote brownfields redevelopment projects by shielding prospective and current owners from potential liability in exchange for cleaning up contaminated property.

Most state voluntary cleanup programs offer some form of liability assurance to prospective purchasers. Some also offer assurances to current owners who successfully complete an approved cleanup. However, because state laws vary, the brownfields project sponsors should review applicable state programs, which are summarized in Chapter 4. Although there are no standard definitions for liability assurances, they can be created in a number of different ways, including by legislative action or administrative action by state environmental authorities.

No-Further-Action Letter

After a site assessment determines that cleanup action is required on a brownfields property, a state can inform a property owner what level of cleanup is necessary for the issuance of a No-Further-Action letter. This letter is only granted after a cleanup has been completed, or a site assessment reveals that no cleanup is required. The letter does not release the new owner from liability, but does guarantee that the state will not take any new enforcement actions at the site, barring discovery of new information unknown at the time the letter is issued. Where an approved cleanup has been completed, a no-further-Action letter is a promise by the state not to require further cleanup. If state cleanup standards change, or new cleanup technologies are developed, the new owner will not be required to do additional cleanup. However, it is important to note that this varies from state to state; some state voluntary cleanup programs severely limit "reopeners" but others do not.

Covenant Not to Sue

A covenant not to sue (CNTS) is granted after cleanup and offers protection from future judicial or administrative enforcement proceedings by state regulators regarding contamination on the property. In some states, the CNTS may not cover conditions or contamination that were unknown at the time the covenant was granted. In some case, the CNTS may be contingent on an approved land use for the property. For example, the state may require that the property be maintained as an industrial use, or that the new use will not exacerbate existing contamination. For example, the Michigan Attorney General has the authority to issue a CNTS to brownfields redevelopment project sponsors who are not affiliated with a potentially responsible party. The CNTS protects the purchaser from all liability to the State of Michigan associated with past releases, known and unknown. It also provides protection from claims by other responsible parties, in exchange for implementation of environmental response activity.

Certificate of Completeness

A certificate of completeness is issued after cleanup if the site meets the agreed-upon state cleanup standards. In some cases, these standards will be individually negotiated for each site, based on a risk assessment. In other cases, the standards will be voluntary cleanup standards that apply to all sites statewide. The certificate of completeness proves to prospective purchasers that the cleanup has occurred and that the state environmental agency participated and was satisfied with the results. In many states, possessing a certificate of completeness limits further liability for both potentially responsible parties and nonresponsible parties.

Liability Release

A liability release shields property owners from liability provided that they are not responsible for any of the original contamination of the site. It is intended to encourage prospective purchasers to clean up brownfields sites without being exposed to the risk of liability for the original contamination. It may be granted prior to cleanup, and may be conditioned on an intention to clean and reuse the site. State laws vary as to the liability protection provided by these releases.

Financial Assurances

Financial assurances are made to assure lenders and capital providers that they will be repaid by another source if the project sponsor should default on a finance agreement. By providing additional guarantees for bond or loan repayment, financial assurances improve the ability of project sponsors to acquire capital, or to acquire capital at a lower cost.

Loan Guarantees

To reassure capital providers regarding the safety of brownfields lending, state, and local governments, and some federal programs, provide loan guarantees to project sponsors. These guarantees assist sponsors in obtaining financing because they provide an additional source of repayment in the event of project bankruptcy. For example, the State of Ohio provides loan guarantees from the state water pollution control fund, the Ohio Water Development Authority, and the Ohio Economic Development Authority. These guarantees are available to parties involved in cleanup or undertaking voluntary actions including assessment, investigation, and remediation, and assist these parties in obtaining project financing.

Bond/Loan Insurance

Bond and loan insurance are credit enhancements that assure lenders and bondholders that interest and principal will be repaid in the event of default by the entity that contracted the debt. States, communities, and private developers can use bond and loan insurance to make debt offerings appear more secure from default, and therefore more attractive to potential investors. These assurances would be particularly important for obtaining debt for brownfields projects. To secure bond or loan insurance, project sponsors can either seek out insurers on the private capital markets who are prepared to insure a brownfields project, or the state or local government could create a bond or loan insurance program specifically for them.

CHAPTER 5

BROWNFIELDS ASSESSMENT PILOTS

Introduction

Since 1993, the U.S. EPA has awarded grants to states, cities, towns, counties, and American Indian Tribes for National and Regional Brownfields Assessment Demonstration Pilots. National Pilots are awarded through a competitive application process under criteria developed by EPA Headquarters. Regional Pilots are selected by EPA Regions, which use their own selection criteria. These pilots, each funded up to $200,000 over a two-year period, are designed to support creative explorations and demonstrations of brownfield solutions. The pilots are intended to provide the EPA, states, municipalities, and communities with useful information and strategies as they continue to seek methods to promote a unified approach to site assessments, environmental cleanup, and redevelopment.

Funding for the brownfields assessment pilots is authorized under Section 104(d)(1) of the Comprehensive Environmental Response, Compensation, and Liability Act (CERCLA), 42 U.S.C. § 9604(d)(1). States, cities, towns, counties, U.S. Territories, and Indian Tribes are eligible to apply. Cooperative agreement funds may only be awarded to an officially recognized political subdivision of a state.

Through a brownfields cooperative agreement, the EPA authorizes an eligible state, political subdivision, Territory, or Indian Tribe to undertake activities that the EPA itself has the authority to pursue under CERCLA Section 104(a) or 104(b). All restrictions on the EPA's use of funding cited in Section 104 of CERCLA also apply to brownfields assessment pilot cooperative agreement recipients. Brownfields demonstration pilots must conform to the following guidelines:

- Pilot activities should be directed toward environmental activities preliminary to cleanup, such as site assessment, site identification, site characterization, and site response or cleanup planning and design areas that have an actual or threatened release of a hazardous substance, pollutant, or contaminant. "Site identification" inn this case means the identification of sites at which such contamination may be an issue of concern. These activities can encompass administration, outreach to stakeholders, or fieldwork associated with site assessment, site identification, site characterization, and site remediation planning and design.

- Brownfields pilot funds may be used to assess, identify, characterize, and plan response or plan cleanup activities at contaminated sites targeted for redevelopment. These funds may not be used to pay for nonenvironmental redevelopment activities (e.g., construction of a new facility).

- All sites targeted in the pilot must present a threatened or actual release of a hazardous substance or a threatened or actual release of a pollutant or contaminant that may present an imminent and substantial endangerment. However, brownfields assessment pilot funds are not intended to be used for activities at any sites listed on the CERCLA National Priorities List.

- Brownfields pilot funds may not be used for actual cleanup or other response activities often associated with such cleanups (e.g., landscaping and groundwater extraction and treatment). Cleanup costs should be funded through other means, such as state voluntary cleanup programs, state government grants, state tax incentive programs, contributions from responsible parties, and prospective purchaser agreements. The EPA does plan to later provide follow-up funding to assessment pilots in a cooperative agreement for capitalization of revolving loan funds.

- Brownfields pilot funds may be used for outreach activities that educate the public about assessment, identification, characterization, or remedial planning activities at a site or set of sites. However, the outreach should be directed toward obtaining more effective public involvement and/or environmental assessment and cleanup of hazardous substances, pollutants, or contaminants at affected sites. These funds may not be used for general education activities (e.g., grants to schools for development of curricula).

- Brownfields pilot funds may not be used for job training. Support for job training activities may be available through the Hazardous Materials Training and Research Institute, EPA programs, other federal agency programs, and state and local programs.

- Brownfields pilot funds may not be used to support "lobbying" efforts of the grantee (e.g., lobbying members of Congress, or lobbying for other federal grants, cooperative agreements or contracts).

- Brownfields pilot funds may not be used for assessment, identification, characterization, or remediation planning at sites contaminated by petroleum products unless they are believed to be co-mingled with a hazardous substance, pollutant, or contaminant (e.g., used oil). CERCLA expressly excludes petroleum from the definition of hazardous substances.

- Brownfields pilot funds may not be used to match any other federal funds without specific statutory authority.

- Brownfields pilot funds may be used to develop creative financing solutions (e.g., tax incentives, revolving loan funds) to brownfields problems. However, federal grant funds may not be used for fund-raising purposes.

The EPA awarded the first brownfields assessment pilot to Cuyahoga County, Ohio in September 1993. In 1994, two additional pilots were awarded to Bridgeport, Connecticut and Richmond, Virginia. Through April 1997, the EPA funded 64 National, and 49 Regional, Brownfields Assessment Pilots. These pilots have been testing redevelopment models, directing efforts at removing regulatory barriers, and bringing together community groups, investors, lenders, developers, and other affected parties to address brownfields issues. The pilots are also serving as models for other states and localities that are struggling with similar problems. This chapter summarizes the ongoing activities of each of the 113 brownfields demonstration pilots selected by the EPA through April 1997.

National Brownfields Assessment Demonstration Pilots

Alabama

Birmingham, AL

The EPA has awarded the City of Birmingham, Alabama a grant for a National Brownfields Assessment Pilot. Activities planned as part of this pilot include establishing a clearinghouse that will serve as a repository for brownfields environmental data on the targeted redevelopment areas and forming a partnership among environmental activists, technical experts, government officials, and business representatives who will support the pilot program with staff and materials. A fundamental goal of the pilot is to develop a comprehensive environmental plan to link approaches to such issues as flood control and groundwater contamination reduction with remediation of soil and site-specific contamination. In addition, Birmingham was selected by the EPA Common Sense Initiative Iron and Steel Sector Brownfield's Workgroup for a special partnership to explore brownfields assessment and redevelopment issues unique to the iron and steel industry sector. For more information, contact Matt Robbins of U.S. EPA Region 4 at (404) 562-8371.

Alaska

Ketchikan Gateway Borough, AK

In April 1997, the EPA awarded Ketchikan Gateway Borough, Alaska a $200,000 grant for a National Brownfields Assessment Pilot. Ketchikan is a community of about 15,000 residents located on the Revillagigedo Island in the southernmost portion of Alaska's panhandle. The site selected for the pilot is the Ward Cove Pulp Mill. The mill was established in 1954 as part of the U.S. Forest Service's decision to develop a forest products industry in southeast Alaska. Previously, the Ketchikan economy was almost entirely dependent on fisheries, tourism. and mining— industries that tend to be highly seasonal and cyclical. At one time, the mill employed up to seven percent of Ketchikan's workforce and offered stable, year-round employment. The current corporate owner of the mill permanently closed it in March 1997.

Ketchikan hopes that this brownfields pilot will be a model for brownfields prevention and remediation. By planning for immediate reuse of the site, the community hopes to avoid the deterioration of buildings, facilities, and equipment. The community is also trying to avoid costs associated with rebuilding infrastructure. Ketchikan also hopes to preserve the scenic beauty and natural resources of the area by directing industrial development to previously developed sites.

Ketchitan's goals for the pilot are: (1) to help maintain a sustainable industrial employment base; (2) to avoid an economy dependent on cyclical and seasonal employment and the problems associated with a transient labor force; and (3) to retain the Ward Cove Pulp Mill workforce in the Ketchikan Gateway Borough community. The brownfield pilot for the Ward Cove Paper Mill site will serve as a model for community planning and redevelopment. Activities planned as part of the pilot include:

- Performing a site survey to inventory the parts of the site can be reused immediately and the parts that should be excluded from immediate reuse consideration;

- Conducting site assessment activities;

- Performing an economic analysis of the property to identify potential industries that may appropriately reuse the site; and

- Planning for site cleanup.

For more information, contact Bob Bright of the Ketchikan Department of Planning and Community Development at (907) 228-6610 or Lori Cohen of U.S. EPA Region 10 at (206) 553-6523 or cohen.lori@epamail.epa.gov.

Arizona

Navajo Nation, AZ

The EPA has awarded the Navajo Nation a grant for a National Brownfields Assessment Pilot. The Navajo Nation's 10-year Forest Management Plan expired in 1992, eliminating access to tribal timber resources and causing the closing of the Navajo Forest Product Industries (NFPI) mill site in Navajo, New Mexico. A site inspection has revealed clear evidence of potentially hazardous substances in the environment. Activities planned as part of the pilot include scoping the local community's needs and concerns, assessing the site to determine the cleanup status of each parcel of the NFPI facility; conducting public meetings to secure a Letter of Decision commitment by the Red Lake Chapter to lease all or part of the site to help finance remediation of the NFPI facility; and preparing a site remediation plan. For more information, contact Thomas Mix of U.S. EPA Region 9 at (415) 744-2378 or mix.tom@epamail.epa.gov.

Tucson, AZ

In April 1997, the EPA awarded the City of Tucson, Arizona a $200,000 grant for a National Brownfields Assessment Pilot. Industrial activity in downtown Tucson that began in the 1880s with the advent of the railroad began to decrease in the 1950s. At that time, rail yards were relocated, a major military base was constructed, and pristine and inexpensive land surrounding the city began drawing development away from the downtown area. A patchwork of vacant, deteriorating, and under-used properties remains. Contamination from various industrial pollutants released over the years threatens the reliability of Tucson's groundwater, the city's only source of drinking water.

The pilot will target one of four designated brownfields areas located within the downtown City Center. The targeted area, known as the Warehouse District/Barraza Aviation Parkway (BAP) Corridor, encompasses approximately 80 acres of warehouse properties, roadways, and vacant sites. The area suffers from potential groundwater and soil contamination resulting from aviation activities, milling operations, the railroad, and other industrial activities. Tucson's areas of highest economical and social stress are located adjacent to these properties. More than 40 percent of City Center residents live in poverty, 11 percent are unemployed, and more than 50 percent of its population is Hispanic.

Tucson's goal is to stimulate sustainable redevelopment of targeted sites. The objectives of the pilot are to complete site assessments, identify funds for cleanup and redevelopment, and begin the redevelopment planning process for brownfields sites within the Warehouse District/BAP Corridor. Activities planned as part of the pilot include:

- Developing a collaborative, community-based process to involve stakeholders;

- Developing brownfields redevelopment planning strategies and waste minimization plans for the Warehouse District/BAP Corridor;

- Establishing a database and mapping system of brownfields in the Warehouse/BAP Corridor, including application to other brownfields sites;

- Identifying funding mechanisms for brownfields cleanup;

- Identifying methods to ensure sustainable redevelopment in the downtown area; and

- Providing outreach and education to minority residents of the City Center.

For more information, contact Jim Hanson of U.S. EPA Region 9 at (415) 744-2237 or Kendall Bert of the City of Tucson at (520) 791-5093.

California

Emeryville, CA

The EPA has awarded the City of Emeryville, California a grant for a National Brownfields Assessment Pilot. The goal of the Emeryville pilot is to encourage redevelopment by building stakeholder confidence in an emerging State of California regulatory policy using area-wide risk management-based approach to environmental cleanups. Activities planned as part of the pilot include compiling existing site information, conducting additional assessments, and creating a geographical information system model. The city plans to convene a broad-based Community Task Force to serve as a forum for community participation in decisionmaking and development of a Mitigation/Risk Management plan. For more information, contact Jim Hanson of U.S. EPA Region 9 at (415) 744-2237.

Richmond, CA

The EPA has awarded the City of Richmond, California a grant for a National Brownfields Assessment Pilot. The goal of the Richmond pilot is to focus on the 900-acre North Richmond Shoreline, which contains a variety of brownfields in a relatively compact area. Activities planned as part of the pilot include providing public recreation; opening the shoreline for public use; establishing zoning standards to limit industrial activities that may endanger human health and the environment; completing preliminary site assessments of two to five sites within the North Richmond Shoreline; developing financing mechanisms; clarifying jurisdictional authority; streamlining the regulatory process; and implementing community education and outreach programs. For more information, contact Wally Woo of U.S. EPA Region 9 at (415) 744-1207.

Sacramento, CA

The EPA has awarded the City of Sacramento, California a grant for a National Brownfields Assessment Pilot. Activities planned as part of the pilot include developing an automated land use permitting process and monitoring system to geographically overlay environmental information onto land use maps to guide cleanup activities and planning; targeting economic redevelopment on brownfields; and developing a cooperative process among federal, state, and local agencies to involve the community in redevelopment and ensure that local land use objectives are reflected in cleanup activities. For more information, contact Thomas Mix of U.S. EPA Region 9 at (415) 744-2378 or mix.tom@epamail.epa.gov.

Santa Barbara County, CA

In April 1997, the EPA awarded Santa Barbara County, California a $200,000 grant for a National Brownfields Assessment Pilot. The Goleta Old Town area has served as an economic, social, and cultural focal point of the Goleta Valley since the early 1900s. During the 1950s and 1960s, military, industrial, and commercial businesses expanded in Old Town. Since that time, however, Goleta Old Town has experienced significant economic decline in the commercial, industrial, and residential sectors of the community. To a large degree, economic redevelopment has been impeded by known and suspected environmental contamination.

The pilot area of Goleta Old Town has a population of approximately 5,000, 44 percent of whom is minority and 12 percent of whom live below the poverty level. Old Town developed a revitalization plan through joint public-private efforts holding more than 25 community meetings. Based on historic and current land uses, the county has identified approximately 50 potential brownfields sites.

Santa Barbara County's goal is to restore the Old Town area as an economically vital social and cultural focus of the Goleta Valley community. Objectives include the creation of effective development partnerships; implementation of sustainable land uses; and encouragement of diverse commerce and business. Activities planned as part of this pilot include:

- Developing cost-effective plans for site assessment, characterization, and future plans for cleanup strategies through a private/public team approach;

- Conducting preliminary and detailed target site assessments, including data compilation, technical interpretations, sampling, drilling, geophysical surveying, hydrogeological testing, and health and safety reviews;

- Determining funding sources and mechanisms for financing future cleanups and revitalization;

- Coordinating the revitalization interests of residents, property owners, businesses, lenders, educational institutions, governments, and other stakeholders; and

- Documenting remediation strategies, revitalization strategies, and pilot progress, including measures of success.

For more information, contact Daniel Gira of County Planning and Development at (805) 568-2068 or Jim Hanson of U.S. EPA Region 9 at (415) 744-2237.

Stockton, CA

The EPA has awarded the City of Stockton, California a grant for a National Brownfields Assessment Pilot. The goal of the Stockton pilot is to encourage economic revitalization of the city's waterfront, which has been designated a state Enterprise Zone. Activities planned as part of the pilot include identifying the sources and scope of brownfields contamination; developing a coordinated partnership that includes the Waterfront Revival Task Force, residents, community groups, businesses, and public entities; developing a comprehensive environmental plan; and participating in California EPA's Expedited Remedial Action Program to develop and implement a remediation strategy. For more information, contact Thomas Mix of U.S. EPA Region 9 at (415) 744-2378 or mix.tom@epamail.epa.gov.

Connecticut

Bridgeport, CT

The EPA has awarded the City of Bridgeport, Connecticut a grant for a National Brownfields Assessment Pilot. Activities planned as part of this pilot include categorizing and prioritizing cleanup sites, developing timeline estimates for duration and methods of cleanup with associated costs, and selecting two to six model sites. Incentives will be identified for effective property assessments, cleanup, and redevelopment for each model site. In addition, the city will coordinate with the Housatonic Community and Technical College to offer environmental science courses to students to prepare them to assist in future redevelopment efforts. For more information, contact John Podgurski of U.S. EPA Region 1 at (617) 573-9681 or podgurski.john@epamail.epa.gov.

Hartford, CT

In April 1997, the EPA awarded the City of Hartford, Connecticut a $200,000 grant for a National Brownfields Assessment Pilot. Of the more than 1,100 acres in the city that were once in productive use, 30 percent have been abandoned since 1986. More than 750 buildings, presenting unknown environmental hazards, are vacant as the result of industrial migration from the city. The industrial exodus has presented serious economic and social problems for the city. In 1995, 62 percent of the city's population of 125,100 was identified as living below federal low-to-moderate income guidelines. Between 1989 and 1995, the number of jobs fell by 22 percent. The city believes that to reverse this decline it must be able to offer inner-city sites of comparable acreage and accessibility as those offered by suburban locations for redevelopment.

The pilot will target blighted and deteriorated sites in three Hartford neighborhoods—Sheldon/Charter Oak, Upper Albany, and Clay Arsenal. Unemployment rates in these target areas range from 15 to 24 percent, and minority population rates range from 80 to 99 percent. Although each of these neighborhoods has attempted to address economic problems through community-based efforts, the perception of environmental contamination has impeded redevelopment. The city believes that, without site investigations, potential purchasers will continue to avoid the unknown environmental risks at these brownfields.

Hartford's goal is to attract manufacturing and commercial industries to brownfields sites. Pilot objectives are to select three brownfields sites for redevelopment, conduct environmental assessments at the three sites, develop site-specific redevelopment strategies, and conduct community outreach. Activities planned for this pilot include:

- Prioritizing and evaluating brownfield sites to determine their redevelopment potential, and selecting three target sites;

- Conducting preliminary environmental assessments at the three target sites;

- Developing site-specific redevelopment strategies for these sites;

- Developing a model for community residents participating in brownfields redevelopment planning; and

- Educating the community about barriers to redevelopment.

For more information, contact Madelyn Cohen of the Hartford Redevelopment Agency at (860) 543-8655 or John Podgurski of U.S. EPA Region 1 at (617) 573-9681 or podgurski.john@epamail. epa.gov.

Delaware

Wilmington, DE

In April 1997, the EPA awarded the City of Wilmington, Delaware a $200,000 grant for a National Brownfields Assessment Pilot. Industrial development in Wilmington began during the industrial revolution of the 1800s and was centered along the Brandywine and Christina Rivers. Recent studies by the Delaware Brownfields Assessment Program have indicated that most of the brownfields located along these rivers are contaminated. Brownfields areas include Cherry Island, the East Seventh Street Peninsula, the Port of Wilmington vicinity, South Madison Street, Bell Alley, Browntown, and Todds Lane. In addition, smaller isolated commercial and industrial properties are potentially contaminated. The communities adjacent to these brownfields areas are comprised of low-to-moderate income families experiencing higher than average unemployment. Poverty rates in these areas range from 12 to 66 percent, and unemployment ranges from 6 to 20 percent.

There are approximately 1,750 acres of vacant, abandoned, underused, and contaminated properties in the city. This reduction in the area available for development limits the amount of tax revenue and employment opportunities that can be generated. The city will conduct an inventory and environmental assessment of the properties as part of the city's plans leading to redevelopment and revitalization of its urban core.

Wilmington's objectives for the pilot are to create an inventory of brownfields sites; increase neighborhood capacity to participate in redevelopment decisionmaking; plan for cleanup funding; and conduct outreach activities to educate site owners and potential developers, investors, and lenders about brownfields redevelopment incentives. Activities planned as part of this pilot include:

- Developing a cleanup and redevelopment planning database that includes an inventory of all industrial and commercial sites at which contamination may be present;

- Encouraging neighborhood participation in redevelopment planning and environmental justice activities; and

- Establishing a brownfields remediation loan program and working to secure Community Reinvestment Act funding for the program.

For more information, contact Emery Graham, Jr. in the City/County Building at (302) 571-4130 or Tom Stolle of U.S. EPA Region 3 at (215) 566-3129 or stolle.tom@epamail.epa.gov.

Florida

Dade County, FL

In April 1997, the EPA awarded Dade County, Florida a $200,000 grant for a National Brownfields Assessment Pilot. Dade County is a large urbanized area situated between two national parks and above a sole source aquifer. It is also within the area targeted for redevelopment as part of the State's "Eastward Ho!" initiative. Dade County's urban expansion into "greenfields" has left older commercial and industrial sites in the urban core vacant and potentially contaminated. The ability of many small service and industrial businesses to pay for site remediation is very limited. As in many cities, actual or perceived contamination of inner-city sites has contributed to the economic decline of these areas.

The pilot will focus on the Poinciana Industrial Center (PIC), which is a 30-acre, county-owned property formerly used for various industrial and commercial purposes. Additional environmental assessment and remediation are required before the site can be effectively redeveloped. The site is located within a federal Community Development Block Grant target area and is adjacent to a public housing development. Area residents are low-income minorities experiencing high levels of underemployment and unemployment. Previous community involvement in similar efforts indicates a high probability of community support for the pilot.

Dade County's goal is to develop incentives and procedures to encourage private sector redevelopment of brownfields throughout the county. The county will use the Poinciana Industrial Center as an example upon which to build a comprehensive brownfields plan. The brownfields redevelopment process will address legal, financial, technical, and community involvement issues. Dade

County believes the area has a strong history of community involvement but that redevelopment has been slow, in part, due to perceptions of site contamination. Activities planned as part of this pilot include:

- Developing a comprehensive process for identification, inventory, assessment, cleanup planning, and reuse of brownfields;

- Creating a database of potential brownfields sites;

- Developing and implementing a community involvement plan; and

- Completing the Poinciana Industrial Center site assessments and developing remediation plans.

For more information, contact Doug Yoder of the Dade County Department of Environmental Resources Management at (305) 372-6766 or Barbara Dick of U.S. EPA Region 4 at (404) 562-8923 or dick.barbara@epamail.epa.gov.

Jacksonville, FL

In April 1997, the EPA awarded the City of Jacksonville, Florida a $200,000 grant for a National Brownfields Assessment Pilot. Historically, Jacksonville's port has served as a major commercial center. Agricultural, petroleum, and paper product industries, in particular, have dominated the commercial market supporting Jacksonville. Commerce flourished for over a century has subsided, leaving over 100 sites in the downtown area with known or suspected soil and groundwater contamination.

Private and public initiatives have begun to revitalize the area. Initiatives include construction of a new sports complex, increased private sector investments, municipal bond funding used for public improvements, and Port Authority efforts to improve and expand the downtown's port facilities. The city anticipates that the EPA's brownfields pilot funding will provide seed money for site assessments and cleanup planning, act as a catalyst for matching funds, motivate partnerships, centralize efforts to address brownfields, and solidify community support.

Jacksonville's objectives are to establish a redevelopment process with defined policies, procedures, and mechanisms that will restore brownfields sites into economically productive properties, create new jobs, and increase quality of life for nearby inner-city neighborhoods. The city anticipates that the pilot will result in a process that can be replicated in other industrial urban core neighborhoods, port cities, and similar waterfront properties. Activities planned as part of this pilot include:

- Evaluating environmental justice concerns in the pilot area and implementing community involvement activities;

- Developing an information repository linked to a geographic information system, and publishing a quarterly brownfields redevelopment newsletter;

- Identifying the roles of cooperating agencies and organizations needed for site redevelopment;

- Identifying public and private funding sources for site restoration and attracting potential investors;

- Taking inventory of private water supplies in the pilot area and developing a groundwater model; and

- Developing approaches for conducting brownfields site assessments and cleanups.

For more information, contact Eric Lindstrom of the Downtown Development Authority at (904) 630-1913 or Barbara Dick of U.S. EPA Region 4 at (404) 562-8923 or dick.barbara@epamail. epa.gov.

Tallahassee, FL

In April 1997, the EPA awarded the City of Tallahassee, Florida a $191,000 grant for a National Brownfields Assessment Pilot. The Gaines Street/Cascades Corridor is currently the focal point for the city's redevelopment efforts. As part of Tallahassee's historical rail corridor, the Gaines Street/Cascades Corridor has supported chemical warehousing, petroleum distribution centers, light industry, animal stockyards, and city-owned coal gasification plant and dump. Seventy-three brownfields properties with known or perceived contamination, scattered across 450 acres, have been identified in the Gaines Street/Cascades Corridor. Adjacent property owners in need of expansion have shown no interest in using these brownfield properties.

Tallahassee believes that properties in the Gaines Street/Cascades Corridor could support increased residential, commercial, and light industrial uses. The properties currently fail to contribute to the vitality of what would otherwise be a vibrant community. Strategically located between the municipal airport and the state capitol complex, the Corridor is poised to become a gateway to downtown Tallahassee.

Tallahassee's goal is to develop an implementable brownfields remediation plan that supports and furthers the broader community redevelopment program for the Gaines Street/Cascades Corridor. The remediation plan will include distinct redevelopment activities, clear roles and responsibilities for stakeholders, and extensive public communication on redevelopment progress. The city anticipates that a measurable objective for the pilot will be the degree to which the public becomes aware of, and involved in, the remediation program planning activities. Activities planned as part of this pilot include:

- Conducting community outreach and sponsoring workshops for stakeholders;

- Completing site and contamination mapping and preparing site assessment reports;

- Developing a remediation plan for cleanup actions in the pilot area; and

- Prioritizing site cleanups and planning redevelopment activities.

For more information, contact Craig Diamond of the Tallahassee-Leon County Planning Department at (904) 891-8621 or Barbara Dick of U.S. EPA Region 4 at (404) 562-8923 or dick.barbara @epamail.epa.gov.

Illinois

Cook County, IL

In April 1997, the EPA awarded Cook County, in partnership with the City of Harvey, Illinois, a $200,000 grant for a National Brownfields Assessment Pilot. The concentration of former industrial facilities that are known or suspected to be contaminated, as well as the presence of landfills, have combined to create a blighted area in Harvey. These areas are characterized by deteriorating housing and infrastructure. In addition, a number of properties are tax delinquent, resulting in declining tax revenues and increasing municipal tax rates to fund basic municipal services. The city is struggling to revitalize its industrial and commercial base, improve housing, and repair its aging infrastructure. Seeking an innovative way to combat these problems, the city joined four neighboring suburban Chicago communities (Dixmoor, Ford Heights, Phoenix, and Robbins) to form the South Suburban Enterprise Communities (SSEC), which is dedicated to the economic redevelopment of the area. The SSEC was designated a federal Enterprise Community in 1995.

The pilot site was selected by the SSEC. It is the former Wyman-Gordon manufacturing facility, a 39-acre parcel in Harvey. The facility is one of many known or suspected brownfields identified during survey conducted in 1991. Although developers have expressed some interest in brownfields, such as the Wyman-Gordon manufacturing facility, redevelopment within the SSEC has not occurred because of concerns about contamination, liability, and unknown remediation costs.

Cook County's goals are to expand its economic base, bring in new businesses, and create new jobs. Redeveloping brownfields is critical step toward achieving these goals. The objectives of the pilot are to conduct a site assessment of the Wyman-Gordon manufacturing facility, involve the community and other stakeholders in redevelopment planning, and begin planning efforts to leverage funds for cleanup through partnerships with developers and investors. Activities planned as part of this pilot include:

- Completing a site assessment of the pilot site;

- Implementing community outreach and education programs to involve the community and other stakeholders in redevelopment planning;

- Planning outreach activities for cleanup and redevelopment, including efforts to leverage redevelopment incentive programs (e.g., the Cook County No Cash Bid Program, the Tax Increment Financing District Program, and tax incentives offered through state and federal enterprise zone programs); and

- Working with community colleges and employment training organizations to link redevelopment of brownfields with job training and business opportunities.

For more information, contact Gwendolyn Clemons at (312) 443-4297 or Mary Beth Tuohy of U.S. EPA Region 5 at (312) 886-7596 or tuohy.marybeth@epamail.epa.gov.

West Central Municipal Conference, IL

The EPA has awarded the West Central Municipal Conference a grant for a National Brownfields Assessment Pilot. Activities planned as part of this pilot include creating a "Rapid Response Team" to provide timely expertise on brownfields redevelopment; establishing a Brownfields Prevention Program to identify ongoing industrial activities that pose a risk of creating new brownfields; supporting redevelopment of at least two public and two private brownfields land parcels; and distributing information about the pilot to the public. For more information, contact Bill Haubold of U.S. EPA Region 5 at (312) 353-3261.

Indiana

Indianapolis, IN

The EPA has awarded the City of Indianapolis, Indiana a grant for a National Brownfields Assessment Pilot. Indianapolis will use the pilot finding to hire a Brownfields Coordinator. The Coordinator will develop and maintain an inventory of brownfields in the city using a geographical information system; develop and coordinate the reuse program, for brownfields redevelopment; coordinate meetings with community groups, prospective property owners, and the city's reuse group; and review additional assessment and cleanup funding mechanisms and approaches to liability issues. For more information, contact Deborah Orr of U.S. EPA Region 5 at (312) 886-7576.

Kansas

Kansas City, KS and MO

The EPA has awarded Kansas City, Kansas and Missouri a grant for a National Brownfields Assessment Pilot. The goal of the Greater Kansas City pilot is to demonstrate economic redevelopment of environmentally contaminated sites in the bi-state Central Industrial District. Existing tools, such as prospective purchaser agreements and financial mechanisms, will be compiled from local and national sources and applied to a few select sites. Activities planned as part of the pilot include conducting an inventory of numerous properties in the Central Industrial District, initiating a community involvement plan, conducting Phase I and Phase II site assessments on four to six sites, integrating public and private interests in the brownfields process at selected sites, and ensuring the involvement of those communities most adversely impacted by the sites. For more information, contact Kerry Herndon of U.S. EPA Region 7 at (913) 551-7286.

Kentucky

Louisville, KY

The EPA has awarded the City of Louisville, Kentucky a grant for a National Brownfields Assessment Pilot. The Louisville Empowerment Zone Brownfields Working Group plans to address a brownfields site in Louisville's heavy industrial corridor. Activities planned as part of the pilot include using a geographical information system to provide information on environmental conditions of property in the corridor; establishing a streamlined process for voluntary cleanup, which will include implementing a "clean closure" mechanism; conducting an area-wide assessment of the Louisville aquifer; and assessing brownfields in the corridor.

For more information, contact Barbara Dick of U.S. EPA Region 4 at (404) 562-8923 or dick.barbara@epamail.epa.gov.

Louisiana

New Orleans, LA

The EPA has awarded the City of New Orleans, Louisiana a grant for a National Brownfields Assessment Pilot. Activities planned as part of the pilot include identifying the city's brownfields; maintaining an inventory of sites on a geographical information system for data analysis; developing criteria for ranking their redevelopment potential; and sponsoring meetings with lenders, developers, city planners, citizens, and agency officials to explore remediation funding mechanisms. In addition, New Orleans will develop additional strategies for community outreach efforts. For more information, contact Stan Hitt of U.S. EPA Region 6 at (214) 665-6736 or hitt.stan@epamail.epa.gov.

Maine

State of Maine

In April 1997, the EPA awarded the State of Maine a $199,017 grant for a National Brownfields Assessment Pilot. Maine's Voluntary Response Action Plan Program has served as the primary vehicle for environmental cleanup by brownfields purchasers. The program does not have sufficient information to assist communities and investors in identifying brownfields opportunities and has not broadly disseminated information regarding existing legal and financial tools. The state intends to use this pilot to fill these critical information and communication gaps.

Although Maine is characterized as rural, 85 towns and cities are centers for jobs, retail trade, and social and cultural services.

The pilot will focus on these 85 service centers/communities that have not experienced the same level of economic growth as surrounding suburban areas. For example, since 1970, housing growth has been 48 percent statewide, as opposed to only 35 percent in the service centers/communities. Twenty-one percent of Maine's service center population is 150 percent below the poverty level.

Maine's goal is to use redevelopment of brownfields as a catalyst for revitalizing many communities. This effort is an outgrowth of the state's Growth Management Program, which calls for orderly residential, commercial, and industrial development that is desirable for communities. The state believes that brownfields redevelopment is a key strategy for channeling development to these growth areas, many of which support historically significant buildings or water frontage. Activities planned as part of this pilot include:

- Creating a geographic information system (GIS) listing of potential brownfields redevelopment opportunities in service center communities;

- Creating GIS profiles of the historic development areas in selected service center communities to assist developers, investors, and decisionmakers in evaluating potential site cleanup issues and additional brownfield sites;

- Implementing outreach and educational programs to ensure better understanding and improved communication; and

- Establishing a municipal revolving loan fund that will assist towns and cities in assessing and planning for redevelopment of brownfields sites.

For more information, contact Fran Rudoff of the Maine State Planning Office at (207) 287-3262 or John Podgurski of U.S. EPA Region 1 at (617) 573-9681 or podgurski.john@epamail.epa.gov.

Maryland

Baltimore, MD

The EPA has awarded the City of Baltimore, Maryland a grant for a National Brownfields Assessment Pilot. Activities planned as part of the pilot include identifying the sources and scope of the brownfields problem; defining the legal and regulatory obstacles to redevelopment; promoting new technologies for remediation; exploring the use of new financing mechanisms to aid site assessment and remediation; conducting at least two demonstration site remediation and development projects, with the potential to create at least fifty new jobs; and promoting voluntary cleanups. For more information contact Tom Stolle of U.S. EPA Region 3 at (215) 566-3129 or stolle.tom@epamail.epa.gov.

Massachusetts

Chicopee, MA

The EPA has awarded the City of Chicopee, Massachusetts a grant for a National Brownfields Assessment Pilot. Activities planned as part of this pilot include conducting a site assessment and designing a remediation strategy; creating an educational program for the neighborhood; identifying specific funding sources; and documenting the redevelopment process. Redevelopment of this site will be lead by the Chicopee Brownfield Task Force, and will create a working model for the cleanup and reuse of the city's other brownfields. Chicopee requested only $59,000 for the two year demonstration pilot, most of which will go to the Phase I and Phase II site assessments and remedial design. For more information, contact John Podgurski of U.S. EPA Region 1 at (617) 573-9681 or podgurski.john @epamail.epa.gov.

Greenfield, MA

In April 1997, the EPA awarded the Town of Greenfield, Massachusetts a $125,000 grant for a National Brownfields Assessment Pilot. Greenfield is the seat of Franklin County and a major regional employment center. The town has experienced a significant decline in its industrial base over the last 20 years as a result of the abandonment of many older industrial/commercial buildings in the town's center. The town also has experienced a 37 percent loss in manufacturing jobs between 1980 and 1990, and estimates that 900 additional jobs were lost between 1990 and 1995. Greenfield and other Franklin County towns have been designated by the Commonwealth as an Economic Target Area. This designation enables Greenfield to receive priority for state capital funding and to offer tax incentives to prospective property developers.

The pilot site consists of an abandoned, 145,000 square-foot, machine tool manufacturing plant located along the Green River and dating back to the 1870s. Since the Greenfield Tap and Dye plant closed in 1993, the site has been vandalized, and open containers of hazardous materials have been identified on the property. Redevelopment of this site could provide needed space for expansion by local manufacturers, and is highly desirable with respect to existing transportation and infrastructure support. The pilot project will develop a partnership between the town, Commonwealth environmental agencies, University of Massachusetts students, and private consultants to prepare an environmental assessment and remediation plan for this site.

Greenfield's goals are to evaluate the environmental concerns at the pilot site, explore an innovative cooperative model for site assessment, create redevelopment opportunities, and plan for the restoration of the site as an asset to a blighted neighborhood. In particular, this pilot will focus on model approaches to reducing site assessment costs, and these models will be evaluated to determine their applicability for use at other sites in the area. Pilot goals also include the determination of future land use options and cleanup levels for the pilot site and are directed toward job training and workforce development for students. Activities planned as part of the pilot include:

- Conducting additional site assessments, characterizing hazardous wastes, and preparing a remediation work plan for the Greenfields Tap and Dye facility;

- Determining future land use options for the facility;

- Identifying funding sources and private sector developers to assist in cleanup and redevelopment; and

- Expanding a cooperative partnership model between the local government, the Commonwealth, and University of Massachusetts.

For more information, contact Teri Anderson of the Office of Planning and Community Development at (413) 772-1548 or John Podgurski of U.S. EPA Region 1 at (617) 573-9681 or via e-mail at podgurski.john@epamail.epa.gov.

Lawrence, MA

The EPA has awarded the City of Lawrence, Massachusetts a grant for a National Brownfields Assessment Pilot. The goal of the Lawrence pilot is to provide long-term stability and a safe environment for its downtown industrial, commercial, and residential centers by employing the existing public/private partnerships created to redevelop three significant contaminated sites. Activities planned for the pilot include taking an inventory of brownfields within the North Canal industrial corridor; expanding the city's existing community advisory committees to encourage meaningful involvement of the community's minority groups and other stakeholders; creating a "one stop" guidance manual for brownfields redevelopment; and coordinating city, state, and federal efforts. For more information, contact John Podgurski of U.S. EPA Region 1 at (617) 573-9681 or podgurski.john@epamail. epa.gov.

Lowell, MA

The EPA has awarded the City of Lowell, Massachusetts a grant for a National Brownfields Assessment Pilot. The Lowell pilot intends to focus efforts on overcoming key obstacles to brownfields redevelopment already identified by the city in previous brownfields projects. Lowell has been designated a federal Enterprise Community. Activities planned as part of the pilot include ranking potential brownfields sites; completing site assessments of priority sites including two North Canal Project sites and three to five other sites; implementing a comprehensive, multilingual, multimedia brownfield education program in the impacted communities; and developing a self-sustaining and secure funding program for continuing to redevelop other contaminated properties. For more information, contact Lynne Jennings of U.S. EPA Region 1 at (617) 573-9634.

New Bedford, MA

In April 1997, the EPA awarded the City of New Bedford, Massachusetts a $172,000 grant for a National Brownfields Assessment Pilot. New Bedford has undergone industrial changes over its history, beginning with the whaling industry that later gave way to textile and apparel manufacturing in the late 1800s. The city is working to diversify and supplement its industrial base, which has eroded due to the departure of manufacturing industries and changes in federal fishing industry policies. The city believes that the fish processing capabilities and transportation facilities in the area provide a setting with great potential for expansion of its aquaculture industry. New Bedford already has begun investigating vacant and underused industrial sites to determine their suitability for aquaculture development.

The pilot will use the city's initial investigations to identify candidate sites, many of which formerly housed mill operations. Many sites may be adapted with few modifications to the aquaculture industry. Growth of the aquaculture business will help alleviate New Bedford's economic and social problems.

New Bedford's goal is to convert area brownfields into productive aquaculture sites in accordance with existing city plans. The pilot also will contribute to the Commonwealth's efforts to develop the city's aquaculture business. Pilot objectives include developing an inventory of appropriate brownfields sites, securing community input, identifying remediation costs, and documenting the process to facilitate replicability at other brownfields areas. Activities planned as part of the pilot include:

- Developing site selection criteria, including tax status of the property and the remedial work required;

- Evaluating potential sites for aquaculture use in accordance with the selection criteria;

- Conducting environmental assessments at two sites, including drilling, field sampling, data analysis, and report preparation; and

- Integrating site-specific data into the city's existing geographic information system.

For more information, contact Gary Gomes of the City of New Bedford Grants Administration at (508) 979-1466 or John

Podgurski of U.S. EPA Region 1 at (617) 573-9681 or podgurski.john@epamail.epa.gov.

Worcester, MA

The EPA has awarded the City of Worcester, Massachusetts a grant for a National Brownfields Assessment Pilot. The goal of the Worcester pilot is to create incentives for the redevelopment of urban industrial sites and ensure the safety and health of the surrounding neighborhoods. Activities planned as part of this pilot include developing a public input mechanism through the creation of the Central Massachusetts Brownfields Advisory Council, selecting and assessing three priority pilot sites, and investigating redevelopment financing options. The city plans to prepare protocols for the identification, analysis, selection, acquisition, and disposition of brownfields sites. For more information, contact John Podgurski of U.S. EPA Region 1 at (617) 573-9681 or podgurski.john@epamail.epa.gov.

Michigan

Detroit, MI

The EPA has awarded the City of Detroit, Michigan a grant for a National Brownfields Assessment Pilot. As part of this pilot, Detroit created the Redevelopment of Urban Sites Action Team (the R.E.U.S. A-Team) to identify and address obstacles to the reuse of abandoned properties. The goals of the A-Team are to educate potential investors about brownfields success stories; to establish a countywide sustainable development community roundtable; and to produce a manual to teach others the "lessons learned" in Detroit. For more information, contact Mike Gifford of U.S. EPA Region 5 at (312) 886-7257.

Minnesota

Chippewa County/Kinross Township, MN

The EPA has awarded Chippewa County/Kinross Township, Minnesota a grant for a National Brownfields Assessment Pilot. Activities planned as part of this pilot include completing Phase I through Phase III site assessments; convening a community task force of public and private stakeholders (including the U.S. Army Corps of Engineers and the Sault Ste. Marie Tribe of Chippewa Indians) to plan redevelopment strategies for each potential brownfield; preparing legal documentation related to land ownership, liability, due care requirements, zoning, and financing; and involving affected communities. For more information, contact Mary Beth Tuohy of U.S. EPA Region 5 at (312) 886-7596 or tuohy.marybeth@epamail.epa.gov.

St. Paul Port Authority, MN

In April 1997, the EPA awarded the Port Authority of St. Paul, Minnesota a $146,000 grant for a National Brownfields Assessment Pilot. Historically, the City of St. Paul's industrial development evolved from its location as both a navigation hub on the Mississippi River and railroad center. No longer dependent on railroads or shipping, facilities moving into St. Paul are locating in areas outside of the urban core.

The City of St. Paul has 4,000 acres of land zoned for industrial use, but nearly 1,000 of these acres are underused or abandoned. Redevelopment of industrial property needed to maintain the city's tax base, increase employment opportunities, and attract suitable industrial facilities has been limited due to either known or suspected contamination. In addition to the public health issues associated with potential contamination, many sites in the urban core have deteriorating structures that attract illegal activities, such as drug trafficking and vagrancy. Such conditions foster further disinvestment in the inner city and investment in undeveloped suburban greenfields, perpetuating a cycle of urban core decline and suburban sprawl.

The goals of the St. Paul Port Authority are to optimize the reuse of abandoned and underused industrial sites within the City of St. Paul, create increased employment opportunities for local residents, and generate sufficient tax revenues to provide services needed for long-term, ecologically sound, industrial growth. The Port Authority will partner with neighborhood organizations to gain support for redevelopment projects and workforce development. The initial work will focus on up to six sites targeted for redevelopment. Activities planned for this pilot include:

- Working with neighborhood organizations to identify up to six target brownfields sites for redevelopment;

- Conducting site assessments at up to six brownfields sites;

- Preparing and publishing reports on the results of the site assessments;

- Preparing response action or cleanup plans for one to three targeted sites; and

- Partner with neighborhood organizations to establish a workforce development plan.

For more information, contact Lorrie Louder of the St. Paul Port Authority at (612) 224-5686 or Mary Beth Tuohy of U.S. EPA Region 5 at (312) 886-7596 or tuohy.marybeth@epamail.epa.gov.

Missouri

St. Louis, MO

The EPA has awarded the City of St. Louis, Missouri grant for a National Brownfields Assessment Pilot. Activities planned as part of the pilot include investigating the Dr. Martin Luther King Business Park to characterize environmental concerns; establishing and building a Brownfields Reinvestment Fund; working with state agencies to implement the recently enacted Abandoned Property Reuse Act; and organizing a voluntary Environmental Consultant Committee to guide selection of cleanup criteria and development of risk-based cleanup standards. In addition, St. Louis will form a Citizens Advisory Council to ensure community involvement in the initiative, and will transfer knowledge gained from the business park efforts to a Brownfields Redevelopment Model for implementation at other sites. For information, contact Kerry Herndon of U.S. EPA Region 7 at (913) 551-7286.

Wellston, MO

In April 1997, the EPA awarded the City of Wellston, Missouri a $200,000 grant for a National Brownfields Assessment Pilot. Wellston is a state-designated Enterprise Zone and a federally designated Enterprise Community in St. Louis County. Wellston's population has declined by 60 percent over the past 50 years, 46 percent of the current residents live below the poverty level, and the city has a 22 percent unemployment rate. Most industries have moved to the suburbs, and a once vibrant retail district has disappeared from the city. The Wellston pilot is focusing on a 100-acre area near the Wellington Metro Link Station. A previous user of a portion of that area was the Wagner Electric Company. It manufactured electrical transformers, electric motors, brake linings, and other components. A portion of the Wagner site was cleaned up under Superfund authority; however, the city believes that other areas at the site also may be contaminated.

The Land Clearance for Redevelopment Authorities of St. Louis County and the City of Wellston plan to redevelop brownfields areas (including portions of the Wagner site) as a Wellston Technology Park (WTP). The WTP would require improvements to infrastructure to facilitate residential and commercial development. The pilot is seen as an opportunity to recapture a long-lost regional asset and to create a new economic base for the city.

Wellston's goal is to create employment and reinvestment opportunities by redeveloping a 100-acre abandoned industrial area into an industrial technology park. Objectives of the pilot are to conduct environmental assessments of properties in the 100-acre area, prepare remediation and redevelopment plans, and develop a community outreach program. Activities planned as part of this pilot include:

- Conducting Phase I environmental assessments on vacant industrial buildings and lots on the 100-acre site;

- Conducting Phase II subsurface investigations on properties identified as suspect during the Phase I assessments, and developing a database of suspect properties;

- Preparing remediation plans;

- Preparing a comprehensive redevelopment plan, including land use strategies; and

- Developing a community outreach program to actively involve residents in the redevelopment efforts.

For more information, contact Dennis Coleman of the Land Clearance for Redevelopment Authorities of St. Louis County and the City of Wellston at (314) 889-7663 or Susan Klein of U.S. EPA Region 7 at (913) 551-7786 or klein.susan@epamail.epa.gov.

New Jersey

Jersey City, NJ

In April 1997, the EPA awarded Jersey City, New Jersey a $200,000 grant for a National Brownfields Assessment Pilot. Located on the Paulus Hook peninsula and in close proximity to New York City, Jersey City served as a magnet to the railroad and shipping industries over the last century. In the 1960s, railroad use began declining and industrial companies began departing from the area. These changes resulted in both environmental and economic problems. Approximately 20 percent of the city's acreage has been identified as potential brownfields sites. The pilot area consist of the former industrialized and rail areas surrounded by the residential communities of Bergen Hill, Greenville, and Lafayette.

Jersey City's brownfields pilot will serve a prototype for development of a standardized redevelopment model. It will focus on methods for the completion of brownfields site inventories, site assessments, and remediation planning. Particular emphasis will be on funding a comprehensive community-based environmental education and participation program.

Jersey City believes the brownfields pilot will encourage redevelopment and reuse of brownfields properties that will lead to an increased municipal tax base, create new industrial jobs, and reduce potential exposure to contaminants by residents of adjacent neighborhoods. Activities planned as part of this pilot include:

- Developing an inventory of brownfields sites in a comprehensive date and graphic information retrieval system;

- Conducting programs for community involvement, environmental education, and public participation, and establishing a mobile educational information center;

- Completing site assessments in the target area; and

- Developing remedial work plans for site cleanups, incorporating innovative technologies whenever possible.

For more information, contact Paul Hamilton of the Jersey City Redevelopment Agency at (201) 547-4799 or Larry D'Andrea of U.S. EPA Region 2 at (212) 637-4314 or dandrea.larry@epamail. epa.gov.

Newark, NJ

The EPA has awarded the City of Newark, New Jersey a grant for a National Brownfields Assessment Pilot. The goal of the Newark pilot is to coordinate New Jersey's innovative legislative and regulatory tools to produce a pipeline of clean, redeveloped sites while inventing a model process replicable in other cities. Newark has been designated a federal Enterprise Community and an Urban Enterprise Zone. Activities planned as part of the pilot include completing a comprehensive GIS-based brownfields inventory; assessing four diverse sites; continuing outreach to the community through the Newark Brownfields Working Group; applying innovative site assessment technologies in cooperation with the New Jersey Institute of Technology and Rutgers University; encouraging private investment; linking redevelopment to revitalization; and producing a brownfields redevelopment plan. For more information, contact Larry D'Andrea of U.S. EPA Region 2 at (212) 637-4314 or dandrea.larry@epamail.epa.gov.

Perth Amboy, NJ

In April 1997, the EPA awarded the City of Perth Amboy, New Jersey a $200,000 grant for a National Brownfields Assessment Pilot. With its close proximity to major water and ground transportation routes, Perth Amboy has served as the industrial and manufacturing hub of central New Jersey for many years. The exodus of industry, disinvestment, and a general suburbanization of the region have resulted in many areas of vacant or underused industrial and commercial property, as well as many substandard buildings in need of rehabilitation or demolition. Industrial decline in the city also has resulted in socio-economic erosion, as shown by a per capita income that is 138 percent lower than the state average. Since 1990, the assessed value of portions of the targeted redevelopment area fell by more than $3.8 million.

The pilot will be conducted on 877 acres of historically heavy industrial property located in the northeast and southwest sections of the city. Currently, 43 percent of this acreage is vacant. Although rich in historical and cultural heritage, the pilot area has been contaminated through many years of industrial activity. The pilot area will complement the city's current redevelopment plan, which includes a unique private/public partnership called Focus 2000. Integration of Focus 2000 with Perth Amboy's Urban Enterprise Zone program and the brownfields pilot will help to provide additional incentives for property development.

Perth Amboy's goal is to provide technical expertise, public/private support, and vision to empower the local community and private developers in remediation and revitalization of the redevelopment area. The city aims to delineate contamination; plan for the use of innovative technologies and site cleanup protocols; improve public accessibility to brownfields and risk information; and develop sustainable insurance coverage programs. Activities planned as part of this pilot include:

- Conducting surveys, inventories, and assessments in the brownfields redevelopment area, and compiling related database information;

- Developing an insurance pool coverage program addressing liability exposure, remediation cost overruns, and third party liability coverage;

- Conducting feasibility studies for innovative technologies that may be used in site cleanups; and

- Developing a public participation and risk communication plan with support from Rutgers University and the New Jersey Institute of Technology.

For more information, contact Melvin Ramos of the City of Perth Amboy at (908) 826-0920 or Larry D'Andrea of U.S. EPA Region 2 at (212) 637-4314 or dandrea.larry@epamail.epa.gov.

Trenton, NJ

The EPA has awarded the City of Trenton, New Jersey grant for a National Brownfields Assessment Pilot. Activities planned as part of this pilot include establishing the Brownfields Environmental Solutions for Trenton (BEST) Advisory Council to advise the city on redevelopment issues; identifying and performing site investigations at key commercial/industrial brownfields sites; raising public awareness of possible issues at sites in residential areas; and evaluating methods and options for encouraging financial institutions to invest in key brownfields sites and neighborhoods to prevent "brownlining." For more information, contact Larry D'Andrea of U.S. EPA Region 2 at (212) 637-4314 or dandrea.larry@epamail.epa.gov.

New York

Elmira, NY

In April 1997, the EPA awarded the City of Elmira, New York a $200,000 grant for a National Brownfields Assessment Pilot. Since 1970, Elmira has lost more than 10,000 manufacturing jobs as industrial employers abandoned urban brownfields sites. These job losses have resulted in a decreased population, increased neighborhood disinvestment and visual blight, increased numbers of vacant sites, and growing percentage of tax-exempt property. Although the city has implemented economic recovery measures, little redevelopment of brownfields has occurred. Environmental assessment and cleanup are required before new jobs can be created at underused or vacant sites.

Elmira has acquired a number of industrial properties, totaling about 50 acres, through abandonment and foreclosure. Eight of these properties, which range in size from 2.4 to 19 acres, have been selected for consideration as potential brownfields redevelopment sites for this pilot/ Past land use of the pilot properties (including railway, dry cleaning, and foundry operations) indicate the potential for contamination. Redevelopment efforts are expected to be facilitated by tax and non-tax incentives and other innovative financing tools offered through the city's status as a state Economic Development Zone. For example, Elmira will examine the feasibility of funding a stop-loss insurance program to cover private remediation costs in excess of cleanup estimates.

Elmira's objective is to assess, plan for cleanup, and redevelop brownfields sites within the city. Successful revitalization of brownfields sites is anticipated to result in increased employment, restored property tax revenues, and improved quality of life in affected neighborhoods. Objectives for the pilot are to complete preliminary site assessments at up to six sites and detailed assessments at up to four sites. Activities planned as part of this pilot include:

- Selecting a focused number of brownfields sites by a technical advisory team composed of representatives of the Chemung County Health Department, local and state environmental and economic development agencies, and potential development firms;

- Conducting preliminary environmental assessments at the selected brownfields;

- Obtaining technical advice from environmental and legal consultants, as needed; and

- Planning for cleanup under the State Voluntary Cleanup Program.

For more information, contact Cheryl Schneider of the Department of Business & Housing Development at (607) 737-5691 or Larry D'Andrea of U.S. EPA Region 2 at (212) 637-4314 or via e-mail at dandrea.larry@epamail.epa.gov.

New York, NY

The EPA has awarded the City of New York a grant for a National Brownfields Assessment Pilot. The goal of the New York City pilot is to mobilize a public/private task force to develop new approaches and performance measures that will accelerate redevelopment of brownfields. Activities planned as part of the pilot include working with communities to quantify the adverse impacts of brownfields, establishing a community outreach and education program, conducting assessments of five priority brownfields sites, and developing technical guidance for testing, sampling, and remediating hazardous wastes on brownfields properties. The city wants to provide the foundation for a policy framework to guide future decisions and cleanup investments in its Empowerment Zone and other disadvantaged communities. For more information, contact Walter Schoepf of U.S. EPA Region 2 at (212) 637-4319.

Niagara Falls, NY

In April 1997, the EPA awarded the City of Niagara Falls, New York a $195,250 grant for a National Brownfields Assessment Pilot. Between 1960 and 1990, the city's population declined substantially, and the manufacturing worker population dropped by one-third. Industries have left the area, leaving idle sites that are a major problem for Niagara Falls. Seventeen of these former industrial sites, encompassing 386 acres, are suspected of containing contaminated soil or groundwater and are unmarketable as a result of the environmental stigma. No tracts of undeveloped, uncontaminated land remain for development within the city; therefore, brownfields cleanup is imperative for economic growth. To promote successful redevelopment of the properties, the environmental risks must be defined accurately to encourage interest by banks and developers.

Of the 17 contaminated sites, four have been targeted for the pilot. Because the four sites are within the state-designated Economic Development Zone, the city will be able to offer tax credits and utility rate reductions to new or expanding businesses. Redevelopment of these sites will provide an opportunity for Niagara Falls to revitalize economically disadvantaged areas, provide jobs, augment the city's dwindling tax base, and limit urban sprawl and infrastructure maintenance costs.

The city's goal is to provide guidance in redeveloping underused and potentially contaminated properties. The city will use a systematic approach toward redevelopment that includes outreach, risk assessment, and environmental education. For each of the four sites targeted in the pilot, the city will develop cost estimates for rehabilitation, demolition, and remediation and will identify potential financing sources. Experience gained from the pilot will be used to address additional sites with contamination concerns and redevelopment potential. Activities planned as part of this pilot include:

- Conducting detailed investigations of four targeted sites to determine the extent of contamination;

- Planning for the cleanup of each of the four targeted sites, and developing cost estimates;

- Creating a comprehensive education and outreach program that addresses the needs of the Economic Development Zone neighborhoods;

- Establishing an Environmental Awareness Center to develop, coordinate, implement, and document environmental education programs; and

- Coordinating pilot activities with ongoing brownfields efforts conducted by the city's Department of Environmental Services.

For more information, contact Dan Gagliardo of the Department of Environmental Services at (716) 286-4460 or Larry D'Andrea of U.S. EPA Region 2 at (212) 637-4314 or dandrea.larry@epamail.epa.gov.

Rochester, NY

The EPA has awarded the City of Rochester, New York a grant for a National Brownfields Assessment Pilot. Activities planned as part of the Rochester pilot include selecting four to five priority sites that are eligible for a revolving loan/grant program and two publicly-owned for additional environmental characterization and redevelopment; preparing marketability criteria for brownfields site selection; and bringing host residential communities into reuse decisionmaking process to develop site-specific property recycling strategies. Creation of these strategies will rely on partnerships with current and future site owners and users, government regulatory agencies, and development staff. For more information, contact Walter Schoepf of U.S. EPA Region 2 at (212) 637-4319.

Rome, NY

The EPA has awarded the City of Rome, New York a grant for a National Brownfields Assessment Pilot. The goal of the Rome pilot is to redevelop a 200-acre industrial area, which is adjacent to the central business district and in a state Economic Development Zone. Innovative site characterization technologies developed at the U.S. Department of Defense's Rome Laboratories will be used in assessments of a 17-acre demonstration site. Activities planned as part of the pilot include conducting environmental site assessments and updating a redevelopment plan for the 17-acre parcel of the industrial park, establishing letters of intent with property owners and regulators, using the Brownfields Task Force to involve the adjacent neighborhoods, and documenting the process for replication at other brownfields sites. For more information, contact D. Mather of U.S. EPA Region 2 at (212) 637-4357.

North Carolina

Charlotte, NC

The EPA has awarded the City of Charlotte, North Carolina a grant for a National Brownfields Assessment Pilot. Activities planned as part of this pilot include assessing two target sites in the South End; resolving barriers to reinvestment and development; creating model lending partnerships, and risk and liability sharing agreements; and stimulating community involvement, input and support. A key element of Charlotte's plan is to develop a cooperative relationship with the financial institutions in the city, which is the third largest financial center in the country. For more information, contact Matt Robbins of U.S. EPA Region 4 at (404) 562-8371.

Fayetteville, NC

In April 1997, the EPA awarded the City of Fayetteville, North Carolina a $200,000 grant for a National Brownfields Assessment Pilot. Downtown Fayetteville has been in decline since the 1970s, when businesses, manufacturers, and other facilities closed or relocated to outlying areas. More than half of the downtown retail space is presently unoccupied. Environmental contamination has been identified at three downtown sites, and more contaminated areas may be identified during the pilot program. By 1996, 52 percent of the residents in the Fayetteville had a standard pf living below the poverty level. The unemployment rate is 16 percent.

Cumberland County, which includes Fayetteville, is the only county in the state that is a federally designated Urban-Distressed Community. Urban redevelopment strategies are being led by a comprehensive vision that identifies the need for public/private partnerships with significant emphasis on brownfields. The pilot will target three areas in downtown Fayetteville, composed of mixed residential, commercial, and retail properties.

The objectives of the pilot are to assess and manage environmental issues related to redevelopment in three targeted areas and inventory brownfields in the downtown area. The city has developed numerous partnerships, including Cumberland County, Fort Bragg, and Fayetteville State University, to identify redevelopment opportunities, including brownfields, that will help to restore over 3,000 downtown acres to residential, recreational, educational, business, and industrial use. The objectives of the pilot are to conduct site assessments, conduct feasibility studies at three sites, develop cleanup and reuse models, and increase community involvement. For more information, contact Roger Stancil of the City of Fayetteville at (910) 433-1990 or Barbara Dick of U.S. EPA Region 4 at (404) 562-8923 or dick.barbara@epamail.epa.gov.

High Point, NC

In April 1997, the EPA awarded the City of High Point, North Carolina a $200,000 grant for a National Brownfields Assessment Pilot. As one of North Carolina's leading industrial centers, High Point maintains an extensive furniture manufacturing industry. The city has undertaken efforts to establish an industrial redevelopment program in the West Macedonia Revitalization Area, southeast of the central business district. The area is characterized by vacant, underused, and deteriorating industrial buildings, small clusters of blighted residential dwellings, and an abundance of undeveloped land.

Redevelopment within the industrial portion of the West Macedonia Revitalization Area has been limited. Opportunities for redevelopment have been hampered by both the availability of ample "greenfield" sites outside of the city, and by known or suspected environmental contamination resulting previous furniture and textile production. Experts from the University of North Carolina's Center for Study of Social Issues will join the city in managing the pilot and conducting economic market analyses.

High Point's goals are to revitalize the West Macedonia Revitalization Area and develop a model for addressing brownfields sites. The pilot will help the city to assess brownfields sites, plan site cleanup, and foster opportunities for public/private partnerships. Activities planned as part of this pilot include:

- Conducting an environmental assessment of vacant industrial properties;

- Determining the feasibility of private redevelopment and revitalization of brownfields sites within the pilot area, and determining the potential of reclaimed property for various industrial and service-related uses;

- Developing innovative approaches for redevelopment of brownfields sites;

- Expanding the city's community-based planning and community involvement program; and

- Identifying potential workforce needs once redevelopment takes place.

For more information, contact H. Lewis Price of the City of High Point at (910) 883-3289 or Barbara Dick of U.S. EPA Region 4 at (404) 562-8923 or dick.barbara@epamail.epa.gov.

Ohio

Cuyahoga County, OH

The EPA has awarded Cuyahoga County, Ohio a grant for a National Brownfields Assessment Pilot. As part of this pilot, the Cuyahoga County Planning Commission (CPC) in Cleveland has selected two sites for cleanup and redevelopment. One site involves securing remediation technologies, and the other involves construction with the intention of encouraging economic growth. Other pilot activities include working with an area community college to provide training in environmental work to local residents; developing high school curricula on environmental issues; establishing a community/business task force, community outreach, and financial support for brownfields assessment; cleanup; and redevelopment. For more information, contact Joe Dufficy of U.S. EPA Region 5 at (312) 886-1960.

Lima, OH

The EPA has awarded the City of Lima, Ohio a grant for a National Brownfields Assessment Pilot. The goal of the Lima brownfields pilot is to transform a 200-acre industrial park that has been hard-hit by industrial closings and defense downsizing into a modernized industrial community. Activities planned as part of the pilot include conducting Phase I site assessment and planning, implementing outreach activities in the community, and crafting legal agreements delineating partnership terms and financial arrangements for the assessment, remediation, and development of the industrial park. Lima's brownfields program will complement the river corridor redevelopment project, enhance water quality of the Ottawa River, and provide adjoining greenspace. The plan requires boundary annexation of 120 acres in the adjacent township of Shawnee, which supports the plan. For more information, contact Andy Warren of U.S. EPA Region 5 at (312) 353-5485.

Oregon

Oregon Mill Sites, OR

The EPA has awarded the Oregon Economic Development Department a grant for a National Brownfields Assessment Pilot. The Oregon Economic Development Department hopes to return vacant Oregon Mill Sites in seven rural communities to productive use. Activities planned as part of the pilot include developing cleanup standards and approaches for remediation; exploring financing options and development risks; and creating a computer model to measure costs and benefits of various cleanup alternatives. In addition, site-specific reuse plans will be developed to be consistent with local land use planning requirements. Local Action Committees will ensure broad community participation in the redevelopment process. For more information, contact Matt Wilkening of U.S. EPA Region 10 at (206) 553-2184.

Portland, OR

The EPA has awarded the City of Portland, Oregon a grant for a National Brownfields Assessment Pilot. The goal of the Portland pilot is to encourage environmental cleanup and redevelopment at specific sites within the Enterprise Community and along the Willamette River waterfront. Activities planned as part of the pilot include conducting education and outreach to involve citizens; creating outreach opportunities for schools; and developing an Internet-accessible online computer information system that will provide data on site assessments, cleanups, and development. A key component of the pilot will be the crafting of partnership agreements with affected neighborhoods on assessment, cleanup, and redevelopment activities at specific sites. For more information, contact Chip Humphry of U.S. EPA Region 10 at (503) 326-2678.

Pennsylvania

Bucks County, PA

In April 1997, the EPA awarded Bucks County, Pennsylvania a $200,000 grant for a National Brownfields Assessment Pilot. Since mid-century, the economic vitality of Bucks County has centered on a manufacturing industrial base located along the Delaware River. The loss of 10,000 jobs at U.S. Steel and industrial downsizing over the past two decades have resulted in the county's high unemployment rate. There are more than three square miles of vacant industrial facilities, underused buildings, and abandoned properties in the county.

Bucks County secured an Enterprise Zone designation from the Commonwealth of Pennsylvania in 1996. Three of the municipalities in the Enterprise Zone are among the county's most populous. County Commissioners are trying to facilitate the revitalization of older, abandoned, and underused buildings within Bucks County, particularly within these Enterprise Zone communities. Businesses that want to locate in the county tend to avoid brownfields and their suspected contamination despite accessibility to a large, high-quality workforce and an established transportation network. Instead, businesses often elect to locate in undeveloped parts of the county, which has exacerbated urban decay and suburban sprawl.

The objective of this brownfield pilot is to initiate a comprehensive assessment of potentially contaminated industrial and commercial properties that would be appropriate for private sector investment. The pilot will focus on brownfields within three Enterprise Zone communities--Bristol Township, Bristol Borough, and Morrisville Borough. Activities planned for this pilot will be implemented in three phases:

- Phase 1: Coordination with Enterprise Zone Plan
  - Forming a Brownfields Task Group;
  - Establishing goals for designated brownfields communities, and identifying the unique cultural, social, historical, and environmental aspects of the communities; and

- • Ensuring community participation and outreach.
- • Phase 2: Site Inventory (and Ranking)
  - • Reviewing available databases and surveys to identify brownfields sites, and creating an inventory of brownfields sites; and
  - • Creating a matrix of ranking criteria, and prioritizing sites for environmental assessment.
- • Phase 3: Environmental Site Assessment
  - • Preparing site assessment work plans for sites, and conducting site assessments;
  - • Preparing site assessment reports;
  - • Evaluating appropriate flow of ownership models for site redevelopment and reuse; and
  - • Presenting recommendations to community leaders.

For more information, contact Robert White of the Bucks County Redevelopment Authority at (215) 860-3313 or Tom Stolle of U.S. EPA Region 3 at (215) 566-3129 or stolle.tom@epamail.epa.gov.

Phoenixville, PA

The EPA has awarded the Borough of Phoenixville, Pennsylvania a grant for a National Brownfields Assessment Pilot. The goal of the Phoenixville pilot is to clean up the abandoned Phoenix Iron and Steel Company site and create an urban greenway that would benefit the environmental justice communities living adjacent to the site. Activities planned as part of the pilot include assessing the scope of contamination, estimating potential remediation costs, developing potential land use options, and determining the feasibility of redevelopment. The Borough plans to build community consensus on reuse of the site, develop a master land use plan, and produce a video journal of the project. For more information, contact Tom Stolle of U.S. EPA Region 3 at (215) 566-3129 or stolle.tom@epamail.epa.gov.

Puerto Rico

Puerto Rico Industrial Development Company

In April 1997, the EPA awarded the Puerto Rico Industrial Development Company (PRIDCO) a $200,000 grant for a National Brownfields Assessment Pilot. PRIDCO was created legislatively in 1942 as a public corporation and government entity to stimulate the economy of Puerto Rico through job creation. PRIDCO, which owns approximately 50 percent of the industrially developed property in Puerto Rico, will administer the grant in cooperation with the Puerto Rico Economic Development Administration.

One site, the former Hato Rey Electroplating Site, has been identified as a target for the pilot. The site is located in the economically depressed Cantera community within the municipality of San Juan. It is now a vacant facility that attracts crime and vagrancy. Interest in redeveloping the facility as a recycling center has arisen, but environmental concerns have prevented redevelopment commitments. Other sites to be targeted for the pilot will be selected based on community need and significant redevelopment and reuse potential.

PRIDCO's goal is to develop a prototype for redevelopment of brownfields through public-private partnerships. These partnerships will be supported by incentives to overcome the typical rejection from developers of environmentally impacted properties and by community outreach and education. PRIDCO also plans to establish a revolving loan fund that will enable prospective developers or tenants to assess potentially impacted properties and determine their redevelopment potential. Puerto

Rico believes that the pilot will facilitate development of an island-wide brownfields program. Activities planned as part of this pilot include:

- Conducting site investigation and remedial planning at the former electroplating site;
- Conducting site investigations and remedial planning at two additional sites to be identified;
- Conducting community outreach programs and bi-lingual educational materials for Hato Rey residents and other community stakeholders; and
- Developing plans for a revolving loan fund program intended to encourage site assessment.

For more information, contact Jose Perez-Hernandez of PRIDCO at (809) 754-7546 or Larry D'Andrea of U.S. EPA Region 2 at (212) 637-4314 or dandrea.larry@epamail.epa.gov.

Rhode Island

State of Rhode Island

The EPA has awarded the State of Rhode Island a grant for a National Brownfields Assessment Pilot. The goal of the Rhode Island pilot is to develop a model ecosystem-based program to bring the vacant and underused contaminated properties in two major urban watersheds back to beneficial use. Activities planned as part of the pilot include conducting a regional survey of both watersheds to identify candidate sites for further assessment; assigning specific contact persons to reach out to affected communities; and facilitating roundtable meetings of all stakeholders. Based on community input, the state will conduct assessments at specific priority sites. For more information, contact

John Podgurski of U.S. EPA Region 1 at (617) 573-9681 or by e-mail at podgurski.john@epamail.epa.gov.

South Carolina

Cowpens, SC

In April 1997, the EPA awarded the Town of Cowpens, South Carolina a $200,000 grant for a National Brownfields Assessment Pilot. Cowpens established a textile mill at the turn of the century and chemicals were increasingly used to advance the industry. In the late 1960s, a major textile dying and finishing company moved into the area. In 1990 the company declared bankruptcy, closed the facility, and left the town, eliminating 400 jobs in the process. The closing of this facility, complicated by possible environmental contamination and on-site vandalism, has had a devastating economic impact on the town.

The pilot site is an abandoned, 228,000 square-foot textile facility located on 70 acres within the town limits. Economic problems faced by Cowpens include unemployment and low earnings. Of the 930 households, 261 have no earnings, and the per capita income is $9,844. For the past seven years, the town has not received property taxes from the abandoned facility. Several industrial prospects have investigated the site, but have not chosen to redevelop it based on initial investigations and unknown environmental conditions, including possible groundwater and soil contamination.

Cowpens' goal is to obtain technical assistance to evaluate and assess environmental contamination in the pilot area. Extensive testing was initiated at the site, but further site assessment is necessary. The town also plans to use the pilot as a means for identifying methods to fund remediation and to develop a comprehensive reuse strategy. Activities planned as part of this pilot include:

- Conducting site assessment and developing a plan for cleanup and redevelopment;

- Installing 10 to 20 groundwater wells to monitor contaminant plumes in two aquifers;

- Conducting community outreach and environmental education, with support from Clemson University and Spartanburg Technical College; and

- Working in partnership with the South Carolina Department of Health and Environmental Control.

For more information, contact Elizabeth Belenchia of the Town of Cowpens at (864) 542-1854 or Barbara Dick of U.S. EPA Region 4 at (404) 562-8923 or dick.barbara@epamail.epa.gov.

Tennessee

Knoxville, TN

The EPA has awarded the City of Knoxville, Tennessee a grant for a National Brownfields Assessment Pilot. Activities planned as part of this pilot include evaluating the feasibility of redeveloping its Center City Business Park, which encompasses many acres of abandoned or underutilized commercial and industrial property; expanding and improving its community involvement activities by integrating the existing Center City Business Park Advisory Council with the Partnership for Neighborhood Improvement; investigating sites that are thought to be contaminated and determining the most cost-effective remediation methods to identify potentially responsible parties for the contamination; and developing a cleanup implementation plan that ensures activities do not aggravate existing environmental threats. For more information, contact Barbara Dick of U.S. EPA Region 4 at (404) 562-8923 or dick.barbara@epamail.epa.gov.

Memphis, TN

In April 1997, the EPA awarded the City of Memphis, Tennessee a $200,000 grant for a National Brownfields Assessment Pilot. Shelby County lacks an agency with countywide responsibility for organized redevelopment of brownfields. To address this need, city, county, and state authorities have agreed to form a quasi-public, nonprofit development corporation, the Memphis Brownfields Restoration Corporation (MBRC). The MBRC will address the high number of tax-delinquent, derelict industrial properties in Shelby County and will help support the city's and county's "balanced growth policy," which seeks to limit sprawl through reuse of urban industrial properties. Preliminary estimates indicate that there are more than 100 brownfields sites in Memphis.

The pilot will target the abandoned Firestone Tire and Rubber Company Site, which occupies 88 acres and 1.5 million square feet of building space in the North Memphis Enterprise Community. Vacant since 1983, the plant significantly contributed to economic distress in the adjacent New Chicago neighborhood. Its closure caused the loss of more than 1,500 manufacturing and precision operator jobs between 1980 and 1990, as well as declines in residential neighborhood populations and reduction of residential property values.

The city's goal is to focus on brownfields redevelopment through the MBRC. The MBRC will take ownership of abandoned, tax-delinquent industrial properties, conduct environmental assessments, secure funds for environmental remediation, undertake reuse and redevelopment planning, and sponsor a series of educational forums on brownfields. Brownfields pilot activities will be coordinated with the MBRC. Activities planned as part of this pilot include:

- Performing an environmental assessment and characterization of the Firestone pilot site;

- developing a plan for remediation and reuse of the Firestone site;

- Conducting community outreach and environmental education; and

- Developing a database of site-specific information on environmental conditions and redevelopment potential.

For more information, contact Corky Neale of City of Memphis Division of Housing and Community Development at (901) 576-7450 or Barbara Dick of U.S. EPA Region 4 at (404) 562-8923 or by e-mail at dick.barbara@epamail.epa.gov.

Texas

Houston, TX

The EPA has awarded the City of Houston, Texas a grant for a National Brownfields Assessment Pilot. The goals of the Houston pilot are to establish a permanent organizational infrastructure for future brownfields redevelopment, revitalize inner-city property, and increase jobs. Activities planned as part of the pilot include identifying candidate sites within the city's Federal Urban Enhanced Enterprise Community; involving stakeholders in decisionmaking through the mechanism of a Land Redevelopment Committee; and conducting environmental assessments of eight candidate sites. Houston plans to develop a model redevelopment process encompassing financial incentives, community outreach, targeted job opportunities, and the new Texas Voluntary Cleanup

Program. For more information, contact Stan Hitt of U.S. EPA Region 6 at (214) 665-6736 or hitt.stan@epamail.epa.gov.

Laredo, TX

The EPA has awarded the City of Laredo, Texas a grant for a National Brownfields Assessment Pilot. Activities planned as part of this pilot include taking inventory of current brownfields; determining the most appropriate and cost-effective remediation methods; developing a plan for the remediation and meeting with current property owners, realtors, prospective purchasers, and lending institutions to expedite environmental revitalization. In addition Laredo will expand and improve the city's community involvement plan by integrating two existing community groups. For more information, contact Monica Smith of U.S. EPA Region 6 at (214) 665-6780.

Vermont

Burlington, VT

The EPA has awarded the City of Burlington, Vermont a grant for a National Brownfields Assessment Pilot. Activities planned as part of this pilot include engaging affected neighborhoods in the brownfields process; assessing the level of contamination at targeted sites; prioritizing redevelopment plans, developing partnerships, and obtaining commitments; implementing redevelopment plans as part of an agricultural industrial park; attracting viable businesses to redeveloped sites; and integrating remediation into a replicable process and disseminating this model. For more information, contact John Podgurski of U.S. EPA Region 1 at (617) 573-9681 or via e-mail at podgurski.john@epamail.epa.gov.

Virginia

Cape Charles-Northampton County, VA

The EPA has awarded Cape Charles-Northampton County, Virginia a grant for a National Brownfields Assessment Pilot. Activities planned as part of this pilot include conducting Phase I and Phase II environmental assessments, developing a study to address applicability, feasibility, and cost of remediation technologies, developing a remediation financing program, and designing an environmental management system to measure levels of performance in excess of legislative standards. In addition, President Clinton's Council on Sustainable Development has chosen this locality as a National Eco-Industrial Park demonstration project. For more information, contact Tom Stolle of U.S. EPA Region 3 at (215) 566-3129 or stolle.tom@epamail. epa.gov.

Richmond, VA

The EPA has awarded the City of Richmond, Virginia a grant for a National Brownfields Assessment Pilot. Activities planned as part of the Richmond pilot include developing a systematic and cost-effective means to inventory and market brownfields sites; identifying environmental mitigation alternatives and costs; evaluating commercial and industrial market reuse options; conducting feasibility studies for brownfields reuse; and using new and existing financial incentives to stimulate interest in redevelopment of brownfields sites. Richmond's Neighborhood Teams Process will bring host residential communities into the reuse decisionmaking process. For more information, contact Tom Stolle of U.S. EPA Region 3 at (215) 566-3129 or stolle.tom @epamail.epa.gov.

Washington

Tacoma, WA

The EPA has awarded the City of Tacoma, Washington a grant for a National Brownfields Assessment Pilot. The goal of the Tacoma pilot is to encourage economic growth and redevelopment in the downtown core by addressing environmental contamination and liability issues. Activities planned as part of this pilot include building on existing community involvement activities associated with an adjacent Superfund site; creating partnerships among the city, public development authority, community, and developers; promoting incentives to assessment and redevelopment; and developing a comprehensive assessment, remediation, and redevelopment process. The city will focus brownfields efforts on sites within the Enterprise Community and adjacent National Priorities List site. For more information, contact Walt Jaspers of U.S. EPA Region 10 at (206) 553-0285.

Wisconsin

Northwest Regional Planning Commission, WI

In April 1997, the EPA awarded the Northwest Regional Planning Commission (NWRPC) in Wisconsin a $195,510 grant for a National Brownfields Assessment Pilot. Northwest Wisconsin contains many abandoned or underused industrial and commercial properties. In addition, area municipalities have declined to take tax deeds on many of the delinquent properties because of environmental concerns, effectively making these properties brownfields. Unemployment in northwest Wisconsin is 1.5 times the state average.

Six sites with known contamination have been targeted for the pilot, and an additional six sites may also be considered for the pilot. The selected sites will include a variety of underused public and private properties. Examples of such sites include a former charcoal factory, grain elevators, and other vacant industrial properties occupying a 75-acre waterfront area in the City of Superior. Development in this area has been inhibited by the presence of brownfields despite its key location near utilities, shipping and rail transportation routes, and skilled labor market.

The NWRPC's goal is to develop a process to assess, clean up, and redevelop brownfields sites. The NWRPC's objectives for the pilot are to: (1) develop tools to finance the cleanup of rural brownfields; (2) encourage economic development of critical community sites while ensuring appropriate cleanups; (3) expand job opportunities for minority and low-income persons in economically distressed communities; and (4) develop a network of economic development and environmental professionals to address brownfields redevelopment. A steering committee made up of five municipalities, two tribes, economic development representatives, and community members will guide the implementation of a brownfields redevelopment process that can be applied throughout northwest Wisconsin. Activities planned as part of this pilot include:

- Educating community leaders and professionals in the brownfields redevelopment process;

- Conducting Phase I and Phase II environmental assessments at six sites with suspected contamination;

- Identifying appropriate future uses for the targeted sites; and

- Implementing site remediation and redevelopment plans.

For more information, contact Dale Cardwell at the Northwest regional Planning Commission at (715) 635-2197 or Mary Beth

Tuohy of U.S. EPA Region 5 at (312) 886-7596 or tuohy.marybeth @epamail.epa.gov.

Regional Brownfields Assessment Demonstration Pilots

Alabama

Prichard, AL

EPA Region 4 has awarded the City of Prichard, Alabama a grant for a Regional Brownfields Assessment Pilot. The most economically disadvantaged community in the state, Prichard suffers from an eroding tax base, industrial and residential migration to nearby Mobile, and contamination from organic pollutants in the water supply. Prichard's objectives include creating a technical assistance team to develop remediation plans, creating an educational consortium and clearinghouse, and developing a comprehensive environmental plan. Prichard will use its status as a state Enterprise Zone to offer tax incentives to encourage redevelopment and cleanup. For more information, contact Matt Robbins of U.S. EPA Region 4 at (404) 562-8371.

California

East Palo Alto, CA

In April 1997, EPA Region 9 awarded the City of East Palo Alto, California a $125,000 grant for a Regional Brownfields Assessment Pilot. The Region has joined with the U.S. Department of Housing and Urban Development (HUD) to provide assistance to the city.

East Palo Alto has an ethically diverse population of approximately 25,000 within a 2.5 square mile area. According to the 1990 census, community residents are 86% minority. Incorporated in 1983, the city inherited an area with inadequate infrastructure, low sales and property tax revenues, no central business district, and the 130-acre Ravenswood Industrial Area. The Ravenswood area overlooks wetlands and the San Francisco Bay, and is located at the gateway to technology-based Silicon Valley, making it an attractive location for local industries. Redevelopment has been hampered, however, by the perception of widespread contamination.

The EPA completed a Phase II site investigation in December 1996, which showed that contamination was far less than originally expected. Pilot activities will include further assessment of properties within the Ravenswood Industrial Area. East Palo Alto's goals are to redevelop a large portion of t he 130-acre Ravenswood complex, create new job opportunities for residents, and increase the city's tax base to improve community services. EPA and HUD have teamed together to assist the city by providing a federal staff liaison to work on brownfields and economic development issues, coordinate federal and state programs to meet the needs of East Palo Alto, and identify assistance programs for which the city qualifies. EPA is also assisting the city in community environmental education and convening a Ravenswood Industrial Area Stakeholders Group, which will make land use recommendations and identify a process for implementation of the redevelopment plan. Activities planned as part of the pilot include:

- Working with the CalEPA's Regional Water Quality Control Board to conduct a screening-level investigation of soil and groundwater contamination;

- Determining the extent of soil and groundwater pollution, and identifying areas where more comprehensive studies may need to be conducted;

246 / Brownfields Redevelopment

- Establishing a Ravenswood Industrial Area Stakeholders Group to determine future land uses with the assistance from EPA and HUD;

- Conducting outreach activities to attract businesses to the area; and

- Conducting community outreach and education meetings to inform residents of the results of EPA investigations.

For more information, contact Sherry Nikzat of the Office of the City Manager of the City of East Palo Alto at (415) 853-3122; Mark Johnson of the CalEPA Regional Water Quality Control Board at (510) 286-0305; or Thomas Mix of U.S. EPA Region 9 at (415) 744-2378 or mix.tom@epamail.epa.gov.

Oakland, CA

EPA Region 9 has awarded the Oakland Redevelopment Agency a $200,000 grant for a Regional Brownfields Assessment Pilot. Oakland plans to select two brownfields that have been identified as catalyst sites for other redevelopment in the city's Central District Redevelopment Area and in East Oakland's Coliseum Redevelopment Area. Most of the Coliseum Area is within a federally designated Enhanced Enterprise Community. The overall goal of this project is to revitalize the selected contaminated properties. Activities planned as part of this pilot include reviewing existing data on two sites and completing site assessments; completing surveys, plans, and summary reports; and developing remedial plans and cost estimates. For more information, contact Wally Woo of U.S. EPA Region 9 at (415) 744-1207.

San Francisco, CA

EPA Region 9 has awarded the City of San Francisco, California a grant for a Regional Brownfields Assessment Pilot. The city's goal is to build a model for redevelopment of the South Bayshore community based on the lessons learned from the closing of the adjacent Hunters Point Naval Shipyard and other military bases. The city will use a risk management model based on the innovative California regulatory Non-Attainment Zone policy. Activities planned as part of this pilot include identifying potential exposure pathways, defining acceptable residual levels of contamination based on proposed zoning and land use, developing a Risk Management Plan, and conducting a community involvement program to address environmental concerns related to land use, zoning, economic development, and environmental justice. For more information, contact Bobbie Kahan of U.S. EPA Region 8 at (415) 744-2191.

Colorado

Englewood, CO

In April 1997, EPA Region 8 awarded the City Englewood, Colorado a $200,000 grant for a Regional Brownfields Assessment Pilot. Early in this century, Englewood was home to many of the Denver area's heavy manufacturing industries. Several of the older facilities have become functionally obsolete, and residents near these sites suffer from below average incomes and population growth. In many cases, the potential for environmental liability has kept prospective businesses from redeveloping these obsolete properties.

The pilot will target two sites that are considered to be essential toward achieving the city's long-range planning goals. General Iron Works is a 280,000 square-foot former iron foundry on an 18-

acre parcel. Almost 20 percent of the residents living near the Iron Works site live below the poverty level. Unemployment and poverty rates in nearby neighborhoods are much higher than city average.

Englewood's goal is to establish a brownfields site assessment revolving loan fund that offers low interest loans as incentives for private sector property owners to assess their properties voluntarily. The city's objectives for the pilot are to encourage assessment, remediation planning, and reuse of known brownfields; evaluate potentially contaminated sites; eliminate negative impacts on health and the environment; and ensure environmental and economic benefits for disadvantaged communities. Activities planned as part of the pilot include:

- Creating a Brownfields Task Force and establishing its administrative guidelines;
- Establishing award criteria for a Brownfields Site Assessment Revolving Loan Fund;
- Continuing outreach efforts to community organizations and other stakeholders;
- Identifying sources of remediation funds and potential developers for the two target sites;
- Evaluating commercial and industrial facilities for environmental risk potential.

For more information, contact Mark Graham of the City of Englewood Office of Neighborhood Business Development at (303) 762-2353 or David Ostrander of U.S. EPA Region 8 at (303) 312-6931 or ostrander.david@epamail.epa.gov.

Sand Creek Corridor, CO

EPA Region 8 has awarded the State of Colorado a $200,000 grant for a Regional Brownfields Assessment Pilot in its Sand Creek Corridor. Activities planned as part of this pilot include identifying barriers to redevelopment resulting from liability concerns; ensuring that pilot project activities complement local development objectives; holding educational seminars for business stakeholders to provide accurate information about sites in order to encourage their redevelopment; and creating a "SWAT" team as a point of contact for community and business representatives with brownfields concerns. For more information, contact David Ostrander of U.S. EPA Region 8 at (303) 312-6931 or ostrander. david@epamail.epa.gov.

Connecticut

Naugatuck Valley, CT

EPA Region 1 has awarded the Naugatuck Valley Regional Planning Agency a $90,000 grant for a Regional Brownfields Assessment Pilot. Naugatuck Valley is an industrial area with at least 168 contaminated sites and a 9.9 percent unemployment rate. Two or three sites in the 45-mile long Valley will be selected for the pilot. The Planning Agency's overall goal is to cleanup and reuse contaminated land and water in the Valley. Activities planned as part of this pilot include hiring personnel to develop site selection criteria, obtaining required authorizations for three pilot sites, developing a revolving loan fund, prepare a regional reuse plan, evaluate ownership mechanisms, and expand community involvement. A key element of this project is streamlining authorization processes that cross-political and town lines. For more information, contact John Podgurski of U.S. EPA Region 1 at (617) 573-9681 or podgurski.john@epamail.epa.gov.

New Haven, CT

EPA Region 1 has awarded the City of New Haven, Connecticut a grant for a Regional Brownfields Assessment Pilot. New Haven contains about 130 acres of industrial land occupied by outmoded or abandoned factories that are known or suspected to be contaminated. The brownfields inhibit the city's ability to generate property tax revenue, create jobs for residents of the Enterprise Community, mitigate environmental health risks, and abate crime and drug abuse. New Haven's goals include remediating contaminated sites; encouraging economic development and job creation; maintaining and augmenting the city's tax base; collecting delinquent taxes; alleviating blight; and improving security in the city. For more information, contact Lynne Jennings of U.S. EPA Region 1 at (617) 573-9634.

Florida

Clearwater, FL

EPA Region 4 has awarded the City of Clearwater, Florida a grant for a Regional Brownfields Assessment Pilot. Clearwater's brownfields problem stems from a former lake filled in as part of urban development 40 years ago. Businesses and residences built on the site are being abandoned due to state regulations mandating property set-asides for stormwater attenuation. The area is a state-designated Enterprise Zone. Clearwater's goal is to instill environmental justice by completing site characterizations, offering economic incentives, and creating job opportunities. The University of South Florida, a brownfields partner, will prepare a flow-of-ownership plan with a novel approach to encourage investment and residential support. For more information, contact Barbara Dick of U.S. EPA Region 4 at (404) 562-8923 or dick. barbara@epamail.epa.gov.

Gainesville, FL

In April 1997, EPA Region 4 awarded the City of Gainesville, Florida a $100,000 grant for a Regional Brownfields Assessment Pilot. Construction of new transportation routes west of the city during the 1960s significantly affected downtown Gainesville's business center. Suburban land availability, opportunities for commercial development, access to new transportation routes, and the emergence of shopping malls has prompted many businesses to leave the downtown area.

A critical need to treat stormwater runoff from the downtown area has prompted the city to pursue efforts to create a stormwater park on a 20-acre downtown parcel. This area, the East Gainesville Sprout Project, will serve as the location of the brownfields pilot. It contains contaminated soil and groundwater and is similar to other downtown brownfields. The target area is located within a state Enterprise Zone, which provides additional redevelopment incentives to developers and financial lenders.

Gainesville's goal is to use the pilot as a model for further brownfields assessment, cleanup, and redevelopment efforts. The East Gainesville Sprout Project will assess properties to forward objectives of reducing on-site soil and groundwater contamination and contaminated runoff, increasing new business development and jobs, increasing the tax base, and reversing trends toward greenfields development. The pilot will serve as a model for two other brownfields areas within the city--the Waldo Road Corridor and the Airport Industrial Park--as well as other future brownfields projects. Activities planned as part of the pilot include:

- Developing a cooperative database and geographic information system (GIS) for environmental data;
- Developing a site assessment plan in cooperation with city environmental engineers;

- Developing a risk assessment plan for brownfields properties that builds in information obtained from Alachua County's environmental program;

- Conducting a feasibility study to determine the need for centralized groundwater treatment in the brownfields area;

- As part of the city's brownfields prevention planning, designing a remediation and stormwater park that would protect downtown business properties; and

- Coordinating an outreach program, and establishing an information center.

For more information, contact Stewart Pearson of the City of Gainesville Public Works Department at (352) 334-2051 or Barbara Dick of U.S. EPA Region 4 at (404) 562-8923 or dick. barbara@epamail.epa.gov.

Miami, FL

EPA Region 4 has awarded the City of Miami, Florida a grant for a Regional Brownfields Assessment Pilot. Miami has identified a number of potential brownfields in the distressed Wynwood neighborhood, where business is over 40 percent light industry and warehousing. Wynwood, a state-designated Enterprise Zone, suffers from environmental contamination from leaking underground tanks, sewers, and industrial chemicals. Miami's goal is to assess potential brownfields and empower residents to participate fully in redevelopment planning. Miami will conduct a brownfields audit, involve the city's Neighborhood Enhancement Teams in community involvement, and identify strategies to overcome obstacles and devise incentives for local investment. For more information, contact Barbara Dick of U.S. EPA Region 4 at (404) 562-8923 or dick.barbara@epamail.epa.gov.

St. Petersburg, FL

EPA Region 4 has awarded the City of St. Petersburg, Florida a $200,000 grant for a Regional Brownfields Assessment Pilot. The city will work with the Brownfields Working Group and its teams (Plan Action, Community Strategies, Finance, and Regulatory) to build a community base of understanding, resources, and support for the Brownfields Redevelopment Project. Ultimately, the city anticipates that its revitalization efforts will create jobs and stimulate economic development. For more information, contact Barbara Dick of U.S. EPA Region 4 at (404) 562-8923 or dick. barbara@epamail.epa.gov.

Georgia

Atlanta, GA

EPA Region 4 has awarded the City of Atlanta a grant for a Regional Brownfields Assessment Pilot. Atlanta has established its own Empowerment Zone (EZ) of 30 neighborhoods (population 50,000) and created the Atlanta Empowerment Zone Corporation to implement the EZ plans. Atlanta's overall goals are to inventory brownfields within the EZ, encourage industry involvement in brownfields redevelopment, provide environmental justice planning, and develop sustainable communities. Activities planned as part of this pilot include undertaking a minimum of three Level I and one Level II environmental audits, building a brownfields inventory database, producing a site identification brochure that will be the beginning of an aggressive public communications strategy and demonstration project, developing remediation processes, and creating a central oversight process for reviewing the technical elements of site remediation. For more information, contact Barbara Dick of U.S. EPA Region 4 at (404) 562-8923 or dick.barbara@epamail.epa.gov.

Idaho

Panhandle Health District, ID

EPA Region 10 has awarded the Panhandle Health District in Silver Valley, Idaho a $100,000 grant for a Regional Brownfields Assessment Pilot. The Valley contains the nation's third largest Superfund site and widespread contamination is the result of years of mining. Over 1,500 residences in the towns of Kellogg, Pinehurst, Smelterville, and Wardner are within the boundary of the site. Heavy metals contamination is widespread, unemployment is 20 percent, and property values have dropped from $1.3 billion to $300 million. The Panhandle Health District's goal is to remove the stigma of contamination, demonstrate the merit and viability of new business development in the Valley, and produce a comprehensive business recruitment communications package and guidelines for overcoming Superfund-related development constraints. For more information, contact Sally Thomas of U.S. EPA Region 10 at (206) 553-2102.

Illinois

Chicago, IL

In April 1997, EPA Region 5 awarded the City of Chicago, Illinois a grant for a Regional Brownfields Assessment Pilot. The West Side of Chicago is characterized by mixed residential and industrial land uses. Abandoned industrial properties have created economic blight and hampered redevelopment. In 1993, representatives from the Chicago Departments of Environmental Planning and Development, Buildings, Law, and the Mayor's Office came together to develop a strategy for promoting cleanup and redevelopment of the city's brownfields. The city developed a three-pronged initiative based on this strategy.

The Brownfields Forum is a broad-based public/private policy group including real estate developers, industrialists, bankers, lawyers, representatives from local, state, and federal government agencies, environmental advocates, and community groups. Between December 1994 and June 1995, over 130 people attended a series of working meetings, developing 65 recommendations for promoting brownfields redevelopment. Forum participants formed project teams and implemented some of the recommendations, including regulatory changes, influencing regional planning, involving communities, and promoting pollution prevention.

Also during this time period, the Brownfields Sites Program invested less than $1 million to investigate, clean up, and prepare five sites for private redevelopment. The city worked with community and business groups and local, state, and federal officials which resulted in private capital investment of over $5.2 million and the creation of over 100 jobs.

The Brownfields Economic Analysis studied a critical connection between economic research, public policy, and the practice of brownfields redevelopment. Research performed by economists at the University of Illinois at Chicago discovered that urban sprawl primarily benefits suburban employers who are being subsidized by taxpayers and commuters.

The objectives of this brownfield pilot are to continue the successful work begun by the City of Chicago in two important ways. The brownfields pilot will: assess the responsiveness of environmental and economic redevelopment policies devised by the City of Chicago; and develop a stakeholder participation process for three brownfields redevelopment sites. Activities planned as part of the pilot include:

- Chicago Brownfields Forum Evaluation

- Performing interviews with Forum participants to assess implementation and effects of the 1995 Action Plan; and

- Recording and assessing accomplishments of the Forum's workgroups to better define future redevelopment goals.

- Stakeholder Participation Process

  - Coordinating with the City's Department of Environment and Department of Planning and Development to develop brownfields site-specific information, including site histories, environmental problems, anticipated redevelopment, and interactions with community members;

  - Interviewing stakeholders to determine concerns with sites, levels of participation desired, and concerns relating to the cleanup and redevelopment process; and

  - Developing and implementing a stakeholder participation plan for each site.

For more information, contact Jessica Rio of the City of Chicago Department of Environment at (312) 744-7606 or Bill Haubold of U.S. EPA Region 5 at (312) 353-6261 or haubold.william @epamail.epa.gov.

East St. Louis, IL

EPA Region 5 has awarded the City of East St. Louis, Illinois a grant for a Regional Brownfields Assessment Pilot. The communities include Alorton, Brooklyn, Cahokia, East St. Louis, National City, Sauget, Washington Park, Madison, and Venice. The goal of the East St. Louis pilot is to develop a sustainable secondary materials manufacturing district on former Alcoa

Aluminum site on 220 acres in a predominantly minority area. Activities planned as part of this pilot include establishing an Advisory Committee; conducting title searches and research; creating and employing a geographic information system; transaction screening of the sites; and preparing reports and presentations. For more information, contact Mary Beth Tuohy of U.S. EPA Region 5 at (312) 886-7596 or tuohy.marybeth @epamail.epa.gov.

State of Illinois

EPA Region 5 has awarded the Illinois Environmental Protection Agency (IEPA) a $150,000 grant for a Regional Brownfields Assessment Pilot. The grant will be used to fund environmental assessments now underway at eight to ten brownfields in Chicago and East St. Louis. In addition, IEPA has been granted the use of a mobile lab to facilitate testing at these sites. The IEPA anticipates that the City of Chicago officials will be involved in facilitating prospective purchaser agreements and redevelopment efforts and will serve as the focal point for communications with prospective purchasers at these sites. The City of Chicago is also considering developing a database that will track the results of environmental site assessments conducted throughout the city. For more information, contact Joe Dufficy of U.S. EPA Region 5 at (312) 886-1960.

Indiana

Northwest Indiana Cities

EPA Region 5 has awarded the Cities of Gary, East Chicago, and Hammond, Indiana (known as Northwest Indiana) a grant for a Regional Brownfields Assessment Pilot in partnership with the EPA's Common Sense Initiative (CSI) Iron and Steel Sector

Brownfields Workgroup. The pilot will conform to the Sector's "Brownfields Guiding Principles" to address assessment and redevelopment issues unique to the iron and steel industries. The cities' goals include identifying and removing threats to health and safety, restoring brownfields to productive use, and creating sustainable economic growth. Activities planned as part of this pilot include conducting site assessments of candidate properties, identifying current and past owners, obtaining technical expertise to evaluate existing remediation legal authorities, and development of remediation plans. To accomplish these goals the cities plan to select three iron and steel brownfields sites to serve as pilots. For more information, contact Ted Smith of U.S. EPA Region 5 at (312) 353-6571.

State of Indiana

EPA Region 5 has awarded the Indiana Department of Environmental Management (IDEM) a $150,000 grant for a Regional Brownfields Assessment Pilot. The grant will be used to fund environmental assessments of approximately ten brownfields in Indianapolis and the communities of Gary, Hammond, and East Chicago. IDEM selected several of the sites for assessment during the Summer of 1995, and is currently assessing many of these sites. EPA Region 5 has loaned the pilot mobile van for field testing. City and state officials will facilitate prospective purchaser agreements and redevelopment efforts. IDEM anticipates that increased information on these sites will make them more attractive to prospective buyers. For more information, contact Joe Dufficy of U.S. EPA Region 5 at (312) 886-1960.

Louisiana

Shreveport, LA

EPA Region 6 has awarded the City of Shreveport, Louisiana a grant for a Regional Brownfields Assessment Pilot. The goal of the city's brownfields program is to increase the economic and environmental viability of Shreveport's urban core neighborhoods. Shreveport's urban core has been selected for the federal National Performance Review program, to demonstrate a comprehensive strategy for enhancing delivery of federal support to troubled neighborhoods. Activities planned as part of this pilot include developing an inventory of city brownfields and criteria for ranking site redevelopment potential, conducting Phase I site assessments, exploring redevelopment options, educating the community about brownfields problems and opportunities, and providing a forum to develop community-based strategies for long-term redevelopment. For more information, contact Stan Hitt of U.S. EPA Region 6 at (214) 665-6736 or hitt.stan@epamail. epa.gov.

Maine

Portland, ME

EPA Region 1 has awarded the City of Portland, Maine a $90,000 grant for a Regional Brownfields Assessment Pilot. Portland's demonstration pilot will focus on a Marginal Way site chosen because of its blighted condition and potential as a gateway and employment center for the city. Portland's goal is to restore the productive capacity of the Marginal Way site. To overcome the environmental risks and uncertainty causing disinvestment in the site, Portland plans to conduct market research and an environmental assessment and involve residents and stakeholders in preparing a redevelopment approach for the site. Other activities planned as part of this pilot include analyzing redevelopment options, developing a property disposition plan, and conducting community education and outreach. For more information, contact John Podgurski of U.S. EPA Region 1 at (617) 573-9681 or podgurski.john@epamail.epa.gov.

Maryland

Baltimore County, MD

In April 1997, EPA Region 3 awarded Baltimore County, Maryland a $200,000 grant for a Regional Brownfields Assessment Pilot. For decades, the economic base of Baltimore County consisted of many large, heavy manufacturing operations that occupied much of the county's East Side. Closures and downsizing by manufacturing employers since 1960 have resulted in a significant reduction in manufacturing jobs. Vacant and underused industrial properties in the area are suspected of environmental contamination.

State and local authority has been enacted to protect rural areas of the County and the Chesapeake Bay. The county is faced with attracting new industrial and commercial development while improving the quality of life for residents and continuing to protect the Chesapeake Bay watershed area. Concerns about know or suspected contamination often impede the use of otherwise valuable sites. The county has redirected staff and resources to improve its older communities and has recently developed a comprehensive community and economic revitalization strategy of which brownfields is a part. The southeast industrial corridor has been designated a state Enterprise Zone.

Baltimore County's goals for the pilot are to access brownfields properties, evaluate potential land uses for the properties, and then match the properties with potential purchasers who would be encouraged to enroll in Maryland's new voluntary cleanup program. The new Maryland program can provide eligible parties with releases from state liability if they complete certified cleanups of brownfields properties, which are then redeveloped. This pilot will coordinate the federal and state programs to better benefit the county's communities. Activities planned as part of this pilot include:

- Identifying sections of the county that are at a higher than average risk for brownfields concerns, using a geographic information system (GIS) analysis;

- Developing an Industrial Redevelopment Opportunity Site Inventory that would identify brownfields properties with significant economic potential;

- Conducting seminars, meetings, and other outreach activities to educate businesses and other stakeholders about brownfields policies; and

- Facilitating the assessment and remediation planning of brownfields properties through participation in Maryland's new voluntary cleanup program.

For more information, contact Sharon Klots of the Baltimore County Department of Economic Development at (410) 887-8023 or Tom Stolle of U.S. EPA Region 3 at (215) 566-3129 or stolle. tom@epamail.epa.gov.

Massachusetts

Boston, MA

EPA Region 2 has awarded the City of Boston a $200,000 grant for a Regional Brownfields Assessment Pilot. Activities planned as part of this pilot include developing a model to identify, map, and gather information on brownfields in the Dudley Street

Neighborhood (DSN), the principal business center for Boston's African-American community; developing a community outreach and education program; and investigating ways to secure additional cleanup funding, engage in cost recovery litigation, and promote environmental compliance assurance. For more information, contact Lynne Jennings of U.S. EPA Region 1 at (617) 573-9634.

Lynn, MA

In April 1997, EPA Region 1 awarded the City of Lynn, Massachusetts a $200,000 grant for a Regional Brownfields Assessment Pilot. Over the past 10 years, 15,000 jobs have been lost due to a steady decline of manufacturing, corporate downsizing, relocation of retail establishments, and the presence of contaminated sites. Lynn has identified a target area that encompasses more than 80 percent of the city's commercial/industrial properties. As a result of the city's economic decline, the target area has a 15 percent unemployment rate and a 32 percent poverty rate.

Three brownfields sites have been identified through community outreach to be addressed in this pilot: a former dry cleaning establishment in a residential neighborhood; a long-time tannery site in an industrial sector; and a 25-acre landfill and utility site on Lynn's underused waterfront. These sites represent the wide range of development problems that confront the city and will provide diverse models for residential, industrial, and recreational reuse. Each site involves different stakeholders and different community elements, as well as varying types of current and future uses.

Lynn's goals are to implement an innovative economic/ environmental process that allows the city to identify and assess brownfields areas; solicit business and grass-roots community participation in determining the best reuse of these areas; and leverage funding with other applicable resources. To accomplish these goals, the city will partner with the Conservation Law Foundation, a regional environmental advocacy, nonprofit organization focused on solving New England's public health and environmental problems. Pilot objectives include the completion of site assessments and reuse plans for three targeted sites, creation of a community-wide outreach process, and development of an inventory of other brownfields in the city. For more information, contact Peter DeVeau of the Economic Development and Industrial Corporation at (617) 581-9399 or John Podgurski of U.S. EPA Region 1 at (617) 573-9681 or podgurski.john@epamail.epa.gov.

Somerville, MA

EPA Region 1 has awarded the City of Somerville, Massachusetts a $100,000 grant for a Regional Brownfields Assessment Pilot. Somerville's Office of Housing and Community Development will be taking the lead in developing a cost-effective program to promote private sector reuse of contaminated properties. The pilot program will remediate and reuse three demonstration sites. The main purpose of the demonstration project is to establish an administrative mechanism that reconciles federal housing and urban development and environmental protection policies and serves as a model for other properties. The grant will be used for conducting site assessments at three sites to estimate the costs of remediation. In addition, the city, using a Community Development Block Grant (CDBG) entitlement, will fund stop-loss insurance to cover remediation costs in excess of estimated costs. For more information, contact Lynne Jennings of U.S. EPA Region 1 at (617) 573-9634.

Westfield, MA

In April 1997, EPA Region 1 awarded the City of Westfield, Massachusetts a $197,000 grant for a Regional Brownfields Assessment Pilot. Four years ago, a major manufacturer with over 300 employees ceased operations, leaving 29 buildings vacant on a 6.25-acre property in the heart of downtown Westfield. The site housed a boiler manufacturer for nearly 150 years, and fear of unknown contamination at the site has prevented its redevelopment.

The Westfield Community Development Corporation (CDC) acquired the former H.B. Smith site in November 1996. The CDC has since been working with a potential developer, members of the community and other key stakeholders to explore reuse options for the site. Westfield has committed approximately $1 million of Community Development Block Grant (CDBG) funding toward the cleanup and demolition costs.

The city believes that problems will arise if the site is not redeveloped soon, including safety hazards, fire hazards, trespassing, unauthorized use as a temporary shelter by homeless individuals, potential use for drug sales and distribution, vandalism, and personal liability and injury litigation. This area of the city currently has an unemployment rate of seven percent and a poverty rate of 14 percent. Twenty percent of the population are elderly residents.

Westfield's goal is to develop strategies for redevelopment of the pilot site with assistance from other economic partners. The pilot will form the basis for future remediation of the site. The city's objectives are to create a working model for cleanup and redevelopment; maximize funding for site assessment, remediation planning, and monitoring; develop criteria and databases to manage information on public/private funds; educate the community on brownfields issues; and initiate strategies for redevelopment of the pilot site. Activities planned as part of the pilot include:

- Completing preliminary and detailed site assessments of the target site, including installation of monitoring wells;

- Designing remediation strategies for the pilot site;

- Identifying resources for redevelopment;

- Designing community-based educational programs;

- Identifying additional public/private funding and technical assistance for the pilot site; and

- Documenting the pilot progress and applicability as a brownfields redevelopment model.

For more information, contact James Boardman of the Department of Community Development at (413) 572-6246 or John Podgurski of U.S. EPA Region 1 at (617) 573-9681 or podgurski.john @epamail.epa.gov.

Michigan

Kalamazoo, MI

EPA Region 5 has awarded the City of Kalamazoo, Michigan a $100,000 grant for a Regional Brownfields Assessment Pilot. Kalamazoo's long-range goal is to prevent future brownfields and retain existing industry while promoting a renewed interest in industrial and commercial investment within the city. Kalamazoo intends to create a systematic approach for redeveloping underused and potentially contaminated properties in the city. An initial data collection phase is complete, maps of the brownfields have been entered into a geographical information system, and preliminary evaluation criteria have been selected. Activities planned as part of this pilot include involving the community in setting redevelopment priorities, assessing up to five sites, preparing land use and marketing analyses, and identifying financial and human resources needed for redevelopment through public-private partnerships. For more information, contact Mary Beth Tuohy of U.S. EPA Region 5 at (312) 886-7596 or tuohy.marybeth @epamail.epa.gov.

Minnesota

Downriver Community Conference, MN

EPA Region 5 has awarded the Downriver Community Conference a $75,000 grant for a Regional Brownfields Assessment Pilot. The Downriver Area Brownfield Consortium (DABC) includes the cities of Monroe, Trenton, and Riverview, which are all suburban communities in the Detroit metropolitan area. Industrial disinvestment has resulted in the creation of over 700 acres of brownfields. About 75 percent of the available industrial property in Riverview, alone, are brownfields. The ultimate goal of the brownfields program is to create a process to market a selected brownfield to a developer who would purchase the site and construct a facility. The applicant intends to use the EPA grant for site identification, site investigation and evaluation, site planning and remediation, site marketing and development, and program management. For more information, contact Mary Beth Tuohy of U.S. EPA Region 5 at (312) 886-7596 or tuohy.marybeth@epamail.epa.gov.

State of Minnesota

EPA Region 5 has awarded the Minnesota Pollution Control Agency (MPCA) a $255,000 grant for a Regional Brownfields Assessment Pilot. The grant, made possible by combining funds with other Superfund resources, will be used to fund the agency's

Voluntary Cleanup Program (VCP). To date, MPCA has targeted owners of 32 CERCLIS sites to participate in the program. Remediation at one site is almost complete and is nearing completion at several other sites. MPCA anticipates that remediation at 10-15 sites will be completed in 1997. Cost recovery actions have been initiated for the resources expended in the review and oversight of voluntary cleanups. For more information, contact Joe Dufficy of U.S. EPA Region 5 at (312) 886-1960.

Missouri

Bonne Terre, MO

EPA Region 7 has awarded the City of Bonne Terre, Missouri a $100,000 grant for a Regional Brownfields Assessment Pilot. Bonne Terre (population 3,800) is located at the northern edge of the Missouri Lead Belt. It has suffered economically from closure of mines more than 20 years ago and environmentally from mining wastes that contaminated soil and surface water. The Bonne Terre community is looking to redevelop three mining waste sites that cover 400 acres within city limits. Activities planned as part of this pilot include forming a Bonne Terre Brownfields Committee, completing marketing studies, developing public participation information, establishing a Pilot City Internet Exchange, conducting environmental assessments, preparing a brownfields redevelopment plan, conducting brownfields engineering studies, and producing legal documentation. For more information, contact Susan Klein of U.S. EPA Region 7 at (913) 551-7786 or klein.susan@epamail.epa.gov.

New Hampshire

Concord, NH

EPA Region 1 has awarded the City of Concord, New Hampshire a $90,000 grant for a Regional Brownfields Assessment Pilot. Concord's overall brownfields goals are to identify contamination in a 440-acre industrial corridor, develop a comprehensive remediation and redevelopment plan, and gain the support of key stakeholders. In addition to generating new revenue, the city estimates that the employment potential in the area, which lies next to the city's lowest income neighborhoods, exceeds 2,500 jobs, or eight percent of the city's total employment. The city hosted a symposium last year that explored the redevelopment potential of the corridor. Activities planned as part of this pilot include completing Phase I assessments for at least half of the corridor and conducting Phase II assessments at three sites. In addition, the city will generate an executive summary of the Phase I study and site-specific fact sheets summarizing the Phase II results for the general public. For more information, contact Diane Kelley of U.S. EPA Region 1 at (617) 573-9672.

New Jersey

Camden, NJ

EPA Region 2 has awarded the City of Camden, New Jersey a grant for a Regional Brownfields Assessment Pilot. Camden is the fifth largest and most economically distressed city in New Jersey, with predominantly minority population, a high unemployment rate, and one in three poverty rate. Manufacturing and related land uses account for a third of Camden's nine square miles, and brownfields constitute more than half of all industrial sites in the city. The goal of Camden's brownfields program is to develop an effective strategy for assessment, cleanup, and reuse of its brownfields. The city proposes a comprehensive approach that will integrate technical, community, government, and financial resources. For more information, contact Larry D'Andrea of U.S. EPA Region 2 at (212) 637-4314 or via e-mail at dandrea.larry @epamail.epa.gov.

New York

Buffalo, NY

EPA Region 2 has awarded the City of Buffalo, New York a $200,000 grant for a Regional Brownfields Assessment Pilot. Activities planned as part of this pilot include inventorying and characterizing the city's brownfields; and finalizing development strategies for two to five brownfields redevelopment projects based on community vision, economic development potential, and health and safety concerns. In addition, the pilot is funding a Brownfields Community Coordinator to conduct environmental justice and community outreach activities targeted to specific brownfields sites; and is supporting a Brownfields Planner to oversee overall program integrity, work with the Buffalo Brownfields Task Force, develop techniques for brownfields development, and encourage developers interested on brownfields to assess sites. For more information, contact Walter Schoepf of U.S. EPA Region 2 at (212) 637-4319.

Ohio

Cincinnati, OH

EPA Region 5 has awarded the City of Cincinnati, Ohio a $200,000 grant for a Regional Brownfields Assessment Pilot. The city's brownfields project is focusing on the industrial corridor within the Mill Creek valley watershed, where there are 500 acres of vacant property affecting a population of about 106,000. The area is characterized by declining employment, poverty, and blight. At least 31 different sites have contamination that threatens water quality. One area within the watershed is a state Enterprise Zone (EZ). Some companies have expressed an interest in locating within the EZ but have not done so because of contamination concerns. The city's overall brownfields goals are to revitalize its existing Port Authority as a brownfields redevelopment authority, develop a Brownfields Community Advisory Committee (BCAC), and clean up Queensgate South and one other brownfield. Activities planned as part of this pilot include conducting site assessments and other implementation planning at two sites, developing a public participation process, conducting an environmental impact pre- and post-development study, and creating an economic redevelopment model. For more information, contact Ted Smith of U.S. EPA Region 5 at (312) 353-6571.

Oklahoma

Tulsa, OK

In April 1997, EPA Region 6 awarded the City of Tulsa, Oklahoma a $200,000 grant for a Regional Brownfields Assessment Pilot. Located in the northeastern quadrant of Oklahoma, Tulsa is the 43rd largest city in the country and is continuing to grow. The economic boom of the late 1970s and early 1980s contributed to rapid expansion in outlying greenfields, pulling businesses and residents from the city core and leaving large tracts of potentially contaminated land in older sections of the city. Numerous redevelopment efforts adjacent to the core area have been delayed due to potential environmental risks. The city faces a shortage of greenfields within the city limits and future industrial development must focus on brownfields for future economic growth.

In March 1996, EPA Region 6 provided the Tulsa Industrial Authority (TIA) with a list of 85 archived CERCLIS sites in Tulsa County. After researching the status of these sites, TIA is focusing on 46 potential brownfields located primarily in the northwest neighborhoods of Tulsa. The sites were used for a wide variety of commercial and industrial activities, including electroplating, transformer repair, and electrical equipment and chemical manufacturing. Tulsa plans to assess, develop cleanup plans, and spur redevelopment at 10 of these properties.

Tulsa's goal is to restore abandoned, idled, or underused industrial and commercial sites to productive use and create jobs through a brownfields redevelopment plan. The pilot is designed to empower the community and other redevelopment stakeholders to work together to prevent, assess, safely clean up, and sustainably reuse brownfields. Activities planned as part of this pilot include:

- Conducting environmental assessments at 10 brownfields that are either tax delinquent or already owned by the city;

- Selecting sites for redevelopment based on the best combination of environmental factors and redevelopment potential;

- Clarifying liability issues by development of a model redevelopment process that uses provisions of the new Oklahoma Brownfields Voluntary Redevelopment Act;

- Exploring methods of financing cleanups through state voluntary cleanup programs, state tax incentive programs, contributions from responsible parties, and prospective purchaser agreements; and

- Generating effective public involvement in the redevelopment planning process.

For more information, contact Mickey Thompson of the Tulsa Industrial Authority at (918) 585-1201 or Stan Hitt of U.S. EPA Region 6 at (214) 665-6736 or hitt.stan@epamail.epa.gov.

Pennsylvania

Philadelphia, PA

EPA Region 3 has awarded the Philadelphia City Planning Commission (PCPC) a $200,000 grant for a Regional Brownfields Assessment Pilot. The PCPC will select ten sites and hire a contractor to perform environmental assessments at these sites. The contractor will also create a formal environmental site assessment review process by establishing an interagency Environmental Audit Review (EAR) team. In addition, PCPC will market the selected sites, and a citywide EAR procedure will be established upon completion of the pilot program. For more information, contact Tom Stolle of U.S. EPA Region 3 at (215) 566-3129 or stolle.tom@epamail.epa.gov.

Pittsburgh, PA

EPA Region 3 has awarded the City of Pittsburgh, Pennsylvania a $200,000 grant for a Regional Brownfields Assessment Pilot. The grant will be used to fund activities including creation of an inventory of sites with development potential; identification of environmental problems, remediation alternatives, and associated costs; exploration of market reuse options; and use of financial incentives to stimulate site assessment, cleanup, and redevelopment. For more information, contact Tom Stolle of U.S. EPA Region 3 at (215) 566-3129 or stolle.tom@epamail.epa.gov.

South Dakota

Sioux Falls, SD

EPA Region 8 has awarded the City of Sioux Falls, South Dakota a $200,000 grant for a Regional Brownfields Assessment Pilot. Sioux Falls has been working to redevelop a mixed industrial and commercial corridor adjacent to the Big Sioux River in the city's central business district. Redevelopment has been slow due to the presence of brownfields and five CERCLIS sites. The city's goal is to implement an effective strategy that facilitates redevelopment and reuse within the corridor. Activities planned as part of this pilot include conducting an inventory of properties, assembling a catalogue of high-interest sites, producing an action plan, and seeking stakeholder input and funding. A list of affected parties (local, civic, private, and regulatory) will be developed and opportunities for collaboration will be proposed. For more information, contact David Ostrander of U.S. EPA Region 8 at (303) 312-6931 or ostrander.david@epamail.epa.gov.

Texas

Dallas, TX

EPA Region 6 has awarded the City of Dallas, Texas a $200,000 grant for a Regional Brownfields Assessment Pilot. Activities planned as part of this pilot include obtaining the assistance of an EPA official through an Intergovernmental Personnel Act (IPA) assignment; organizing the Brownfields Initiative program; holding community meetings to obtain input from neighborhood associations, real estate developers, the financial community, chambers of commerce, and interested business associations regarding site selection and potential redevelopment; and providing public resources to businesses wishing to relocate to a redeveloped brownfields site. For more information, contact Stan Hitt of U.S. EPA Region 6 at (214) 665-6736 or by e-mail at hitt.stan@epamail.epa.gov.

Utah

Murray City, UT

EPA Region 8 has awarded the Murray City, Utah a $178,000 grant for a Regional Brownfields Assessment Pilot. The city's brownfields surround the former Murray smelter, a 141-acre site in Murray City (population 31,282) and a designated Superfund Accelerated Cleanup Model (SACM) site. The area is surrounded by schools, single-family and multiple-unit residential areas, and office complexes. The city would like to develop the area to complement adjacent land uses, improve light rail transportation, and construct an extension of Main Street needed for reconstruction of a major transportation corridor. Activities planned as part of this pilot include formulating a land reuse plan that deals with liability concerns of property owners, lenders, and redevelopers; establishing implementation agreements; documenting the process; and identifying lessons learned. For more information, contact David Ostrander of U.S. EPA Region 8 at (303) 312-6931 or ostrander.david@epamail.epa.gov.

Ogden City, UT

In April 1997, EPA Region 8 awarded the Odgen City, Utah a $200,000 grant for a Regional Brownfields Assessment Pilot. With the completion of the transcontinental railroad in 1869, Ogden City grew from a small frontier town into a major industrial center. The railroads and associated industries closed their Ogden City operations in the 1970s and 1980s, leaving behind high unemployment, unskilled workers, and environmental pollution.

The pilot will focus on three sites within a five-block area of Ogden City's central business district where vacant rail yards a former tannery, and large warehouses are typical of the area's properties. In the area that will be targeted for the pilot, 80 percent of the property is vacant and only five businesses are operating. A large railroad property covers half of the central business district. The poverty rate in this district is almost twice the city's average, unemployment exceeds 25 percent, and almost half of the adults have less than a high school education.

Ogden City's goal is to revitalize the central business district by removing barriers to economic development and reclaiming potentially valuable properties for mixed use development. The city's pilot objectives are to assess contamination in the pilot area, demonstrate the viability of redeveloping obsolete facilities, attain the highest and best use of priority properties, and regain the city's progressive image by cleaning up gateway areas. Activities planned as part of the pilot include:

- Evaluating historically significant data on past land use;

- Conducting field sampling and analyses, focusing on at least three priority sites within the central business district;

- Developing remediation plans for the three priority sites;

- Implementing a public education program on brownfields; and

- Locating sources of remediation funding.

For more information, contact Jon Ruiz of the Ogden City Public Works Department at (801) 629-8970 or David Ostrander of U.S. EPA Region 8 at (303) 312-6931 or ostrander.david@epamail. epa.gov.

Provo, UT

EPA Region 8 has awarded the Provo City Ironton Economic Redevelopment Project a grant for a Regional Brownfields Assessment Pilot.the project is the site of a former steel mill that constitutes the largest tract of undeveloped and unused property in the city. Redevelopment of the former steel mill site and surrounding property has been blocked by concerns over contamination and liability. The objective of the project is to create an environmentally sensitive development and address environmental justice concerns for the surrounding community. Redevelopment of the site will provide employment opportunities for the community, increase surrounding property values, and increase the city's tax base. For more information, contact David Ostrander of U.S. EPA Region 8 at (303) 312-6931 or ostrander.david@epamail.epa.gov.

Salt Lake City, UT

EPA Region 8 has awarded Salt Lake City, Utah a $200,000 grant for a Regional Brownfields Assessment Pilot. Salt Lake City's 650-acre Gateway District is a former industrial center on the western edge of the city bordering the central business district. The area has been severely impacted by abandoned industrial sites and changing transportation networks. The city's overall goal is to support an accelerated redevelopment of the Gateway District to allow for expansion of downtown mixed use development and provide support facilities for the 2002 Winter Olympic Games. Activities planned as part of this pilot include identifying and characterizing potentially contaminated sites; conducting field sampling and analysis; developing site-specific, risk-based corrective actions for at least one site within each category of contamination; developing prototype reuse processes for each category of contamination; developing standard voluntary cleanup documentation; and identifying cleanup funding sources. For more information, contact David Ostrander of U.S. EPA Region 8 at (303) 312-6931 or ostrander.david@epamail.epa.gov.

West Jordan, UT

EPA Region 8 has awarded the City of West Jordan, Utah a $200,000 grant for a Regional Brownfields Assessment Pilot. The grant will be used to begin the detailed planning required to reverse the stigma of developing brownfields. Through cooperative agreements with county, state, and federal agencies, business, and industry, West Jordan intends to leverage brownfields funds to redevelop former industrial properties to create a "high image" business and industrial park along the Jordan River Parkway Corridor. This effort is viewed as an initial step in revitalizing the city's central core, which suffers from heavy industrialization and declining residential and commercial uses. For more information, contact David Ostrander of U.S. EPA Region 8 at (303) 312-6931 or ostrander.david@epamail.epa.gov.

Washington

Bellingham, WA

EPA Region 10 has awarded the Port of Bellingham, Washington a $100,000 grant for a Regional Brownfields Assessment Pilot. The Port has initiated a Central Waterfront Redevelopment Project to clean up and revitalize a 67-acre area in the core of this small coastal community. Current property owners have not been able to effectively address environmental problems. Potential environmental liability and huge cleanup costs are discouraging business interest in the waterfront. The Port proposes to facilitate participation of cooperative partners, consolidate property management, develop a conceptual design for the overall project, and plan construction of a warehouse to lease to Georgia Pacific. For more information, contact Walt Jaspers of U.S. EPA Region 10 at (206) 553-0285.

Duwamish Coalition, WA

EPA Region 10, with co-funding from EPA's Office of Underground Storage Tanks, has awarded the Washington Department of Ecology (WDOE) a $200,000 grant to fund a Regional Brownfields Assessment Pilot. The pilot is backed by the Duwamish Coalition, a group of commercial, environmental, and community representatives. Activities planned as part of this pilot include developing a decision-tree methodology as a model for risk evaluation and remedy selection, which will be incorporated into a new WDOE guidance document for contaminated sites; and evaluating fate and transport, leachability tests of contaminated soils, and adaptation of national efforts regarding risk-based corrective action guidance. For more information, contact Nancy Harney of U.S. EPA Region 10 at (206) 553-2141.

Puyallup Tribe of Tacoma, WA

EPA Region 10 has awarded the Puyallup Tribe of American Indians a $100,000 grant for a Regional Brownfields Assessment Pilot. The Puyallup Tribe plans to develop a marine terminal in the Tacoma, Washington industrial waterfront area on one of its Trust lands and an adjacent property that is currently being remediated under a RCRA corrective action permit. The Tribe is working with the property owner and proposes to coordinate a cleanup and redevelopment plan, develop drainage and wetlands mitigation plan consistent with that for the Tribe's surrounding properties, and involve students at the Tribal College in the pilot activities. The project area encompasses about 80 acres. For more information, contact Robbie Heeden of U.S. EPA Region 10 at (206) 553-0201.

Wisconsin

Milwaukee County, WI

EPA Region 5 has awarded the Milwaukee County, Wisconsin a grant for a Regional Brownfields Assessment Pilot. This pilot represents a unique collaborative effort between the County of Milwaukee, the City of Milwaukee, and the 30th Street Industrial Corridor Corporation (ICC). The ICC is a nonprofit organization, focusing on economic redevelopment, with close ties to the business community, job training alliances, and community groups. The pilot will focus efforts on the five-mile long segment of active rail line in the urban center of Milwaukee, commonly identified as the 30th Street Industrial Corridor. The ICC will focus on day-to-day pilot activities, including site selection, oversight of technical studies and remedial plans, and loan fund management, while the City of Milwaukee and the County will provide general guidance and oversight. For more information, contact Mike Anastasio of U.S. EPA Region 5 at (312) 886-7951.

Wisconsin Department of Natural Resources

EPA Region 5 has awarded the Wisconsin Department of Natural Resources (WDNR) a grant for a Regional Brownfields Assessment Pilot. The WDNR's objective in this brownfields effort is to encourage redevelopment by providing no-cost environmental site assessments to interested municipalities. WDNR will provide a common approach and analysis for each site. This will eventually form the basis for decisions regarding community health issues, property marketability, and long-term environmental liability implications. For more information, contact Joe Dufficy of U.S. EPA Region 5 at (312) 886-1960.

CHAPTER 6

Brownfields Redevelopment Case Studies[*]

Introduction

One of the advantages of development of a brownfields site is that the planned land use can truly be considered in the development of cleanup options. This advantage can best be appreciated when one considers that environmental agencies traditionally have required that sites be remediated to natural background levels if the site was proposed for future use. This was usually cost-prohibitive. As an alternative to background conditions, owners and/or prospective purchasers can use risk assessments to identify cleanup levels that would be protective of human health under worst case exposure scenarios. However, historic regulatory requirements were based on unrealistic exposure periods (i.e., a lifetime) and overly conservative exposure conditions (i.e., children ingesting soil). This yielded unrealistic and overstated risk. By applying good science (i.e., realistic exposure assumptions and the most current toxicological parameters) and real planned land use, sites can be remediated and be beneficially reused at a fraction of the cost.

A primary driver for brownfields is economic growth. Considering that development of a brownfield site is often much

---

[*] Written by Jack D. Riggenbach, ERM-Southeast, Inc., Kennesaw, Georgia; Dan Hinds, Frontier Environmental Services, Inc., Golden, Colorado; and Ronald Fender, ERM, Inc, Exton, Pennsylvania. This chapter is based on a paper presented by the authors at the 1996 Annual Meeting of the Air and Waste Management Association, entitled "Application of Land Use Planning to Three Brownfield Cleanup Projects." Reprinted here with permission of the authors.

less costly than development of a greenfield site, the fact remains that the highest and best use of property historically used for commercial or industrial purposes will, in many instances, be continued use as commercial or industrial property. The skyrocketing cost of site remediation over the past 15 years and the failure of Superfund and many state cleanup programs to promote cleanup has caused the emergence of more practical approaches to use of these contaminated sites.

This chapter describes three projects that incorporate brownfields concepts. The role of past, current, and possible future land use and land use planning is described for each. The first project is a part of a state superfund site where a former large industrial facility was redeveloped for alternate industrial use by a number of smaller tenant industries. The second project is being conducted at the location of a federal Superfund site and is currently being developed commercially as a retail store. The third project is a low income housing complex that is in the remedial planning stages and located near property that was used for waste disposal.

Case Study #1: Redevelopment for Industrial Use

Avtex Fibers Site, Meadville, Pennsylvania

The Avtex Fibers Site is located in northwest Pennsylvania, in the town of Meadville. The site is approximately 170 acres in size (nearly 35 acres under roof) and has been used for fiber manufacturing for almost 60 years until it was closed in 1986. At full capacity, the facility employed nearly 2,000 workers. Market decline during the 1980s reduced employment to approximately 850 when the facility closed.

During the production period, the site was owned and operated by the Viscose Company (later known as American Viscose

Company), Avtex Fibers Corporation, and another company. Portions of the site are currently owned by the Crawford County Industrial Redevelopment Agency. Avtex Fibers, now in bankruptcy, owns the remainder of the site.

Beginning in 1982, when operations were declining, the Crawford County Industrial Redevelopment Authority took an interest in the site for continued industrial use. When operations ceased in 1986, the Meadville Redevelopment Authority (MRA) leased portions of the former manufacturing facility to promote industrial reuse and increased employment.

Byproducts from the fiber manufacturing process were disposed on-site in several waste management units including surface impoundments, pits, and landfills. Based on these historical waste management practices, the U.S. EPA conducted a Preliminary Assessment and Site Investigation in 1988 to assess whether the site warranted further action under the federal Superfund program. That assessment concluded that there was not sufficient risk to human health and the environment to warrant formal listing on the National Priorities List.

The Pennsylvania Department of Environmental Resources (PDER) conducted its own assessment in 1989 and listed the site for purposes of the state superfund program. In 1990 and 1991, PDER conducted a Remedial Investigation/Feasibility Study (RI/FS) and recommended a $29 million remedy. That remedy would have taken two to three years to implement and would have been disruptive of the redevelopment operations of the MRA, which were in the early stage of development.

Contamination Assessment

The primary contaminants of concern at the site were polychlorinated biphenyls (PCBs) and carcinogenic polynuclear aromatic hydrocarbons (CPAHs). Some volatile organics (VOCs) and arsenic were also identified during the RI/FS. Contaminants were found in 17 separate locations on the site based on historic waste disposal practices.

Evaluation of the site investigation data showed that the PCB and CPAH contamination was in shallow soils with no evidence of vertical migration toward groundwater. CPAH contamination was predominantly concentrated in storm water discharge locations from runoff from the asphalt-paved production areas. Arsenic was initially of potential concern because of the historic storage and disposal of fly ash from coal-fired boilers. However, only very low levels were detected in very isolated locations in groundwater, which was not migrating further and was cross-gradient from the nearest water supply wells. The concern over groundwater quality was so minimal that even the PDER did not recommend groundwater remediation.

Applicable Regulations

In 1989, the state listed the site as a state superfund site under authority of the Pennsylvania Hazardous Sites Cleanup Act (HSCA). This law was established to allow the state to require remediation of sites that are contaminated but do not pose a significant enough risk to human health or the environment to qualify for listing under the federal Superfund program.

It is significant to note that the 1990/1991 RI/FS conducted by PDER was executed under the philosophy of a former Governor and PDER Administration and prior passage of Pennsylvania's Land Recycling and Environmental Remediation Standards Act (LRERSA), which was signed into law on May 19, 1995. Additional discussion of this new law is provided in Chapter 2. This new "brownfields" legislation paved the way for the ultimate resolution at this site. There are three levels of remediation addressed by LRERSA: (1) Background; (2) Statewide Standards; and (3) Site Specific Cleanup. This project was conducted pursuant to the site-specific concept which is the most flexible regarding planned reuse, but is also the most burdensome regarding technical documentation, risk assessment, and community involvement.

With a new state administration, a renamed and more practical state environmental agency—now called the Pennsylvania Department of Environmental Protection (PDEP)—and a new brownfields law, the opportunity to balance environmental protection with economic growth presented itself for the first time. One of the former owners of the site successfully negotiated a remediation plan, which provided adequate protection of human health and the environment, was supported by the community, and promoted—rather than disrupted—industrial redevelopment at the site.

It is noteworthy that Pennsylvania's Brownfields Program is being touted as an excellent example for other states to follow to best balance environmental and economic growth concerns. This project provides a wonderful example of how the program can succeed in promoting job creation and reuse of industrial property.

Remedial Planning

The initial concept of remediation proposed by the former PDER envisioned excavation of some 28,000 cubic yards of soil for on-site treatment through solvent extraction. This concept was flawed by several factors, not the least of which was that the treatment process was not proven on any previous full-scale remediation for similar soil contamination. Also, the potential risk of a residual extraction solvent in the post-treated soil could be higher that the risk posed by the contamination itself. The calculated risk from the contaminants found at the site was significantly overstated and did not incorporate the most current risk and toxicological parameters. The areas delineated for excavation and treatment were based on field data that were insufficient to support the delineation, yielding a high probability for cost escalation once remediation commenced. Some areas were identified as requiring remediation where the data showed no need for remediation.

Under the more practical LRERSA, and with aggressive community relations and support, a remedy was designed that targeted selected areas for excavation and disposal in a new disposal cell constructed within the existing fly ash landfill, and containment of the remaining soil contamination. Containment included soil cover or asphalt paving. Containment was appropriate because the contaminants were not migrating off-site or onto groundwater, direct contact was precluded by the cover/paving, and the planned land use was industrial—with certain areas having limited or restricted access consistent with the planned land use. On an area of the site not involved in former industrial operations, a playground was constructed to support a day care center created to serve workers of the new industrial operations.

The remedy has been successfully constructed. Remediation took less than six months and reduced the originally proposed remediation cost by an order of magnitude. PDEP issued a Certificate of Substantial Completeness in December 1995.

Land Use Planning Issues

The MRA has a 10-year build-out plan for the tenant reuse of the former fiber manufacturing buildings. These are masonry buildings with glazed brick interior walls in some locations and concrete floors designed for heavy equipment. An on-site wastewater treatment plant exists as well, although it is not currently in use.

During the planning and design of the remedy, one of the former owners and the MRA cooperated so that the remedy supported the redevelopment plans. In areas where additional parking or road construction was needed to support planned redevelopment, impacted soil was covered with asphalt paving with sufficient bearing and wear coats to support truck traffic where necessary. In other areas, impacted soil was covered with clean backfill to facilitate planned landscaping.

This project is an example of the successful integration of environmental remediation with planned industrial reuse of industrial property. Current tenant operations include injection molding for mini-van dashboards, assembly of surgical steel valve components, and plastic diaper recycling. Employment is now over 1,200 from approximately 15 tenant operations. Full redevelopment will provide nearly as many jobs as during full capacity operations of the former fiber manufacturing operations.

Case Study #2: Redevelopment for Commercial Use

Robinson Brick Company Site, Denver, Colorado

The Robinson Brick Company (ROBCO) Site covers 17.3 acres in an area of Denver, Colorado zoned for industrial use. The site is on the National Priorities List (NPL) of Superfund sites. The EPA completed remedial investigation for the ROBCO Site in April 1986 and a Feasibility Study in September 1986. The EPA Record of Decision (ROD) for cleanup of radium-contaminated portions of the site was issued on September 30, 1986. The remedy for cleanup of the site called for excavation of radium-contaminated soil to meet cleanup levels provided for in 40 C.F.R. § 192. Remedial action of radium-contaminated areas began in May 1988 and was completed in March 1991. An area currently undergoing remediation for heavy metal contamination is the site under consideration for this project.

Site History

Since the late 1800s, significant changes have occurred both in physical features and type of industrial operations conducted at the

ROBCO site. The Bailey Milling, Amalgamating, and Mining Company was incorporated in 1884. By 1885, the Bailey Reduction Company was also incorporated and the Bailey Smelter had been constructed as early as 1882. The smelter processed carbonate ores from Leadville mines until operations ceased in 1893 because of the "silver panic" and "mining crash." The Bailey Smelter was dismanteled around 1900.

By 1903, the Colorado Zinc Company had constructed a mill on, and just east of, the site of the Bailey Smelter. By 1908, the size of the original mill building had doubled. Ore processed by this operation continued to be lead-, zinc-, and cadmium-rich carbonate ores from the Leadville area mines. Zinc milling operations continued until about 1910. However, by 1913, the zinc mill had burned and was in ruins.

The Sutton, Steele, and Steele Mining and Milling Company (SSS) operated a dry concentration process and custom mill from 1911 to 1917 at the far north end of the ROBCO site. Waste materials from SSS operations may be present as fill material in old Merchant's Mill Ditch at the north end of the site and on railroad property to the northeast.

The National Radium Institute (NRI) operated its ore extraction facility at the ROBCO site. Radium, vanadium, and uranium were extracted from carbonate ore at the facility. By June 1914, the NRI plant had begun full-scale production; in 1916, radium operations ceased. However, some fractioning operations at the NRI plant may have continued until 1918. The NRI operations ceased shortly thereafter. Minerals Recovery Company purchased the NRI plant late in 1918 but went out of business by 1920.

Prest-O-Lite Company used a part of the site in the mid- and late-1920s to manufacture and service storage batteries. The company also made carbide and acetylene by a process that involved calcium carbide and hydrochloric acid. During approximately the same time period, the old NRI facility was occupied by the Minerals Products Company which was in the business of treating and sacking metallic ore insulation. From 1927 to about 1930, U.S. Gasoline Corporation used the NRI facility as an oil reclamation plant. Security Petroleum used the site (specific use unknown) from 1932 to 1936. Dated materials found during the 1988 EPA Remedial Action activities indicate that a part of the site was used as a landfill in the early 1930s (primarily the south part of the main site west trench). By 1942, the Colfax Pressed Brick Company had begun operations on the site. This company was the predecessor of the Robinson Brick and Tile Company, which is now the Robinson Brick Company, the current owner of the site. ROBCO occupied the site through the 1980s until production ceased in 1984.

Applicable Cleanup Standards

The closure documents established the method by which the ROBCO site was effectively and safely closed with respect to identified areas of metal contamination. The areas of contamination are areas within the boundaries of the site that exhibit metal contamination above risk-based cleanup standards established by the U.S. EPA and Colorado Department of Public Health and Environment (CDPHE). According to a baseline risk assessment prepared by the EPA and presented in the OU-9 ROBCO Site Record of Decision, dated October 1991, the only contaminants present in soils on the site in concentration levels that pose significant risks are arsenic, lead, and zinc.

The area of contamination by these metals was largely confined to fill material. The discolored soil and fill material comprising the area of contamination has been identified as consisting of sand mixed with cinders, charred lumber, glass shards, rubble, brick material, and metal shavings. The fill material that exceeds the site screening criteria within the area of contamination is distinctively dark brown to black in color. The total quantity of contaminated materials exceeding the risk-based cleanup standards is 58,000 cubic yards.

Remedial Planning

As indicated in the ROD, the selected remedial action is designed to prevent direct contact with, or inhalation or ingestion of, metals-contaminated soils, in part by covering the affected areas with a soil cover. This remedial action will consist of consolidating 58,000 cubic yards of contaminated soil in parking lot areas of the site. It will also involve moving 120,000 cubic yards of uncontaminated on-site soils in order to carry out the remedy. The contaminated materials that will be consolidated under the parking areas will be covered by a subsurface layer of geotextile and geonet that will provide a permeable drainage layer and that will also serve as an identification barrier. All utilities will be placed into utility trenches that will be covered with uncontaminated materials to an estimate of $2.5 million for the non-brownfield approach.

In addition, the remedial action includes the continuation of downgradient groundwater monitoring as a means of checking for contaminant migration toward the South Platte River via groundwater. Institutional controls implemented by the EPA and CDPHE are also a part of the selected remedy. These controls consist of off-site groundwater monitoring and deed restrictions for those on-site areas where the contaminated materials will be consolidated.

Home Depot U.S.A., Robinson Brick Company, U.S. EPA Region 8, and the CDPHE agreed to perform the ROBCO Site Closure in a defined "shared" and "phased" manner. Environmental Resources Management, Inc (ERM) provided environmental consulting services in assisting Home Depot, Robinson Brick Company, EPA Region 8, and the CDPHE in negotiating a Prospective Purchaser Agreement, closure documents, closure design criteria, and closure sequencing, and in performing on-site Construction Quality Assurance (CQA) oversight. ERM was contracted to perform environmental consulting, design, engineering, and on-site remedial support for the implementation of the ROBCO Site Remedial Response Action.

In a separate agreement between Home Depot U.S.A. and Robinson Brick Company, Robinson Brick Company contracted with ERM for implementation of the Phase I and Phase III "shared" scope of work. EPA Region 8 contracted with its Contractor, Sverdrup Environmental, to perform Phase II "Shared" Scope of Work.

Prospective Purchaser and Future Land Use of the Site

The chief issue in land use planning was to have a party that saw value in the site if it could be remediated in a way that would enable the party to use the site. Home Depot became interested as a prospective purchaser and would like to redevelop the site for commercial use, in part for a retail store. The prospective purchaser's interest in the site and the EPA's and CDPHE's interest in arriving at a remedy that would enable the site to be used in the future put the project into an attractive light. In effect, Home Depot will use the full 17.3-acre site and it will purchase the site from ROBCO. This will enable ROBCO to remove itself from the site. The prospective purchaser agreement that was signed will give Home Depot assurances that it will not be buying future liabilities. Institutional controls will provide both agencies with assurance that the public and environment will be protected in the future.

Case Study #3: Redevelopment for Residential Use

Herndon Homes Site, Atlanta, Georgia

The Herndon Homes Site is a low-income housing development that was built in the early 1940s. It is owned by the Atlanta Housing Authority. It covers approximately 20 acres and has 54 apartment buildings. Prior to development as an apartment complex, the southern half of the development had been undeveloped and partially used as a waste disposal area, presumably by a number of industries operating in the area. During 1993, renovations were undertaken including removal of lead-based paint, remodeling of building interiors and exteriors, and installation of a new storm sewer. Trenching operations for the sewer on a portion of the 20-acre development exposed buried wastes. Sewer construction workers complained of the wastes and the U.S. EPA conducted an initial investigation. The agency found lead, arsenic, and polynuclear aromatic hydrocarbons (PAHs) in soil and waste samples from the southern one-half of the development. This finding slowed the installation of the sewer and building rehabilitation since hazardous waste training was required for the sewer contractor's workers once the contamination was detected. Ambient air monitoring and oversight slowed progress further, relative to normal construction. At the present time, the northern half of the development has been renovated and is currently occupied. The southern half of the development has been partially renovated and is currently unoccupied. The unoccupied area was fenced to prevent unauthorized access. This has met with some success although vagrants have been found in some of the unoccupied buildings at times.

Contamination Assessment

After the initial discovery of wastes, a complete site investigation was undertaken of the project site. Numerous surface and subsurface soil samples and groundwater samples were collected, both around and under the apartment buildings. What was found supported initial observations from the storm sewer contractor that the southern half of the development contained wastes that extended to depths greater than 15 feet below grade in some places. The wastes were below the water table in some places as well. While chemical analyses of soil and waste samples showed elevated concentrations of lead, arsenic, and benzo(a)pyrene on the unoccupied areas, groundwater contamination was not widespread. In fact, the only well in the unoccupied area that showed any evidence of groundwater contamination was a well on the upgradient portion of the unoccupied area. This well showed evidence of low part-per-billion concentrations of several PAHs. A groundwater sample obtained from a location upgradient to the on-site well suggested that groundwater contamination might be migrating onto the site. Beryllium in the low part-per-billion range is the only contaminant that has been detected on a consistent basis above proposed cleanup levels in wells in the occupied portion of the development.

Applicable Regulations Governing Remediation

Investigation and remediation of this project are governed by Georgia's Hazardous Sites Response Act (HSRA). Enacted in 1994, HRSA specifies that a site must be remediated to one of five cleanup levels denoted "Risk Reduction Standards." Type 1 and 2 Risk Reduction Standards are for residential land use. Types 3 and 4 are for commercial and industrial land use. These four types of Risk Reduction Standards represent concentrations that the soil and groundwater must attain after remediation is complete. Types 1 and 3 are lookup values based primarily on standard exposure assumptions. Types 2 and 4 are based on site-specific exposure assumptions. Type 5 Risk Reduction Standards do not specify a cleanup concentration. Rather, Type 5 is used when wastes will be left in place. Under a Type 5 cleanup, the wastes on the site must be contained to prevent exposure and to prevent continued groundwater contamination. According to the Georgia Environmental Protection Division, at the present time, a Type 5 site cannot be used for residential purposes.

Remedial Planning

Initial remedial planning in late 1995 envisioned that the northern half of the site could continue to be used for residential purposes. This is because the concentration of chemicals in the soils on the northern half that exceeded the residential Risk Reduction Standards was restricted to shallow soils. Furthermore, wastes were not noted per se on the northern half. The southern half of the development presents a different scenario. Because the Atlanta Housing Authority needs to use as many of the remaining apartment buildings as possible for residential purposes, seven of the apartments on the southern half have currently been designated for residential use. These seven buildings lie on the outer part of the southern half in an area that can be remediated to Type 1 and 2 residential Risk Reduction Standards. The remainder of the southern half has wastes that are too extensive to be remediated to residential Risk Reduction Standards to enable its continued use for apartments.

The seven apartment buildings slated for residential use on the southern half will serve a dual purpose. First, they will be used for temporary relocation of residents from the northern half during remediation of the northern half. This is extremely important. Without this use, it would be necessary to relocate residents to an off-site location during remediation. This presents difficulties because the residents currently have transportation arrangements for school and work. If relocated off-site, the Atlanta Housing Authority would be responsible for providing transportation. Second, the seven apartment buildings will be used for normal residential purposes after all remediation is complete.

Several alternatives have been evaluated for the nonresidential portion of the southern half. These alternatives were examined to see which would provide the appropriate level of protection for nonresidential use at the least cost. The alternatives considered were: (1) complete removal of wastes (for comparison) which would have restored the area to residential use; and (2) waste containment through the use of concrete slabs, grass pavers (a honeycomb-like concrete structure that is filled with soil and grass) or a subsurface geotextile barrier. The costs for these alternatives ranged from a high of $15 million for complete removal of the estimated 375 million tons of wastes on the southern half of the development to $1.9 million for the use of grass pavers to effectuate the containment. A slurry wall for control of groundwater was considered with the use of concrete slabs. Complete removal was deemed too costly for the return of investment.

Land Use Planning Issues

Many land use planning issues emerged during the initial stages of remedial planning. Perhaps the most important is the use of the nonresidential portion of the southern half of the development. The Atlanta Housing Authority's mission is to provide safe, affordable housing to low income families. Since 17 apartment buildings may be lost for further residential use, the Housing Authority is now faced with the task of evaluating possible nonresidential uses of these 17 buildings. One possible solution is to use the existing apartment buildings in some way. Short-term housing has been considered but the Georgia Environmental Protection Division has stated that the Type 5 Risk

Reduction Standard cannot be used for any type of residential use. Conversion of the buildings by remodeling the interiors is possible; for example, change from apartments to offices. This raises the question of location. Is the location attractive enough to entice businesses to relocate in sufficient numbers to use fully the available space? This question has not yet been answered. Another possible use under consideration is for training.

Perhaps the biggest impediment to development of the nonresidential portions of the site thus far is the uncertainty over what it actually might be used for. The primary focus of remedial planning activities has been to move as quickly as possible to remediate the northern portion of the site in order for the residents of those apartments to return their lives to some semblance of normalcy. This has required a tremendous amount of energy and time in considering the details necessary to move the remediation forward. Furthermore, remediation of the currently occupied areas can proceed without having a defined plan for the nonresidential portion of the southern half. However, the nonresidential part of the site cannot remain unused for too long because of its proximity to the residential buildings. Since the unoccupied buildings are magnets for vagrants and the homeless, members of the community do not feel completely safe with the vacant buildings at present. In the long-term, the Atlanta Housing Authority will need to define a permanent use for these buildings that will blend with the residential nature of the development. This may mean that the Housing Authority will have to form an alliance with some partner who has the necessary skills to develop these buildings for some creative use.

Comparison of the Three Projects

Comparison of the three projects shows important differences and significant similarities. Regarding differences, two of the three projects are superfund-type projects on old industrial areas, while the third is currently a residential use. Type of contamination, contaminant concentration, and cleanup levels are different for all three, as is the proposed redevelopment land use. These three projects demonstrate how brownfields concepts have been successfully used in cases where three different land uses—industrial, commercial, and residential—were major factors in the redevelopment and reuse of the site. The nonresidential portion of the Herndon Homes site may be developed by leaving in place materials that contain chemical concentrations that are higher than would be permitted under a no restriction reuse scenario. This is similar to the ROBCO site in Denver. The former site owner had the active involvement of a redevelopment authority which was absent in the other two cases.

Perhaps the most significant similarity is that in all three cases, the environmental agencies expressed an interest in seeing the land redeveloped for some future use and were cooperative in reaching those goals. A spirit of cooperation between affected parties—owner, prospective purchaser, redevelopment authorities, the community, and regulatory agencies—is essential for the successful reuse of brownfield properties. All three cases demonstrate that brownfield sites can be remediated at substantially less cost than may have otherwise been possible. Finally, these projects support the observation that many environmental agencies are beginning to include a strong element of common sense initiatives that will be of ever increasing importance in order to continue to protect human health and the environment, but also promote beneficial reuse of brownfield sites.

Conclusions

These three projects lend evidence to the emergence of the brownfield redevelopment concept. They demonstrate that environmental agencies, landowners, prospective purchasers, and other parties can work together to redevelop sites that can be remediated to other than natural background conditions and then be beneficially reused. This lends support to the belief, held by many in industry and the environmental consulting business, that by applying practical knowledge based on realistic technical considerations and market realities, the economic vitality and environmental protection can be managed in a win-win context such that society does not have to be forced to choose one over the other.

As can be expected, some may be opposed to brownfield redevelopment, believing that remediation to less stringent levels is not protective of human health and the environment. However, the fact remains that a good deal of common sense, current technical/scientific knowledge, and effective land use planning support the belief that former industrial facilities can be safely redeveloped in property that does not meet the overly stringent and often unnecessary criteria previously held as cleanup goals. By skillfully integrating environmental realities with planned land use, these industrial areas can be reused safely and to the economic benefit of communities across the country.

APPENDIX A

U.S. EPA Brownfield Program Contacts

U.S. EPA HEADQUARTERS

Katherine Dawes
Brownfields Coordinator
U.S. EPA Headquarters
401 M Street, S.W. (5101)
Washington, DC 20460
(202) 260-8394
(202) 260-6606 (Fax)

U.S. EPA Regional Offices

EPA Region 1 - *Connecticut, Massachusetts, Maine, New Hampshire, Rhode Island, Vermont*

Brownfields Coordinator
U.S. EPA Region 1
JFK Federal Building
One Congress Street
Boston, MA 02203
(617) 573-9681
(617) 573-9662 (Fax)

EPA Region 2 - *New Jersey, New York, Puerto Rico, Virgin Islands*

Brownfields Coordinator
U.S. EPA Region 2
290 Broadway - 18th FL
New York, NY 10007
(212) 637-4314
(212) 637-4360 (Fax)

EPA Region 3 - *Delaware, Maryland, Pennsylvania, Virginia, West Virginia, District of Columbia*

Brownfields Coordinator
U.S. EPA Region 3
841 Chestnut Street
Philadelphia, PA 19107
(215) 566-3129
(215) 566-3001 (Fax)

EPA Region 4 - *Alabama, Florida, Georgia, Kentucky, Mississippi, North Carolina, South Carolina, Tennessee*

Brownfields Coordinator
U.S. EPA Region 4
Atlanta Federal Center
100 Alabama Street, S.W.
Atlanta, GA 30303
(404) 562-8923
(404) 562-8370 (Fax)

EPA Region 5 - *Illinois, Indiana, Michigan, Minnesota, Ohio, Wisconsin*

Brownfields Coordinator
U.S. EPA Region 5
77 West Jackson Boulevard
Chicago, IL 60604
(312) 886-7596
(312) 886-2737 (Fax)

EPA Region 6 - *Arkansas, Louisiana, New Mexico, Oklahoma, Texas*

Brownfields Coordinator
U.S. EPA Region 6
First Interstate Bank Tower at
Fountain Place
1445 Ross Avenue - Suite 1200
Dallas, TX 75202
(214) 665-6736
(214) 665-6660 (Fax)

EPA Region 7 - *Iowa, Kansas, Missouri, Nebraska*

Brownfields Coordinator
U.S. EPA Region 7
726 Minnesota Avenue
Kansas City, KS 66101
(913) 551-7786
(913) 551-7063 (Fax)

EPA Region 8 - *Colorado, Montana, North Dakota, South Dakota, Utah, Wyoming*

Brownfields Coordinator
U.S. EPA Region 8
One Denver Place
999 18th Street - Suite 500 (EPR)
Denver, CO 80202
(303) 312-6931
(303) 312-6071 (Fax)

EPA Region 9 - *Arizona, California, Hawaii, Nevada, American Samoa, Guam, Trust Territories of the Pacific*

Brownfields Coordinator
U.S. EPA Region 9
75 Hawthorne Street, H-1
San Francisco, CA 94105
(415) 744-2237
(415) 744-2180 (Fax)

EPA Region 10 - *Alaska, Idaho, Oregon, Washington*

Brownfields Coordinator
U.S. EPA Region 10
1200 Sixth Avenue
Seattle, WA 98101
(206) 553-6523
(206) 553-0124 (Fax)

U.S. EPA Brownfields Internet Homepage

The U.S. EPA's Brownfields Internet homepage went on-line in January 1996. The EPA developed the homepage to maximize distribution of brownfields information, increase the timeliness of the information, and reduce document distribution costs. The homepage is an effective vehicle for providing local governments, businesses, affected community members, and other brownfields stakeholders with access to the brownfields information and tools that they need to become involved in local brownfields dialogue across organizations, communities, and media to understand, address, and solve brownfields problems.

The Brownfields homepage provides the user with access to a range of brownfields information, including several key brownfields documents. The brownfields homepage is updated frequently to ensure that users have access to the most current brownfields information and redevelopment tools. Future versions of the homepage may allow users to query information pertaining to their specific information needs; access more in-depth pilot information, including maps, photographs, and updates of ongoing activities; and access cleanup and redevelopment tools, such as the CERCLIS archive list and the LandView database.

The homepage information is organized into the following four categories: general information; tools; other brownfields-related EPA sites; and brownfields initiative information.

1. General Information—Provides general information about the Brownfields Initiative and includes:

   - Mission Statement
   - Brownfields Action Agenda
   - Major Milestones/Accomplishments
   - Frequently Asked Questions
   - Announcements/What's New

2. Tools—Provides information on available brownfields tools and includes:

   - Index of Brownfields Publications
   - Brownfields in the News
   - Endorsements
   - Starting a Brownfields Effort
   - Contacts
   - Tools

3. Other Brownfields-Related EPA Sites—Provides information on and links to related EPA Web sites, including:

   - Superfund
   - Office of Enforcement and Compliance Assurance
   - Office of Environmental Justice
   - Environmental Finance Advisory Board
   - Common Sense Initiative Iron and Steel Sector
   - Subcommittee

Additional state and non-EPA sites will be linked to the Brownfields homepage in the future.

4. Brownfields Initiative—Provides detailed information on:

   - Regional Brownfields Initiatives
   - Liability and Cleanup Issues
   - Partnerships and Outreach

- Job Development and Training
- Brownfields Pilots

The Brownfields Pilot page gives the user additional information on pilot announcements, application information, pilot fact sheets, and tools for new pilot participants. These pilot tools include organizations and publications of interest, advice from other pilot participants, available funding mechanisms, and a discussion of various brownfields stakeholders.

The Brownfields homepage can be accessed in any of the following ways:

1. Type the URL address: http://www.epa.gov/swerosps/bf/
2. From EPA's homepage (http://www.epa.gov/), choose the highlighted link "Offices," then "Solid Waste and Emergency Response," then "Outreach Programs, Special Projects, and Initiatives," then "Brownfields".
3. From EPA's homepage (http://www.epa.gov/), choose the highlighted link "Initiatives," then "Brownfields Home Page".

For more information about the Brownfields homepage, contact Jim Mass of U.S. EPA at (202) 260-8927 or mass.james@epamail.epa.gov.

APPENDIX B

State Brownfield Program Contacts

Alaska

Director, Voluntary Cleanup/Brownfields Program
Alaska Department of Environmental Conservation
Division of Environmental Quality
P.O. Box #O
Juneau, AK 99801

Arkansas

Director, Voluntary Cleanup/Brownfields Program
Arkansas Department of Pollution Control and Ecology
ADDC&E (Bldg. D)
8001 National Drive
Little Rock, AR 72209

Arizona

Director, Voluntary Cleanup/Brownfields Program
Arizona Department of Environmental Quality
2005 N. Central Avenue
Phoenix, AZ 85004

California

Director, Site Mitigation Program
Department of Toxic Substances Control
California Environmental Protection Agency
400 P Street, 4th FL
P.O. Box 806
Sacramento, CA 95812-0806
(916) 323-3376

Colorado

Director, Voluntary Cleanup/Brownfields Program
Colorado Department of Public Health and Environment
4300 Cherry Creek Drive South
Denver, CO 80222

Connecticut

Director, Urban Site Remedial Action Program
Connecticut Department of Environmental Protection
79 Elm Street
Hartford, CT 06106-5127
(860) 424-3705

Delaware

Director, Voluntary Cleanup/Brownfields Program
Site Investigation & Restoration Branch
Waste Management Section
Delaware Department of Natural Resources and Environmental Control
715 Grantham Lane
New Castle, DE 19720-4801
(302) 323-4540

Illinois

Director, Site Remediation Program
Illinois Environmental Protection Agency
2200 Churchill Road
Springfield, IL 62794-9276
(217) 782-6760

Indiana

Director, Voluntary Cleanup/Brownfields Program
Indiana Department of Environmental Management
105 S. Meridian Street
P.O. Box 6015
Indianapolis, IN 46225

Kansas

Director, Voluntary Cleanup/Brownfields Program
Kansas Department of Health and Environment
Forbes Field, Building 321
Topeka, KS 66620

Louisiana

Director, Voluntary Cleanup/Brownfields Program
Office of Solid and Hazardous Waste
Louisiana Department of Environmental Quality
P.O. Box 82178
Baton Rouge, LA 70884-2178
(504) 765-0249   (504) 765-0299 (Fax)

Maine

Director, Voluntary Cleanup/Brownfields Program
Maine Department of Environmental Protection
State House Station #17
Augusta, ME 04333

Maryland

Director, Voluntary Cleanup/Brownfields Division
Waste Management Administration
Maryland Department of the Environment
2500 Broening Highway
Baltimore, MD 21224
(410) 631-3437

Massachusetts

Director, Voluntary Cleanup/Brownfields Program
Massachusetts Department of Environmental Protection
One Winter Street - 5th FL
Boston, MA 02108

Michigan

Director, Voluntary Cleanup/Brownfields Program
Site Reclamation Information & Funding Section
Environmental Response Division
Michigan Department of Environmental Quality
Knapps Centre
P.O. Box 30426
Lansing, MI 48909
(517) 335-3397   (517) 373-9657 (Fax)

Minnesota

Director, Voluntary Investigation and Cleanup Unit
Site Response Section
Groundwater and Solid Waste Division
Minnesota Pollution Control Agency
520 Lafayette Road, North
St. Paul, MN 55155
(612) 296-8407   (612) 296-9707 (Fax)

Missouri

Director, Voluntary Cleanup/Brownfields Program
Missouri Department of Natural Resources
205 Jefferson St.
P.O. Box 176
Jefferson City, MO 65102

Montana

Director, Voluntary Cleanup/Brownfields Program
Environmental Remediation Division
Montana Department of Environmental Quality
2209 Phoenix Avenue
P.O. Box 200901
Helena, MT 59620
(406) 444-0478   (406) 444-1901 (Fax)

New Hampshire

Director, Voluntary Cleanup/Brownfields Program
New Hampshire Department of Environmental Services
Health and Welfare Building
6 Hazen Drive
Concord, NH 03301
(603) 271-6778

New Jersey

Director, Voluntary Cleanup/Brownfields Program
New Jersey Department of Environmental Protection
401 East State Street - 5th FL
CN 028
Trenton, NJ 08625
(609) 633-1480

New York

Director, State Brownfields Program
Division of Environmental Remediation
New York Department of Environmental Conservation
50 Wolfe Road, Room 260A
Albany, NY 12233-7010
(518) 457-5861

North Carolina

Director, Voluntary Cleanup/Brownfields Program
Department of Environment, Health and Natural Resources
Division of Environmental Management
P.O. Box 2091
Raleigh, NC 27602

Ohio

Director, Voluntary Action Program
Ohio Environmental Protection Agency
1800 Watermark Drive
Columbus, OH 43215
(614) 644-2056

Oklahoma

Director, Voluntary Cleanup/Brownfields Program
Waste Management Division
Oklahoma Department of Environmental Quality
1000 Northeast 10th Street
Oklahoma City, OK 73117
(405) 271-7071   (405) 271-8425 (Fax)

Oregon

Director, Voluntary Cleanup Program
Waste Management and Cleanup Division
Oregon Department of Environmental Quality
811 Southwest 6th Avenue
Portland, OR 97204
(503) 229-6834   (503) 229-6977 (Fax)

Pennsylvania

Director, Land Recycling Program
Pennsylvania Department of Environmental Protection
P.O. Box 8471
Harrisburg, PA 17105-8471
(717) 783-7816   (717) 787-1904 (Fax)

Tennessee

Director, Voluntary Cleanup/Brownfields Program
Tennessee Department of Environment and Conservation
L & C Tower
401 Church Street
Nashville, TN 37243

Texas

Director, Voluntary Cleanup Section
Pollution Cleanup Division
Texas Natural Resource Conservation Commission
P.O. Box 13087, MC 221
Austin, TX 78711-3087
(512) 239-2498

Utah

Director, Voluntary Cleanup/Brownfields Program
Utah Department of Environmental Quality
P.O. Box 16700
288 North, 1460 West Street
Salt Lake City, UT 84116-0700

Vermont

Director, Voluntary Cleanup/Brownfields Program
Vermont Department of Environmental Conservation
103 South Main Street
Waterbury, VT 05671-0404
(802) 241-3491

Virginia

Director, Waste Division
Virginia Department of Environmental Quality
629 East Main Street
Richmond, VA 23219
(800) 698-4147   (804) 698-4500 (Fax)

Washington

Director, Toxics Cleanup Program
Washington Department of Ecology
Mail Stop PV-11
Olympia, WA 98504
(360) 407-7185

Wisconsin

Director, Voluntary Cleanup/Brownfields Program
Contaminated Land Recycling - SW/3
Bureau of Remediation and Redevelopment
Department of Natural Resources
101 S. Webster Street
Madison, WI 53707-7921
(608) 264-6020

Model Prospective Purchaser Agreement
60 Fed. Reg. 34792 (July 3, 1995)

Region ____

In the matter of: [name] [Docket Number] under the authority of the Comprehensive Environmental Response, Compensation, and Liability Act of 1980, 42 U.S.C. § 9601, et seq., as amended. [state law, if appropriate] Agreement and Covenant Not To Sue [Insert Settling Respondent's Name]

I. Introduction

This Agreement and Covenant Not to Sue ("Agreement") is made and entered into by and between the United States Environmental Protection Agency ("EPA") [state of ___] and _____ [insert name of Settling Respondent] (collectively the "Parties"). EPA enters into this Agreement pursuant to the Comprehensive Environmental Response, Compensation, and Liability Act of 1980, as amended ("CERCLA"), 42 U.S.C. § 9601, et seq. [If the state is a party, insert "The State of _____, enters into this Agreement pursuant to [cite relevant state authority.]" and make appropriate reference to state with respect to affected provisions, including payment or work to be performed].

[Provide introductory information, consistent with Definitions and Statement of Facts, about the party purchasing the contaminated property including, name ("Settling Respondent"), address, corporate status if applicable and include proposed use of the property by prospective purchaser. Provide name, location and description of Site.]

The Parties agree to undertake all actions required by the terms and conditions of this Agreement. The purpose of this Agreement is to settle and resolve, subject to reservations and limitations contained in Sections VII, VIII, IX, and X [If this Agreement contains a separate section for Settling Respondent's reservations, add section number], the potential liability of the Settling Respondent for the Existing Contamination at the Property which would otherwise result from Settling Respondent becoming the owner of the property. The Parties agree that the Settling Respondent's entry into this Agreement, and the actions undertaken by the Settling Respondent in accordance with the Agreement, do not constitute an admission of any liability by the Settling Respondent. The resolution of this potential liability, in exchange for provision by the Settling Respondent to EPA [and the state] of a substantial benefit, is in the public interest.

II. Definitions

Unless otherwise expressly provided herein, terms used in this Agreement which are defined in CERCLA or in regulations promulgated under CERCLA shall have the meaning assigned to them in CERCLA or in such regulations, including any amendments thereto.

1. "EPA" shall mean the United States Environmental Protection Agency and any successor departments or agencies of the United States.

2. "Existing Contamination" shall mean any hazardous substances, pollutants or contaminants, present or existing on or under the Site as of the effective date of this Agreement.

3. "Parties" shall mean EPA, [State of _____], and the Settling Respondent.

4. "Property" shall mean that portion of the Site which is described in Exhibit 1 of this Agreement.

5. "Settling Respondent" shall mean _____.

6. "Site" shall mean the [Superfund] Site, encompassing approximately _____ acres, located at [address or description of location] in [name of city, county, and State], and depicted generally on the map attached as Exhibit 2. The Site shall include the Property, and all areas to which hazardous substances and/or pollutants or contaminants, have come to be located [provide a more specific definition of the Site where possible; may also wish to include within Site description structures, USTs, etc].

7. "United States" shall mean the United States of America, its departments, agencies, and instrumentalities.

III. Statement of Facts

8. [Include only those facts relating to the Site that are relevant to the covenant being provided the prospective purchaser. Avoid adding information that relates only to actions or parties that are outside of this Agreement.]

9. The Settling Respondent represents, and for the purposes of this Agreement EPA [and the state] relies on those representations, that Settling Respondent's involvement with the Property and the Site has been limited to the following:

[Provide facts of any involvement by Settling Respondent with the Site, for example performing an environmental audit, or if Settling Respondent has had no involvement with the Site so state.].

IV. Payment

10. In consideration of and in exchange for the United States' Covenant Not to Sue in Section VIII herein [and Removal of Lien in Section XXI herein if that is part of the consideration for the agreement], Settling Respondent agrees to pay to EPA the sum of $_____, within ___ days of the effective date of this Agreement. [A separate section should be added if the consideration is work to be performed.] The Settling Respondent shall make all payments required by this Agreement in the form of a certified check or checks made payable to "EPA Hazardous Substance

Superfund," referencing the EPA Region, EPA Docket number, and Site/Spill ID#____ [insert 4-digit no.; first 2 numbers represent Region, second 2 numbers are Region's Site/Spill ID no.], [DOJ case number ___, if applicable] and name and address of Settling Respondent. [insert Regional Superfund Lockbox address where payment should be sent]. Notice of payment shall be sent to those persons listed in Section XV (Notices and Submissions) and to EPA Region ___ Financial Management Officer [insert address].

11. Amounts due and owing pursuant to the terms of this Agreement but not paid in accordance with the terms of this Agreement shall accrue interest at the rate established pursuant to Section 107(a) of CERCLA, 42 U.S.C. § 9607(a), compounded on an annual basis.

[___.] [Work To Be Performed] [Include this section and other appropriate provisions relating to performance of the work, such as financial assurance, agency approvals, reporting, etc., where work to be performed is the consideration for the Agreement. ___. Statement of Work attached as Exhibit 3.]

V. Access/Notice to Successors in Interest

12. Commencing upon the date that it acquires title to the Property, Settling Respondent agrees to provide to EPA [and the state] its authorized officers, employees, representatives, and all other persons performing response actions under EPA [or state] oversight, an irrevocable right of access at all reasonable times to the Property and to any other property to which access is required for the implementation of response actions at the Site, to the extent access to such other property is controlled by the Settling Respondent, for the purposes of performing and overseeing response actions at the Site under federal [and state] law. EPA agrees to provide reasonable notice to the Settling Respondent of the timing of response actions to be undertaken at the Property. Notwithstanding any provision of this Agreement, EPA retains all of its authorities and rights, including enforcement authorities related thereto, under CERCLA, the Solid Waste Disposal Act, as amended by the Resource Conservation and Recovery Act, 42 U.S.C. § 6901, ("RCRA")

et seq., and any other applicable statute or regulation, including any amendments thereto.

13. Within 30 days after the effective date of this Agreement, the Settling Respondent shall record a certified copy of this Agreement with the Recorder's Office [or Registry of Deeds or other appropriate office], _____ County, State of _____. Thereafter, each deed, title, or other instrument conveying an interest in the Property shall contain a notice stating that the Property is subject to this Agreement. A copy of these documents should be sent to the persons listed in Section XV (Notices and Submissions).

14. The Settling Respondent shall ensure that assignees, successors in interest, lessees, and sublessees, of the Property shall provide the same access and cooperation. The Settling Respondent shall ensure that a copy of this Agreement is provided to any current lessee or sublessee on the Property as of the effective date of this Agreement and shall ensure that any subsequent leases, subleases, assignments or transfers of the Property or an interest in the Property are consistent with this Section, and Section XI (Parties Bound/Transfer of Covenant), of the Agreement [and where appropriate, Section ___ (Work to be Performed)].

VI. Due Care/Cooperation

15. The Settling Respondent shall exercise due care at the Site with respect to the Existing Contamination and shall comply with all applicable local, State, and federal laws and regulations. The Settling Respondent recognizes that the implementation of response actions at the Site may interfere with the Settling Respondent's use of the Property, and may require closure of its operations or a part thereof. The Settling Respondent agrees to cooperate fully with EPA in the implementation of response actions at the Site and further agrees not to interfere with such response actions. EPA agrees, consistent with its responsibilities under applicable law, to use reasonable efforts to minimize any interference with the Settling Respondent's operations by such entry and response. In the event the Settling Respondent becomes aware of any action or occurrence which causes or threatens a release of hazardous substances,

pollutants or contaminants at or from the Site that constitutes an emergency situation or may present an immediate threat to public health or welfare or the environment, Settling Respondent shall immediately take all appropriate action to prevent, abate, or minimize such release or threat of release, and shall, in addition to complying with any applicable notification requirements under Section 103 of CERCLA, 42 U.S.C. § 9603, or any other law, immediately notify EPA of such release or threatened release.

VII. Certification

16. By entering into this agreement, the Settling Respondent certifies that to the best of its knowledge and belief it has fully and accurately disclosed to EPA [and the state] all information known to Settling Respondent and all information in the possession or control of its officers, directors, employees, contractors and agents which relates in any way to any Existing Contamination or any past or potential future release of hazardous substances, pollutants or contaminants at or from the Site and to its qualification for this Agreement. The Settling Respondent also certifies that to the best of its knowledge and belief it has not caused or contributed to a release or threat of release of hazardous substances or pollutants or contaminants at the Site. If the United States [and the state] determines that information provided by Settling Respondent is not materially accurate and complete, the Agreement, within the sole discretion of the United States, shall be null and void and the United States [and the state] reserves all rights it [they] may have.

VIII. United States' Covenant Not To Sue[*]

17. Subject to the Reservation of Rights in Section IX of this Agreement, upon payment of the amount specified in Section IV (Payment), of this Agreement [if consideration for Agreement is work to be performed, insert, as appropriate, "and upon completion of the work specified in Section ___ (Work to Be Performed) to the satisfaction of EPA"], the United States [and the state] covenants not to sue or take any other civil or administrative action against Settling Respondent for any and all civil liability for injunctive relief or reimbursement of response costs pursuant to Sections 106 or 107(a) of CERCLA, 42 U.S.C. § 9606 or 9607(a) [and state law cite] with respect to the Existing Contamination.

IX. Reservation of Rights

18. The covenant not to sue set forth in Section VIII above does not pertain to any matters other than those expressly specified in Section VIII (United States' Covenant Not to Sue). The United States [and the State] reserves and the Agreement is without prejudice to all rights against Settling Respondent with respect to all other matters, including but not limited to, the following:

(a) claims based on a failure by Settling Respondent to meet a requirement of this Agreement, including but not limited to Section IV (Payment), Section V (Access/Notice to Successors in Interest), Section VI (Due Care/Cooperation), Section XIV (Payment of Costs, [and, if appropriate, Section ___ (Work to be Performed)];

(b) any liability resulting from past or future releases of hazardous substances, pollutants or contaminants, at or from the Site caused or

---

[*] Since the covenant not to sue is from the United States, Regions negotiating these Agreements should advise the Department of Justice of any other federal agency involved with the Site, or which may have a claim under CERCLA with respect to the Site and use best efforts to advise such federal agency of the proposed settlement.

contributed to by Settling Respondent, its successors, assignees, lessees or sublessees;

(c) any liability resulting from exacerbation by Settling Respondent, its successors, assignees, lessees or sublessees, of Existing Contamination;

(d) any liability resulting from the release or threat of release of hazardous substances, pollutants or contaminants, at the Site after the effective date of this Agreement, not within the definition of Existing Contamination;

(e) criminal liability;

(f) liability for damages for injury to, destruction of, or loss of natural resources, and for the costs of any natural resource damage assessment incurred by federal agencies other than EPA; and

(g) liability for violations of local, State or federal law or regulations.

19. With respect to any claim or cause of action asserted by the United States [or the state], the Settling Respondent shall bear the burden of proving that the claim or cause of action, or any part thereof, is attributable solely to Existing Contamination.

20. Nothing in this Agreement is intended as a release or covenant not to sue for any claim or cause of action, administrative or judicial, civil or criminal, past or future, in law or in equity, which the United States [or the state] may have against any person, firm, corporation or other entity not a party to this Agreement.

21. Nothing in this Agreement is intended to limit the right of EPA [or the state] to undertake future response actions at the Site or to seek to compel parties other than the Settling Respondent to perform or pay for response actions at the Site. Nothing in this Agreement shall in any way restrict or limit the nature or scope of response actions which may be taken or be required by EPA [or the state] in exercising its authority under federal [or state] law. Settling Respondent acknowledges that it is purchasing property where response actions may be required.

X. Settling Respondent's Covenant Not To Sue

22. In consideration of the United States' Covenant Not To Sue in Section VIII of this Agreement, the Settling Respondent hereby covenants not to sue and not to assert any claims or causes of action against the United States [or the state], its authorized officers, employees, or representatives with respect to the Site or this Agreement, including but not limited to, any direct or indirect claims for reimbursement from the Hazardous Substance Superfund established pursuant to the Internal Revenue Code, 26 U.S.C. § 9507, through CERCLA Sections 106(b)(2), 111, 112, 113, or any other provision of law, any claim against the United States, including any department, agency or instrumentality of the United States under CERCLA Sections 107 or 113 related to the Site, or any claims arising out of response activities at the Site, including claims based on EPA's oversight of such activities or approval of plans for such activities.

23. The Settling Respondent reserves, and this Agreement is without prejudice to, actions against the United States based on negligent actions taken directly by the United States, not including oversight or approval of the Settling Respondent's plans or activities, that are brought pursuant to any statute other than CERCLA or RCRA and for which the waiver of sovereign immunity is found in a statute other than CERCLA or RCRA. Nothing herein shall be deemed to constitute preauthorization of a claim within the meaning of Section 111 of CERCLA, 42 U.S.C. § 9611, or 40 CFR 300.700(d).

XI. Parties Bound/Transfer of Covenant

24. This Agreement shall apply to and be binding upon the United States, [and the state], and shall apply to and be binding on the Settling Respondent, its officers, directors, employees, and agents. Each signatory of a Party to this Agreement represents that he or she is fully authorized to enter into the terms and conditions of this Agreement and to legally bind such Party.

25. Notwithstanding any other provisions of this Agreement, all of the rights, benefits and obligations conferred upon Settling Respondent under this Agreement may be assigned or transferred to any person with the prior written consent of EPA [and the state] in its sole discretion.

26. The Settling Respondent agrees to pay the reasonable costs incurred by EPA [and the state] to review any subsequent requests for consent to assign or transfer the Property.

27. In the event of an assignment or transfer of the Property or an assignment or transfer of an interest in the Property, the assignor or transferor shall continue to be bound by all the terms and conditions, and subject to all the benefits, of this Agreement except as EPA [the state] and the assignor or transferor agree otherwise and modify this Agreement, in writing, accordingly. Moreover, prior to or simultaneous with any assignment or transfer of the Property, the assignee or transferee must consent in writing to be bound by the terms of this Agreement including but not limited to the certification requirement in Section VII of this Agreement in order for the Covenant Not to Sue in Section VIII to be available to that party. The Covenant Not To Sue in Section VIII shall not be effective with respect to any assignees or transferees who fail to provide such written consent to EPA [and the state].

XII. Disclaimer

28. This Agreement in no way constitutes a finding by EPA [or the state] as to the risks to human health and the environment which may be posed by contamination at the Property or the Site nor constitutes any representation by EPA [or the state] that the Property or the Site is fit for any particular purpose.

XIII. Document Retention

29. The Settling Respondent agrees to retain and make available to EPA [and the state] all business and operating records, contracts, site studies

and investigations, and documents relating to operations at the Property, for at least ten years, following the effective date of this Agreement unless otherwise agreed to in writing by the Parties. At the end of ten years, the Settling Respondent shall notify EPA [and the state] of the location of such documents and shall provide EPA [and the state] with an opportunity to copy any documents at the expense of EPA [or the state]. [Where work is to be performed, consider providing for document retention for ten years or until completion of work to the satisfaction of EPA, whichever is longer.]

XIV. Payment of Costs

30. If the Settling Respondent fails to comply with the terms of this Agreement, including, but not limited to, the provisions of Section IV (Payment), [or Section____ (Work to be Performed)] of this Agreement, it shall be liable for all litigation and other enforcement costs incurred by the United States [and the state] to enforce this Agreement or otherwise obtain compliance.

XV. Notices and Submissions

31. [Insert names, titles, and addresses of those to whom notices and submissions are due, specifying which submissions are required.]

XVI. Effective Date

32. The effective date of this Agreement shall be the date upon which EPA issues written notice to the Settling Respondent that EPA [and the state] has fully executed the Agreement after review of and response to any public comments received.

XVII. Attorney General Approval

33. The Attorney General of the United States or her designee has issued prior written approval of the settlement embodied in this Agreement.

XVIII. Termination

34. If any Party believes that any or all of the obligations under Section V (Access/Notice to Successors in Interest) are no longer necessary to ensure compliance with the requirements of the Agreement, that Party may request in writing that the other Party agree to terminate the provision(s) establishing such obligations; provided, however, that the provision(s) in question shall continue in force unless and until the party requesting such termination receives written agreement from the other party to terminate such provision(s).

XIX. Contribution Protection

35. With regard to claims for contribution against Settling Respondent, the Parties hereto agree that the Settling Respondent is entitled to protection from contribution actions or claims as provided by CERCLA Section 113(f)(2), 42 U.S.C. § 9613(f)(2) for matters addressed in this Agreement. The matters addressed in this Agreement are [all response actions taken or to be taken and response costs incurred or to be incurred by the United States or any other person for the Site with respect to the Existing Contamination].

36. The Settling Respondent agrees that with respect to any suit or claim for contribution brought by it for matters related to this Agreement it will notify the United States [and the state] in writing no later than 60 days prior to the initiation of such suit or claim.

37. The Settling Respondent also agrees that with respect to any suit or claim for contribution brought against it for matters related to this Agreement it will notify in writing the United States [and the state] within 10 days of service of the complaint on them.

XX. Exhibits

38. Exhibit 1 shall mean the description of the Property which is the subject of this Agreement.

39. Exhibit 2 shall mean the map depicting the Site.

[___. Exhibit 3 shall mean the Statement of Work.]

XXI. Removal of Lien

40. [Use this provision only when appropriate.] Subject to the Reservation of Rights in Section IX of this Agreement, upon payment of the amount specified in Section IV (Payment) [or upon satisfactory completion of work to be performed specified in Section ___ (Work to be Performed)], EPA agrees to remove any lien it may have on the Property under Section 107(l) of CERCLA, 42 U.S.C. § 9607(l), as a result of response action conducted by EPA at the Property.

XXII. Public Comment

41. This Agreement shall be subject to a thirty-day public comment period, after which EPA may modify or withdraw its consent to this Agreement if comments received disclose facts or considerations which indicate that this Agreement is inappropriate, improper or inadequate.

It is So Agreed:

United States Environmental Protection Agency

By:

Regional Administrator, Region _____   Date_____

It is So Agreed:

By:

Name_____   Date_____

Sample EPA Comfort/Status Letters
62 Fed. Reg. 4624 (January 30, 1997)

SAMPLE NO PREVIOUS SUPERFUND INTEREST LETTER

Addressee

Re: [Insert name or description of property/site]

Dear [Insert name of party]:

    I am writing in response to your letter dated --/--/-- concerning the property referenced above. My response is based upon the facts presently known to the U.S. Environmental Protection Agency ("EPA") and is provided solely for informational purposes. The federal Superfund Program, established to cleanup hazardous waste sites, is administered by EPA in cooperation with individual states and local and tribal governments. Sites are discovered by citizens, businesses, and local, state or federal agencies. When a potential hazardous waste site is reported, EPA records the available information in its database, the Comprehensive Environmental Response, Compensation, and Liability Information System ("CERCLIS"). [Note: if a region practices pre-CERCLIS screening procedures, please include language indicating that the procedures exists, whether or not the property is in the process of being "pre-screened", and what this means to the inquirer. Adjustments may be needed to the sample language contained in this letter.] The fact that a site is listed in CERCLIS, however, does not mean that an EPA response action will occur at the site or that ownership or operation of the site is restricted or may be associated with liability. The fact that a

328 / *Brownfields Redevelopment*

property is not listed in CERCLIS does mean that EPA is not currently planning to take any action under the federal Superfund program to evaluate the site for inclusion on the National Priorities List (NPL) or to conduct removal or remediation activities. The above-referenced property was not identified in a search of the active and archived records in the CERCLIS database. Please note that its absence from CERCLIS does not represent a finding that there are no environmental conditions at this property that require action or that are being addressed under another federal or state program. The absence of the property from CERCLIS means that, at this time, EPA is not aware of any information indicating that there has been a release or threat of release of hazardous substances at or from the facility that needs to be assessed by the federal Superfund program and that no such assessment has been performed by EPA in the past. I encourage you to contact [insert name of state or local agency] to determine if they have information regarding the property and its environmental condition. [Regions also are encouraged to check with other program offices to determine whether EPA is addressing this site under another statute such as RCRA]. If you would like more comprehensive information on current or historical CERCLIS data or to request an additional search, please contact the National Technical Information Service ("NTIS"), a publishing clearinghouse for government information. The address is: U.S. Department of Commerce, 5285 Port Royal Road, Springfield, VA 22161 (telephone: (703) 487-4650; fax: (703) 321- 8547.) CERCLIS information is also available on the Internet at http:// www.epa.gov/superfund/index.html#Products. Should you have any further questions about Superfund, please feel free to contact me at [insert phone number/address.]

Sincerely,

Regional Contact

cc: State contact

SAMPLE NO CURRENT SUPERFUND INTEREST LETTER

Addressee

Re: [Insert name or description of property]

Dear [Insert name of party]:

I am writing in response to your letter dated --/--/-- concerning the property referenced above. My response is based upon the facts presently known to the United States Environmental Protection Agency ("EPA") and is provided solely for informational purposes. For the reasons stated below, EPA does not presently contemplate additional Superfund action for this property. In response to growing concern over health and environmental risks posed by hazardous waste sites, Congress enacted the Comprehensive Environmental Response, Compensation, and Liability Act of 1980, as amended ("CERCLA"), establishing the Superfund program to clean up these sites. The Superfund program is implemented by EPA in cooperation with individual states and local and tribal governments. Sites are discovered by citizens, businesses, and local, state, or federal agencies. After a potential hazardous waste site is reported to EPA, the available information is recorded in the Comprehensive Environmental Response and Liability Information System ("CERCLIS"), EPA's data management system for Superfund. Sites are added to CERCLIS when EPA believes that there may be contamination that warrants action under Superfund.

I. [FOR ARCHIVED SITES]

If, after an initial investigation, EPA determines that the contamination does not warrant Superfund action, or if an appropriate Superfund response action has been completed, EPA will archive that site from CERCLIS. This means that EPA believes no further federal response is appropriate. Archived sites may be returned to the CERCLIS site inventory if new information necessitating further Superfund consideration is discovered. EPA has archived the above-referenced property from the CERCLIS site inventory because [choose one of the following (a, b, or c) to complete the sentence] [a.] , following site evaluation activities, EPA determined that either no contamination was found or conditions at the property did not warrant further federal Superfund involvement. [b.] a federal removal action was completed and no further Superfund action is planned for this property. [c.] environmental conditions at the property are subject to requirements of [RCRA, UST, OPA, etc.], however, no further interest under the federal Superfund program is warranted. For further information concerning these requirements, please contact [name and telephone number]. [Add to previous sentence] EPA, therefore, anticipates no need to take additional Superfund enforcement, investigatory, cost recovery, or cleanup action at this archived site unless new information warranting further Superfund consideration or conditions not previously known to EPA regarding the site are discovered. EPA will maintain a dialogue with the states and will continue to refer archived sites to the states for their review and consideration. You may want to contact [insert state contact, address and telephone number] for further information.

II. [FOR PARTIAL OR FULL DELETIONS FROM NPL OR FOR A SITE BOUNDARY SITUATION]

CERCLIS does not describe sites in precise geographical terms primarily because the boundaries of the contamination and available information on those boundaries can be expected to change over time. Once enough information regarding the nature and extent of the release of the hazardous substances is gathered, EPA can more accurately delineate the boundaries of a site.

[Choose either (a), (b) or (c)].

(a) [If the property was included in a partial deletion from the NPL] The above-referenced property [is/appears to be] situated within the [name of NPL site] which is included on EPA's list of high priority hazardous waste CERCLIS sites known as the National Priorities List

("NPL"). EPA, however, has determined that no further investigatory or cleanup action is appropriate at the property under the federal Superfund program. With the [insert State Agency] concurrence, EPA has decided to delete the portion of the NPL site which contains the above-referenced property in accordance with the Agency's "Procedures for Partial Deletions at NPL Sites" (OERR Directive Number 9320.2- 11, August 30, 1996).

(b) [If the property is contained within the NPL site or is defined as the NPL site and the site has been deleted from the NPL] The identified property [is/appears to be] [select one: situated within the defined geographical borders of the [name of NPL site] or defined as the [name of the NPL site]] which is included on EPA's list of high priority hazardous waste CERCLIS sites known as the National Priorities List ("NPL"). EPA, however, has determined that no further investigatory or cleanup action is appropriate at the property. In consultation with the [insert State Agency], EPA has decided to delete this property from the NPL in accordance with "Deletion from the NPL" 40CFR 300.425(e).

(c) [If the property is not part of the CERCLIS site but is nearby] The above-referenced property is located [near or adjacent to] the [name of CERCLIS Site]. At this time, [statement as to the status of the site at present time: e.g., preliminary assessment, site investigation, removal, remedial investigation or feasibility study is underway or is completed]. Based upon available information, the property is not presently considered by EPA to be a part of the [name of the CERCLIS site].

[Add to end of paragraph (a), (b), or (c)]

EPA, therefore, anticipates no need to take [any/additional] [Superfund enforcement--include if PRP search and cost recovery are complete] investigatory or cleanup action at this property unless new information warranting further Superfund consideration or conditions not previously known to EPA regarding the property are discovered. You may want to contact [insert state agency information] for further information. [If appropriate, enclose a copy of the fact sheet on the CERCLIS site].

III. [IF ADMINISTRATIVE RECORD HAS BEEN COMPILED]

EPA has compiled an administrative record for the [name of CERCLIS or NPL Site] which provides information on the nature and extent of the contamination found at the site. This record is available at EPA Region--and at [location nearby to the site]. If you have any additional questions, or wish to discuss this information, please feel free to contact [insert EPA contact and address].

Sincerely yours,

Regional Contact

cc: State contact

SAMPLE FEDERAL SUPERFUND INTEREST LETTER

Addressee

Re: [insert name or description of property/site]

Dear [Insert name of party]:

I am writing in response to your letter dated --/--/-- concerning the property referenced above. My response is based upon the facts presently known to the United States Environmental Protection Agency ("EPA") and is provided solely for informational purposes. In response to growing concern over health and environmental risks posed by hazardous waste sites, Congress passed the Comprehensive Environmental Response Compensation and Liability Act ("CERCLA") and established the Superfund program to clean up these sites. The Superfund program is implemented by EPA in cooperation with individual states and local and tribal governments. Sites are discovered by citizens, businesses, and local, state and federal agencies. After a potential hazardous waste site is reported to EPA, the site-specific information is recorded in the Superfund database, the Comprehensive Environmental Response and Liability Information System ("CERCLIS"). Sites are added to CERCLIS when EPA believes that there may be contamination that warrants action under Superfund. EPA initially screens a potential hazardous waste site to determine what type of action, if any, is necessary. The Superfund program may then perform a preliminary assessment and site investigation to determine whether contamination at a property is likely to require a federal cleanup response, an evaluation to determine if a short term response action to eliminate or reduce contamination is needed, and add the site to EPA's list of high priority hazardous waste sites known as the National Priorities List ("NPL"). EPA is examining [and/or addressing] the property referenced above in connection with the [insert name of CERCLIS/NPL site] under the authority of CERCLA.

[Insert appropriate paragraphs from Sections I and/or II below. Use III for requests regarding the applicability of a specific policy. Section IV represents the closing paragraph for all the Federal Superfund Interest letters].

I. STATUS OF THE IDENTIFIED PROPERTY:

a. The above-referenced property is presently part of [or is] the [insert name of site.] [Add paragraph from Section II for further information concerning the site.]

b. The above-referenced property may be part of the [insert name of site.] [Add paragraph from Section II for further information concerning the site.]

II. STATUS OF EPA ACTIVITIES

a. The site has been placed in the Comprehensive Environmental Response, Compensation and Liability Information System ("CERCLIS") site inventory, but no studies or investigations have been performed to date. Accordingly, EPA has not developed sufficient information relating to the nature and extent of contamination to presently determine whether further federal action is appropriate under Superfund. Additionally, EPA has not yet determined which properties may be considered part of the site.

b. A Superfund site evaluation is planned at the [insert name of site] to investigate possible contamination, and where it may be located. Accordingly, EPA has not yet determined which properties may be considered part of the [insert name of site.] [Add description of site evaluation activity or attach relevant documents, if available.]

c. A Superfund site evaluation activity is underway at the [insert name of site] to investigate possible contamination, and where it may be located. Accordingly, EPA has not yet determined which properties may be considered part of the [insert name of site.] [Add description of site evaluation activity or attach relevant documents, if available.]

d. The [insert name of site] has been proposed to [or placed on] the Superfund National Priorities List ("NPL"). [Refer to and/or attach Federal Register notice.] The description of [insert name of site] contains EPA's preliminary evaluation of which properties are affected, although the actual borders of the Superfund site could change based on further information regarding the extent of contamination and appropriate remedy.

e. A Superfund Remedial Investigation/Feasibility Study ("RI/FS") is planned at [insert name of site.] [Add description of RI/FS and ensuing activities or attach relevant documents, if available].

f. A Superfund Remedial Investigation/Feasibility Study ("RI/FS") is underway at [insert name of site.] [Add description of RI/FS and ensuing activities or attach relevant documents, if available].

g. A Superfund Remedial Investigation/Feasibility Study ("RI/FS") has been completed at [insert name of site.] [Add description of RI/FS and ensuing activities or attach relevant documents, if available].

h. EPA is planning a Superfund Remedial Design/Remedial Action ("RD/RA") at [insert name of site.] [Insert pertinent information such as a description of the ROD and RD/RA, such as date of issuance of the ROD, schedule for cleanup; Fund lead or PRP implementation, cleanup progress to date; a schedule for future cleanup, especially a final completion date, cleanup levels to be achieved, and anticipated future land use of the Site, or attach relevant informational documents].

i. EPA has commenced a Superfund Remedial Design/Remedial Action ("RD/RA") at [insert name of site.] [Insert pertinent information such as a description of the ROD and RD/RA, such as date of issuance of the ROD, schedule for cleanup; Fund lead or PRP implementation, cleanup progress to date; a schedule for future cleanup, especially a final completion date, cleanup levels to be achieved, and anticipated future land use of the Site, or attach relevant informational documents].

j. Superfund Remedial Design/Remedial Action ("RD/RA") has been completed at insert name of site.] [If possible provide information on cleanup achievements, whether it was PRP or Fund-lead, etc., or attach relevant informational documents, if available] A Five-year Review will [will not] be necessary at [insert name of site.] [Also, describe status with respect to deletion from the NPL.]

k. A removal action is planned at [insert name of site.] [provide information on cleanup achievements, whether it was PRP or Fund-lead, and contact number for On-Scene Coordinator, cost recovery staff, or ORC attorney, or attach relevant informational documents, if available.]

l. A removal action is ongoing at [insert name of site.] [provide information on cleanup achievements, whether it was PRP or Fund-lead, and contact number for On-Scene Coordinator, cost recovery staff, or ORC attorney, or attach relevant informational documents, if available.]

m. A removal action has been completed at [insert name of site.] [provide information on cleanup achievements, whether it was PRP or Fund-lead, and contact number for On-Scene Coordinator, cost recovery staff, or ORC attorney, or attach relevant informational documents, if available.]

III. FOR PARTIES OR SITES COVERED BY AN EPA POLICY/STATUTE/

REGULATION

Dear [Insert name of party]:

I am writing in response to your letter dated --/--/-- concerning the property referenced above. My response is based upon the facts presently known to the United States Environmental Protection Agency ("EPA"). As you may know, the above-referenced property is located within or near the [insert name of CERCLIS site.] EPA is currently taking [insert description of any action that EPA is taking or plans to take and any contamination problem.]

[Choose either paragraph [a] or [b]]:

[a. For situations when a party provides information showing that 1) a project found to be in the public interest is hindered or the value of a property is affected by the potential for Superfund liability, and 2) there is no other mechanism available to adequately address the party's concerns] The [insert policy citation/statutory/regulatory provision], provides that EPA, in an exercise of its enforcement discretion, will not take an enforcement action against parties who meet the conditions and criteria described in the [insert policy/statute/regulation]. Based upon the information currently available to EPA, EPA believes that the [policy/statutory/regulatory provision] applies to [you/your] situation. I am enclosing a copy of the [policy/statutory or regulatory provision and fact sheet, if appropriate] for your review.

[b. For situations when a party does not provide information showing that 1) a project found to be in the public interest is hindered or the value of a property is affected by the potential for Superfund liability, and 2) there is no other mechanism available to adequately address the party's concerns, attach the appropriate policy/statutory or regulatory language and insert the following language]:

The [insert policy citation/statutory/regulatory provision], provides that EPA, in an exercise of its enforcement discretion, will not take an enforcement action against parties who meet the conditions and criteria described in the [insert policy/statute/regulation]. [EPA currently does not have enough information available to determine whether the [insert policy/statutory/regulatory citation] applies to your situation OR EPA, based upon the current information available, believes that you/your circumstances do not meet the criteria/provisions of the [policy/statute/regulation]. I, however, have enclosed a copy of the [policy/statutory or regulatory language] for your own review and determination of its applicability to you [or your situation].

IV. CLOSING PARAGRAPH

EPA hopes that the above information is useful to you. [Optional--In addition, we have included a copy of our latest fact sheet for the (insert name of site.)] Further, we direct your attention to the [insert location of site local records repository] at which EPA has placed a copy of the Administrative Record for this site. [Include for section C letters only: This letter is provided solely for informational purposes and does not provide a release from CERCLA liability.] If you have any questions, or wish to discuss this letter, please feel free to contact [insert EPA contact and address].

Sincerely,

Regional Contact

Enclosure

SAMPLE STATE ACTION LETTER

Addressee

Re: [Insert name or description of site/property]

Dear [Insert name of party]:

I am writing in response to your letter dated --/--/-- concerning the property referenced above. My response is based upon the facts presently known to the United States Environmental Protection Agency ("EPA") and is provided solely for informational purposes. The problem of investigating, responding to, and cleaning property contaminated by hazardous substances is a complex one. In an effort to maximize resources and ensure timely responses, EPA and the states work together in responding to properties posing threats of environmental contamination. Although the Comprehensive Environmental Response Compensation and Liability Act ("CERCLA", also known as "Superfund") is a federal law that establishes a federal program, the law also envisions and provides for state involvement at sites handled under the Superfund program. CERCLA explicitly describes scenarios under which a state may have a significant and prominent role in site activities.

I. [INSERT THIS SECTION FOR SITES DESIGNATED STATE-LEAD IN CERCLIS]

The site about which you have inquired, [site name], is a site that falls under the federal Superfund program, but has been designated a state-lead. A state-lead designation means that although the site remains in EPA's inventory of sites and may be on EPA's list of highest priority sites, the National Priorities List ("NPL"), implementing responsibilities to investigate and cleanup that site rest with the state of [insert name of state]. Specifically, [insert name of state] is responsible for the day-to-day activities at the site and will ultimately recommend the cleanup for the site. EPA's role is to review some of [insert name of state]'s milestone documents, if appropriate, provide technical assistance if needed, and, in most cases, approve the final cleanup method recommended by the state.

The state and EPA work together closely, pursuant to the terms of a Memorandum of Agreement ("MOA") to ensure that site responses are conducted in a timely manner and that interested parties are included in site activities. Because EPA's day-to-day role at the [insert name of site] is somewhat limited, you should check with the [your state or state's environmental program] for more detailed information on site activities. [insert name of state] is best able to provide you with detailed information about the site and public documents regarding site activity. [Regions should include the state RPM name and number, or at least the state's applicable department name and number].

II. [INSERT THIS SECTION FOR SITES DESIGNATED "DEFERRED TO STATE AUTHORITIES" PURSUANT TO EPA'S SUPERFUND DEFERRAL POLICY]

The site about which you have inquired, [site name], is a site that falls under the federal Superfund program, but for which EPA does not have the day- to-day responsibility. Specifically, the [site name] site is not proposed for or listed on the NPL. EPA has agreed not to propose or list the [site name] site on the NPL while the state of [name of state] addresses the environmental conditions at the property under its own state authorities. While the [site name] cleanup is being conducted, EPA intends to act in accordance with "Guidance on Deferral of NPL Listing Determinations While States Oversee Response Actions" (OSWER Dir. 9375.6-11, May 3, 1995). A copy of this guidance is enclosed for your review and should help you to better understand EPA's role and intentions at sites for which activities are deferred to state authorities.

III. [INSERT FOR A SITE DESIGNATED "DEFERRED" THAT NOW HAS BEEN ARCHIVED]

The conditions at the above-referenced property were addressed by [name of state] pursuant to EPA's "Guidance on Deferral of NPL Listing Determinations While States Oversee Response Actions" (OSWER Dir. 9375.6-11, May 3, 1995). Upon completion of cleanup activities at the [site name], the property has been removed from EPA's inventory of hazardous waste sites, the Comprehensive Environmental Response, Compensation, and Liability Information System ("CERCLIS"). Consistent with EPA's state deferral guidance, EPA does not intend to further consider the property for listing on the NPL [or to take additional Superfund enforcement, investigatory, cost recovery, or clean up action at the property] unless EPA receives new information about site conditions that warrants reconsideration. A copy of EPA's "Guidance on Deferral of NPL Listing Determinations While States Oversee Response Actions" is enclosed for your review, so that you may better understand the nature of EPA's role at the [site name]. For detailed information about site activities and conditions, you may wish to contact [insert name of state or state's environmental department], the agency responsible for overseeing activities on the property.

IV. [INSERT FOR A SITE ADDRESSED UNDER A STATE VCP THAT HAS AN MOA IN PLACE]

The site about which you have inquired, [site name], is a site contained in EPA's inventory of hazardous waste sites, the Comprehensive Environmental Response, Compensation, and Liability Information System. The [site name] site is not, however, proposed for or listed on EPA's list of highest priority sites, the National Priorities List ("NPL"). EPA and the state of [insert name of state] have agreed, pursuant to a memorandum of agreement ("MOA") between the two agencies, to place the site under the authorities of [insert name of state]'s Voluntary Cleanup Program. For specific details regarding the activities at [site name] or the MOA, you may wish to contact the [state name or department responsible for implementing the MOA]. If you have any additional questions, or wish to discuss this information, please feel free to contact [insert EPA contact and address].

Sincerely yours,

Regional Contact:

cc: State contact

APPENDIX E

CERCLA Enforcement against Lenders and Government Entities That Acquire Property Involuntarily
60 Fed. Reg. 63517 (December 11, 1995)

SUMMARY: This policy memorandum sets forth the Environmental Protection Agency ("EPA") and the Department of Justice's ("DOJ") policy regarding the government's enforcement of the Comprehensive Environmental Response, Compensation and Liability Act ("CERCLA") against lenders and against government entities that acquire property involuntarily. As an enforcement policy, EPA and DOJ intend to apply as guidance the provisions of the "Lender Liability Rule" promulgated in 1992, thereby endorsing the interpretations and rationales announced in the Rule. See "Final Rule on Lender Liability Under CERCLA," 57 Fed. Reg. 18344 (April 29, 1992). This rule was vacated by the Circuit Court of Appeals for the District of Columbia in 1994.

The purpose of the memorandum is to provide guidance within EPA and DOJ on the exercise of enforcement discretion in determining whether particular lenders and government entities that acquire property involuntarily may be subject to CERCLA enforcement actions. The memorandum advises EPA and DOJ personnel to consult both the regulatory text of the Rule and the accompanying preamble language in exercising their enforcement discretion under CERCLA as to lenders and government entities that acquire property involuntarily.

FOR FURTHER INFORMATION CONTACT: Laura Bulatao, Office of Site Remediation Enforcement, 401 M St. SW. (Mail Code 2273A), Washington, DC 20460 (202-564-6028), or the RCRA/Superfund Hotline at 800-424-9346 (in Washington, DC area at 703-412-9810).

Note: The memorandum below has been altered from the original memorandum issued on September 22, 1995 to reflect updated information about obtaining additional copies and whom to contact for further information. No other changes were made to the text of the policy. The original memorandum issued on September 22, 1995 was not published in the Federal Register.

Dated: November 30, 1995.

Jerry Clifford, Director, Office of Site Remediation Enforcement, U.S. Environmental Protection Agency.

MEMORANDUM

Subject: Policy on CERCLA Enforcement Against Lenders and Government Entitles that Acquire Property Involuntarily

From: Steven A. Herman, Assistant Administrator, Office of Enforcement and Compliance Assurance, United States Environmental Protection Agency

Lois J. Schaffer, Assistant Attorney General, Environmental and Natural Resources Division, United States Department of Justice

To: Regional Administrators, Regions I-X, EPA, Regional Counsel, Regions I-X, EPA, Waste Management Division Directors, Region I-X, EPA, Chief, Environmental Enforcement Section, DOJ, Assistant Section Chiefs, Environmental Enforcement Section, DOJ

This memorandum sets forth the Environmental Protection Agency's ("EPA") and the Department of Justice's ("DOJ") policy regarding the government's enforcement of the Comprehensive Environmental Response, Compensation and Liability Act ("CERCLA") against lenders and against government entities that acquire property involuntarily. As an enforcement policy, EPA and DOJ intend to apply as guidance the provisions of the "Lender Liability Rule" promulgated in 1992, thereby endorsing the interpretations and rationales announced in the Rule. See "Final Rule on Lender Liability under CERCLA," 57 Fed. Reg. 18,344 (April 29, 1992).[1] (This rule has been vacated by a court, as described below in the "Background" section).

---

[1] This guidance does not address lender liability under any statutory or regulatory authority, rule, regulation, policy, or guidance, other than CERCLA. Specifically, this guidance does not cover lender liability determinations as they relate to the Resource Conservation and Recovery Act ("RCRA") and RCRA's Underground Storage Tank program.

ADDRESSES: Additional copies of this policy statement can be ordered from the National Technical Information Service (NTIS), U.S. Department of Commerce, 5285 Port Royal Rd., Springfield, Va. 22161. Orders must reference NTIS accession number PB95-234498. For telephone orders or further information on placing an order, call NTIS at 703-487-4650 for regular service or 800-553-NTIS for rush service. For orders via email/Internet send to the following address: orders(A)ntis.fedworld.gov.

FOR FURTHER INFORMATION CONTACT: Laura Bulatao, Office of Site Remediation Enforcement (Mail Code 2273A), U.S. Environmental Protection Agency, 401 M Street, SW., Washington, DC 20460 (202-564-6028), or the RCRA/Superfund Hotline at 800-424-9346 (in Washington, DC area at 703-412-9810).

I. Background

This policy guidance establishes EPA's and DOJ's position regarding possible enforcement actions against lenders and government entitites who are associated with property that may be subject to a CERCLA response action. EPA and DOJ recognize CERCLA's unintended effects on lenders and government entities and the relative concern from these parties regarding the consequences of potential enforcement. In light of these concerns, lenders may refuse to lend money to an owner or developer of a contaminated or potentially contaminated property or they may hesitate in exercising their rights as secured parties if such loans are made. Additionally, government entities that involuntarily acquire property may be reluctant to perform certain actions related to contaminated or potentially contaminated property.

The language of Section 101(20)(A) leaves lenders and other interested parties uncertain as to which types of actions -- such as "monitoring vessel" or "facility operations", requiring compliance with applicable laws, and refinancing or undertaking loan workouts -- they may take to protect their security interests without risking EPA enforcement under CERCLA. Courts have not always agreed on when a lender's actions are "primarily to protect a security interest," and what degree of "participation in the management" of the property will forfeit the lender's eligibility for the exemption. This uncertainty was heightened by dicta in the Fleet Factors[2] opinion, where the circuit court suggested that a lender participating in the management of a vessel or facility "to a degree indicating a capacity to influence the corporation's treatment of hazardous waste" could be considered liable under CERCLA.[3]

The lack of legislative history on and consistent court treatment of the CERCLA Section 101(20)(A) security interest exemption prompted EPA to address potential lender liability for cleanup costs at CERCLA sites in the Lender Liability Rule, which was promulgated in April 1992.

Regarding the exemption for government entitles, neither the legislative history of CERCLA Sections 101(20)(D) and 101(35)(A) nor the case law provide sufficient explanation of when a property acquisition or transfer is considered involuntary. Thus, in the Rule, EPA also clarified the language of these sections, describing when a government entity was exempted from CERCLA enforcement as an owner or operator or was protected from third party actions.

However, in Kelley v. EPA,[4] the Circuit Court of Appeals for the District of Columbia vacated the Rule on the ground that EPA lacked authority to issue the Rule as a binding regulation. Nevertheless, the Kelley decision did not preclude EPA and DOJ from following the provisions of the Rule as enforcement policy, and the agencies have generally done so.

II. Policy Statement

This memorandum reaffirms EPA's and DOJ's intentions to follow the provisions of the Lender Liability Rule as enforcement policy. EPA and DOJ endorse the interpretations and rationales announced in the Rule

---

[2]United States v. Fleet Factors Corp., 901 F.2d 1550, 1557 (11th Cir. 1990), cert. denied, 111 S Ct. 752 (1991).

[3]Fleet, 901 F.2d at 1557.

[4]15 F.3d 1100 (D.C. Cir. 1994), reh. denied, 25 F.3d 1088 (D.C. Cir. 1994), cert. denied, American Bankers Ass'n v. Kelly, 115 S.Ct. 900 (1995).

and its preamble. The purpose of this memorandum is to provide guidance within EPA and DOJ on the exercise of enforcement discretion in determining whether particular lenders and government entities that acquire property involuntarily may be subject to CERCLA enforcement actions. In making such determinations, EPA and DOJ personnel should consult both the regulatory text of the Rule and the accompanying preamble language in exercising their enforcement discretion under CERCLA as to lenders and government entities that acquire property involuntarily.[5]

After the promulgation of the Lender Liability Rule, but prior to its invalidation, several district and circuit courts adhered to the terms of the Rule or interpreted the statute in a manner consistent with the Rule.[6]

Moreover, notwithstanding the Rule's invalidation in Kelley, since that decision several courts have also interpreted the statute in a way that is consistent with the Rule.[7] EPA and DOJ believe that this case law is further evidence of the reasonableness of the agencies' interpretation of the statute, as embodied formerly in the Rule and now in this policy statement.

III. Use of This Policy

The policies and procedures established in this document and any internal procedures adopted for its implementation are intended solely as guidance for employees of EPA and DOJ. They do not constitute rulemaking and may not be relied on to create a right or benefit,

---

[5] *See* 57 Fed. Reg. 18,344 (April 29, 1992) (text and preamble).

[6] *See* Northeast Doran, Inc. v. Key Bank of Maine, 15 F.3rd 1 (1st Cir. 1994); United States v. McLamb, 5 F.3d 69 (4th Cir. 1993); Waterville Indus., Inc. v. Finance Authority of Maine, 984 F. 2d 549 (1st Cir. 1993); United States v. Fleet Factors, 901 F.2d 1150 (11th Cir. 1990), on remand, 821 F. Supp. 07 (S.D. Ga. 1993); Kelley v. Tiscornia, 810 F. Supp. 901 (W.D. Mich. 1993); Grantors to the Silresim Site Trust v. State Street Bank & Trust Co., 23 ELR 20428 (D. Mass. Nov. 24, 1992).

[7] *See* Z & Z Leasing, Inc. v. Graying Reel, Inc., 873 F.Supp. 51 (E.D. Mich. 1995); Kemp Industries, Inc. v. Safety Light Corp., 857 F.Supp. 373 (D.N.J. 1994).

substantive or procedural, enforceable at law, or in equity, by any person. EPA and DOJ reserve the right to act at variance with this guidance or its internal implementing procedures.

APPENDIX F

Brownfields Bibliography

1. Abrams, Superfund and the Evolution of Brownfields, 21 *Wm. & Mary Envtl. L. & Pol'y Rev.* 265 (Winter 1997)

2. Berger, Campbell, Crolle, Solo & Stephens, Recycling Industrial Sites in Erie County: Meeting the Challenge of Brownfield Redevelopment, 3 *Buff. Envtl. L.J.* 69 (Spring 1995)

3. Buzbee, Brownfields, Environmental Federalism, and Institutional Determinism, 21 *Wm. & Mary Envtl. L. & Pol'y Rev.* 1 (Winter 1997)

4. Campbell, Accounting for the Brownfields: Writing-Off Urban Environmental Remediation Expenses, 3 Hastings W.-N.W. *J. Envtl. L. & Pol'y* 483 (Spring 1996)

5. Clokey, Wisconsin's Land Recycling Act: From Brownfield to Greenfield, 2 *Wis. Envtl. L.J.* 35 (Winter 1995)

6. Creenan & Lewis, Pennsylvania's Land Recycling Program: Solving the Brownfields Problem with Remediation Standards and Limited Liability, 34 *Duq. L. Rev.* 661 (Spring 1996)

7. DuSold, Clarifying Cost Recovery Concepts: Toward Adoption of a Brownfields Program for Indiana, 40-JUL *Res Gestae* 12 (July 1996)

8. Eisen, "Brownfields of Dreams"?: Challenges and Limits of Voluntary Cleanup Programs and Incentives, 96 *U. Ill. L. Rev.* 883 (1996)

9. Glaser, Economic and Environmental Repair in the Shadow of Superfund: Local Government Leadership in Building Strategic Partnerships, 8(4) *Economic Development Quarterly* 345-352 (Nov. 1994)

10. Johnson, The Brownfields Action Agenda: A Model for Future Federal/State Cooperation in the Quest for Environmental Justice? 37 *Santa Clara L. Rev.* 85 (1996)

11. Kamlet, Turning Brownfields Green: New EPA Guidance, 10-JUNE *Prob. & Prop.* 20 (May/June 1996)

12. Laughlin & Digirolamo, A Market-Based Approach to Development Finance: Case Study of the Capital Access Program, 8(4) *Economic Development Quarterly* 315-324 (Nov. 1994)

13. Leigh, Focus: Environmental Constraints to Brownfield Redevelopment, 8(4) *Economic Development Quarterly* 325-328 (Nov. 1994).

14. Markell, Some Overall Observations about the 1996 New York State Environmental Bond Act and a Closer Look at Title 5 and its Approach to the "Brownfields" Dilemma, 60 *Alb. L. Rev.* 1217 (1997)

15. Michel, CERCLA Paradox and Ohio's Response to the Brownfield Problem: Senate Bill 221, 26 *U. Tol. L. Rev.* 435 (Winter 1995)

16. Murphy, Brownfields Sites: Removing Lender Concerns as a Barrier to Redevelopment, 113 *Banking L.J.* 440 (May 1996)

17. Page & Rabinowitz, "Potential for Development of Contaminated Brownfield Sites," 8(4) *Economic Development Quarterly* 353-363 (Nov. 1994)

18. Poindexter, Addressing Morality in Urban Brownfield Redevelopment: Using Stakeholder Theory to Craft Legal Process, 15 *Va. Envtl. L.J.* 37 (Fall 1995)

19. Poindexter, Separate and Unequal: A Comment on the Urban Development Aspect of Brownfields Programs, 24 *Fordham Urb. L.J.* 1 (Fall 1996)

20. *Profiles of Existing Voluntary Cleanup Programs*, The Greenfields Group, Arlington, VA, 1996

21. *Protecting "Greenfields": The State Voluntary Cleanup Program Alternative*, The Greenfields Group, Arlington, VA, 1995

22. Reisch, Reaping "Green" Harvests from "Brownfields": Avoiding Lender Liability at Contaminated Sites: Part II, 26-FEB *Colo. Law.* 9 (Feb. 1997)

23. Reisch, Reaping "Green" Harvests from "Brownfields": Avoiding Lender Liability at Contaminated Sites: Part I, 26-JAN *Colo. Law.* 3 (Jan. 1997)

24. Rieser, Brownfields Bill Promotes Sweeping Changes, 16 *N. Ill. U. L. Rev.* 621 (Summer 1996)

25. Rimer, Environmental Liability and the Brownfields Phenomenon: An Analysis of Federal Options for Redevelopment, 10 *Tul. Envtl. L.J.* 63 (Winter 1996)

26. Swartz, Michigan's Approach to Urban Redevelopment Involving Contaminated Properties, 8(4) *Economic Development Quarterly* 329-337 (Nov. 1994)

27. Sweeney, Brownfields Restoration and Voluntary Cleanup Legislation, 2 *Envtl. Law.* 101 (September 1995)

28. Tondro, Reclaiming Brownfields to Save Greenfields: Shifting the Environmental Risks of Acquiring and Reusing Contaminated Land, 27 *Conn. L. Rev.* 789 (Spring 1995)

29. Trigger, Tripp & Gilezan, Making Brownfields Green Again: How Efforts to Give Urban Centers an Economic Facelift Have Changed the Face of Environmental Policy, 76 *Mich. B.J.* 42 (Jan. 1997)

30. Walsh, Seeding the Brownfields: A Proposed Statute Limiting Environmental Liability for Prospective Purchasers, 34 *Harv. J. Legis.* 191 (Winter, 1997)

31. Wells, Brownfields for Beginners, 71-MAY *Fla. B.J.* 74 (May, 1997)

32. Yount & Meyer, Bankers, Developers, and New Investment in Brownfield Sites: Environmental Concerns and Social Psychology of Risk, 8(4) *Economic Development Quarterly* 338-344 (Nov. 1994)

GLOSSARY

Abatement. Reducing the degree or intensity of, or eliminating, pollution.

Aboveground Storage Tank. A device situated so that the entire surface area of the tank is completely above the plane of the adjacent surrounding surface and the entire surface area of the tank (including the tank bottom) is able to be visually inspected.

Acidic. The condition of water or soil that contains a sufficient amount of acid substances to lower the pH below 7.0

Activated Carbon. A highly adsorbent form of carbon used to remove odors and toxic substances from liquid or gaseous emissions. In waste treatment it is used to remove dissolved organic matter from waste water. It is also used in motor vehicle evaporative control systems.

Acute Exposure. A single exposure to a toxic substance which results in severe biological harm or death. Acute exposures are usually characterized as lasting no longer than a day, as compared to longer, continuing exposure over a period of time.

Acute Toxicity. The ability of a substance to cause poisonous effects resulting in severe biological harm or death soon after a single exposure or dose. In addition, any severe poisonous effect resulting from a single short-term exposure to a toxic substance.

Acutely Hazardous Waste. Commercial chemical products and manufacturing intermediates having the generic names listed in 40 CFR 261.33; off-specification commercial chemical products and manufacturing chemical intermediates which, if they met specifications, would have the generic names listed; and any residue or contaminated soil, water, or other debris resulting from the cleanup of a spill of any of these substances.

Administrative Order. A legal document signed by EPA directing an individual, business, or other entity to take corrective action or refrain from an activity. It describes the violations and actions to be taken, and can be enforced in court. Such orders may be issued, for example, as a result of an administrative complaint whereby the respondent is ordered to pay a penalty for violating a statute.

Administrative Record. All documents which EPA considered or relied on in selecting the response action at a Superfund site, culminating in the record of decision for remedial action or, an action memorandum for removal actions.

Adsorption. An advanced method of treating waste in which activated carbon removes organic matter from wastewater

Aeration. A process which promotes biological degradation of organic matter in water. The process may be passive (as when waste is exposed to air), or active (as when a mixing or bubbling device introduces the air).

Agricultural Pollution. Farming wastes, including runoff and leaching of pesticides and fertilizers; erosion and dust from plowing; improper disposal of animal manure and carcasses; crop residues, and debris.

Air Contaminant. Any particulate matter, gas, or combination thereof, other than water vapor.

Air Pollutant. Any substance in air that could, in high enough concentration, harm man, other animals, vegetation, or material. Pollutants may include almost any natural or artificial composition of airborne matter capable of being airborne. They may be in the form of solid particles, liquid droplets, gases, or in combination thereof. Generally, they fall into two main groups: (1) those emitted directly from identifiable sources and (2) those produced in the air by interaction between two or more primary pollutants, or by reaction with normal atmospheric constituents, with or without photoactivation. Exclusive of pollen, fog, and dust, which are of natural origin, about 100 contaminants have been identified and fall into the following categories: solids, sulfur compounds, volatile organic chemicals, nitrogen compounds, oxygen compounds, halogen compounds, radioactive compounds, and odors.

Air Pollution Control Device. Mechanism or equipment that cleans emissions generated by an incinerator by removing pollutants that would otherwise be released to the atmosphere.

Air Pollution. The presence of contaminant or pollutant substances in the air that do not disperse properly and interfere with human health or welfare, or produce other harmful environmental effects.

Air Quality Control Region. Federally designated area that is required to meet and maintain federal ambient air quality standards. May include nearby locations in the same state or nearby states that share common air pollution problems.

Air Quality Criteria. The levels of pollution and lengths of exposure above which adverse health and welfare effects may occur.

Air Quality Standards. The level of pollutants prescribed by regulations that may not be exceeded during a given time in a defined area.

Air Stripping. A treatment system that removes volatile organic compounds (VOCs) from contaminated ground water or surface water by forcing an airstream through the water and causing the compounds to evaporate.

Air Toxics. Any air pollutant for which a national ambient air quality standard (NAAQS) does not exist (i.e., excluding ozone, carbon monoxide, PM- 10, sulfur dioxide, nitrogen oxide) that may reasonably be anticipated to cause cancer, developmental effects, reproductive dysfunctions, neurological disorders, heritable gene mutations, or other serious or irreversible chronic or acute health effects in humans.

Airborne Particulates. Total suspended particulate matter found in the atmosphere as solid particles or liquid droplets. Chemical composition of particulates varies widely, depending on location and time of year. Airborne particulates include: windblown dust, emissions from industrial processes, smoke from the burning of wood and coal, and motor vehicle or non-road engine exhausts, exhaust of motor vehicles.

Alkaline. The condition of water or soil which contains a sufficient amount of alkali substance to raise the pH above 7.0.

Alternate Concentration Limit (ACL). An alternative to the concentration limit set by EPA or a state for a particular hazardous substance or waste. Proposing an ACL is a way of introducing site-specific considerations to the cleanup process. You must provide evidence to show that the ACL will not have adverse effects on human health and the environment. You must also include an analysis showing that concentrations of contaminants moving between the contamination source and receptors would present an acceptable level of risk to any person in contact with the water, soil, or air. Few ACLs have been permitted under RCRA. SARA has been even more stringent. EPA is currently debating the acceptable cancer risk rates for approval of ACLs.

Alternative Remedial Contract Strategy Contractors. Government contractors who provide project management and technical services to support remedial response activities at National Priorities List sites.

Ambient Air. Any unconfined portion of the atmosphere: open air, surrounding air.

Anaerobic Decomposition. Reduction of the net energy level and change in chemical composition of organic matter caused by microorganisms in an oxygenfree environment.

Anaerobic. A life or process that occurs in, or is not destroyed by, the absence of oxygen.

Animal Studies. Investigations using animals as surrogates for humans with the expectation that the results are pertinent to humans.

Anti-Degradation Clause. Part of federal air quality and water quality requirements prohibiting deterioration where pollution levels are above the legal limit.

Applicable or Appropriate Requirements (ARARs). ARARs include the federal standards and more stringent state standards that are legally applicable or relevant and appropriate under the circumstances. ARARs include cleanup standards, standards of control, and other environmental protection requirements, criteria, or limitations. RCRA has frequently been used as an ARAR for cleanup of Superfund sites.

Aqueous. Something made up of, similar to, or containing water; watery.

Aquifer. An underground geological formation, or group of formations, containing usable amounts of groundwater that can supply wells and springs.

Architectural Coatings. Coverings such as paint and roof tar that are used on exteriors of buildings.

Area Source. Any small source of non-natural air pollution that is released over a relatively small area but which cannot be classified as a point source. Such sources may include vehicles and other small engines, small businesses and household activities.

Aromatic. A type of hydrocarbon, such as benzene or toluene, added to gasoline in order to increase octane. Some aromatics are toxic.

Artesian (Aquifer or well). Water held under pressure in porous rock or soil confined by impermeable geologic formations.

Asbestos Abatement. Procedures to control fiber release from asbestos-containing materials in a building or to remove them entirely, including removal, encapsulation, repair, enclosure, encasement, and operations and maintenance programs.

Asbestos Program Manager. A building owner or designated representative who supervises all aspects of the facility asbestos management and control program.

Asbestos. A mineral fiber that can pollute air or water and cause cancer or asbestosis when inhaled. EPA has banned or severely restricted its use in manufacturing and construction.

Asbestosis. A disease associated with inhalation of asbestos fibers. The disease makes breathing progressively more difficult and can be fatal.

Asbestos-Containing Materials (ACM). Any waste that contains commercial asbestos and is generated by a source subject to an asbestos abatement project. It includes asbestos mill tailings, asbestos waste from control devices, friable asbestos from control devices, and bags or containers that previously contained commercial asbestos.

Attainment Area. An area considered to have air quality as good as or better than the national ambient air quality standards as defined in the Clean Air Act. An area may be an attainment area for one pollutant and a non-attainment area for others.

Attenuation. The process by which a compound is reduced in concentration over time, through absorption, adsorption, degradation, dilution, and/or transformation.

Background Level. In toxic substances monitoring, the average presence in the environment, originally referring to naturally occurring phenomena.

Bench-scale Tests. Laboratory testing of potential cleanup technologies.

Best Available Control Measures (BACM). A term used to refer to the most effective measures (according to EPA guidance) for controlling small or dispersed particulates from sources such as roadway dust, soot and ash from woodstoves and open burning of rush, timber, grasslands, or trash.

Best Available Control Technology (BACT). For any specific source, the necessary technology that would produce the greatest reduction of each pollutant regulated byu the Clean Air Act, taking into account energy, environmental, economic and other costs.

Best Demonstrated Available Technology (BDAT). The technology EPA establishes for a land-banned hazardous waste to reduce overall toxicity or mobility of toxic constituents in the waste. BDAT must be applied to such a waste prior to land disposal unless one can successfully demonstrate the validity of an equivalent treatment method.

Best Management Practice (BMP). Methods that have been determined to be the most effective, practical means of preventing or reducing pollution from nonpoint sources.

Bioassay. Study of living organisms to measure the effect of a substance, factor, or condition by comparing before-and-after exposure or other data.

Biochemical Oxygen Demand (BOD). A measure of the amount of oxygen consumed in the biological processes that break down organic matter in water. The greater the BOD, the greater the degree of pollution.

Biodegradable. Capable of decomposing rapidly under natural conditions.

Biological Oxygen Demand (BOD). An indirect measure of the concentration of biologically degradable material present in organic wastes. It usually reflects the amount of oxygen consumed in five days by biological processes breaking down organic waste.

Biomass. All of the living material in a given area; often refers to vegetation.

Bioremediation. A hazardous waste site remediation technique that utilizes microorganisms to metabolize hazardous organic constituents in waste to nonhazardous compounds. Environmental conditions are carefully controlled in an attempt to create optimum growth conditions for the organisms.

Biota. The animal and plant life of a given region.

Bog. A type of wetland that accumulates appreciable peat deposits. Bogs depend primarily on precipitation for their water source, and are usually acidic and rich in plant residue with a conspicuous mat of living green moss.

Bottom Land Hardwoods. Forested freshwater wetlands adjacent to rivers in the southeastern United States, especially valuable for wildlife breeding, nesting and habitat.

Brackish. Mixed fresh and salt water.

Brownfield. Abandoned, idled, or underused industrial and commercial property that has been taken out of productive use as a result of actual or perceived risks from environmental contamination.

Buffer Strips. Strips of grass or other erosion-resisting vegetation between or below cultivated strips or fields.

By-product. Material, other than the principal product, generated as a consequence of an industrial process.

Cap. A layer of clay, or other impermeable material installed over the top of a closed landfill to prevent entry of rainwater and minimize leachate.

Capacity Assurance Plan. A statewide plan which supports a state's ability to manage the hazardous waste generated within its boundaries over a twenty year period.

Carbon Absorber. An add-on control device that uses activated carbon to absorb volatile organic compounds from a gas stream. (The VOCs are later recovered from the carbon.)

Carbon Adsorption. A treatment system that removes contaminants from ground water or surface water by forcing it through tanks containing activated carbon treated to attract the contaminants.

Carcinogen. Any substance that can cause or aggravate cancer.

CAS Registration Number. A number assigned by the Chemical Abstracts Service to identify a chemical.

Categorical Exclusion. A class of actions which either individually or cumulatively would not have a significant effect on the human environment and therefore would not require preparation of an environmental assessment or environmental impact statement under the National Environmental Policy Act (NEPA).

Categorical Pretreatment Standard. A technology-based effluent limitation for an industrial facility discharging into a municipal sewer system. Analogous in stringency to Best Availability Technology (BAT) for direct dischargers.

Cathodic Protection. A technique to prevent corrosion of a metal surface by making it the cathode of an electrochemical cell.

Characteristic Waste. A solid waste that is a hazardous waste because it exhibits one or more of the following hazardous characteristics: ignitability, corrosivity, reactivity, or toxicity.

Chemical Oxygen Demand (COD). A measure of the oxygen required to oxidize all compounds, both organic and inorganic, in water.

Chlorinated Hydrocarbons. These include a class of persistent, broad-spectrum insecticides that linger in the environment and accumulate in the food chain. Among them are DDT, aldrin, dieldrin, heptachlor, chlordane, lindane, endrin, mirex, hexachloride, and toxaphene. Other examples include TCE, used as an industrial solvent.

Chlorinated Solvent. An organic solvent containing chlorine atoms, e.g., methylene chloride and 1,1,1-trichloromethane, used in aerosol spray containers and in highway paint.

Chlorofluorocarbons (CFCs). A family of inert, nontoxic, and easily liquified chemicals used in refrigeration, air conditioning, packaging, insulation, or as solvents and aerosol propellants. Because CFCs are not destroyed in the lower atmosphere they drift into the upper atmosphere where their chlorine components destroy ozone.

Class I Area. Under the Clean Air Act, a Class I area is one in which visibility is protected more stringently than under the national ambient air quality standards; includes national parks, wilderness area, monuments and other areas of special national and cultural significance.

Clean Air Act (CAA). The law that authorizes regulations governing releases of airborne contaminants from stationary and non-stationary sources. The regulations include National Ambient Air Quality Standards for specific pollutants.

Clean Water Act (CWA). The law that authorizes establishment of the regulatory program to restore and maintain the physical and biological integrity of the nation's waters. The CWA established, among other things, the National Pollutant Discharge Elimination System (NPDES) to regulate industrial and municipal point-source discharges.

Cleanup. Actions taken to deal with a release or threat of release of a hazardous substance that could affect humans and/or the environment. The term "cleanup" is sometimes used interchangeably with the terms remedial action, removal action, response action, or corrective action.

Closure. The procedure a landfill operator must follow when a landfill reaches its legal capacity for solid waste: ceasing acceptance of solid waste and placing a cap on the landfill site.

Closure Plan. A written plan (subject to approval by authorized regulatory agencies) which the owner/operator of a hazardous waste management facility must submit with the RCRA permit application or for interim status closure. The approved plan becomes part of the permit conditions subsequently imposed on the applicant. The plan identifies steps required to (1) completely or partially close a hazardous waste management unit at any point during its intended operating life, and (2) completely close the unit at the end of its intended operating life.

Coastal Zone. Lands and waters adjacent to the coast that exert an influence on the uses of the sea and its ecology, or whose uses and ecology are affected by the sea.

Combined Sewer Overflows. Discharge of a mixture of storm water and domestic waste when the flow capacity of a sewer system is exceeded during rainstorms.

Combined Sewers. A sewer system that carries both sewage and storm-water runoff. Normally, its entire flow goes to a waste treatment plant, but during a heavy storm, the volume of water may be so great as to cause overflows of untreated mixtures of storm water and sewage into receiving waters. Storm-water runoff may also carry toxic chemicals from industrial areas or streets into the sewer system.

Comment Period. Time provided for the public to review and comment on a proposed EPA action or rulemaking after publication in the Federal Register.

Composite Sample. A series of water samples taken over a given period of time and weighted by flow rate.

Comprehensive Environmental Response, Compensation, and Liability Act (CERCLA). Also known as Superfund, it is a program to identify sites where hazardous substances have been or might have been released into the environment and to ensure that they are cleaned up. CERCLA is primarily concerned with abandoned sites.

Comprehensive Environmental Response, Compensation, and Liability Information System (CERCLIS). EPA database which identifies hazardous waste sites that require investigation and possible remedial action to mitigate potential negative impacts on human health or the environment.

Conditionally Exempt Small Quantity Generator (CESQG). Those who generate no more than 100 kilograms of hazardous waste per month. Other than the hazardous waste determination requirement in 40 CFR 262.11, CESQGs are exempt from RCRA provided they do not exceed certain quantity limits for hazardous waste storage or generation.

Consent Decree. A legal document, approved by a judge, that formalizes an agreement reached between EPA and potentially responsible parties (PRPs) through which PRPs will conduct all or part of a cleanup action at a Superfund site; cease or correct actions or processes that are polluting the environment; or otherwise comply with EPA initiated regulatory enforcement actions to resolve the contamination at the Superfund site involved. The consent decree describes the actions PRPs will take and may be subject to a public comment period.

Construction and Demolition Waste. Waste building materials, dredging materials, tree stumps, and rubble resulting from construction, remodeling, repair, and demolition of homes, commercial buildings and other structures and pavements. May contain lead, asbestos, or other hazardous substances.

Contaminant. Any physical, chemical, biological, or radiological substance or matter that has an adverse affect on air, water, or soil.

Contamination. Introduction into water, air and soil of microorganisms, chemicals, toxic substances, wastes, or wastewater in a concentration that makes the medium unfit for its next intended use. Also applies to surfaces of objects and buildings, and various household and agricultural use products.

Contingency Plan. A document setting out an organized, planned, and coordinated course of action to be followed in case of a fire, explosion, or release of hazardous waste constituents which could threaten human health or the environment.

Corrective Action Reporting System (CARS). EPA's national data base of information on corrective action permits and enforcement actions.

Corrective Action. Action to remedy releases from hazardous waste management units, solid waste management units, or any other sources or release(s) at or from a TSD facility. For hazardous waste management units, the owner or operator of a TSD facility must implement corrective action to ensure that these regulated units comply with the ground water protection standard in the facility permit. Corrective action for solid waste management units and for releases beyond the facility boundary may be required in a corrective action permit if necessary to protect human health and the environment. Corrective action for any releases from unpermitted TSD facilities can be accomplished through an enforcement action pursuant to RCRA §3008(h).

Corrective Measures Implementation (CMI). The fourth and final step in the RCRA corrective action process. Includes designing, constructing, operating, maintaining, and monitoring selected corrective measures that have been approved by the regulatory agency. This stage combines activities that are often segregated under Superfund as remedial design (RD) and remedial assessment (RA).

Corrective Measures Study (CMS). The third step in the RCRA corrective action process. If the RCRA facility investigation (RFI) reveals a potential need for corrective measures, the agency requires the owner to perform a CMS to identify and recommend specific measures to correct the releases. Although analogous to the Superfund feasibility study (FS) stage, this study is usually less complicated.

Corrosion. The dissolution and wearing away of metal caused by a chemical reaction such as between water and the pipes, chemicals touching a metal surface, or contact between two metals.

Corrosive. A chemical agent that reacts with the surface of a material causing it to deteriorate or wear away.

Cost Recovery. A legal process by which potentially responsible parties who contributed to contamination at a Superfund site can be required to reimburse the Trust Fund for money spent during any cleanup actions by the federal government.

Cost Sharing. A publicly financed program through which society, as a beneficiary of environmental protection, shares part of the cost of pollution control with those who must actually install the controls. In Superfund, the government may pay part of the cost of a cleanup action with those responsible for the pollution paying the major share.

Cost-Effective Alternative. An alternative control or corrective method identified after analysis as being the best available in terms of reliability, performance, and cost. Although costs are one important consideration, regulatory and compliance analysis does not require EPA to choose the least expensive alternative. For example, when selecting or approving a method for cleaning up a Superfund site the Agency balances costs with the long-term effectiveness of the methods proposed and the potential danger posed by the site.

Cost/benefit Analysis. A quantitative evaluation of the costs which would be incurred versus the overall benefits to society of a proposed action such as the establishment of an acceptable dose of a toxic chemical.

Cover Material. Soil used to cover compacted solid waste in a sanitary landfill.

Criteria Pollutants. The 1970 amendments to the Clean Air Act required EPA to set National Ambient Air Quality Standards for certain pollutants known to be hazardous to human health. EPA has identified and set standards to protect human health and welfare for six pollutants: ozone, carbon monoxide, total suspended particulates, sulfur dioxide, lead, and nitrogen oxide. The term, "criteria pollutants" derives from the requirement that EPA must describe the characteristics and potential health and welfare effects of these pollutants. It is on the basis of these criteria that standards are set or revised.

Discharge. Flow of surface water in a stream or canal or the outflow of ground water from a flowing artesian well, ditch, or spring. Can also apply to discharge of liquid effluent from a facility or of chemical emissions into the air through designated venting mechanisms.

Disposal. The discharge, deposit, injection, dumping, spilling, leaking, or placing of any hazardous waste or hazardous substance into or on any land or water so that such waste or substance may enter the environment or be emitted into the air or discharged into any waters, including ground water.

Downgradient. The direction that groundwater flows; similar to "downstream" for surface water.

Ecological Risk Assessment. The application of a formal framework, analytical process, or model to estimate the effects of human actions(s) on a natural resource and to interpret the significance of those effects in light of the uncertainties identified in each component of the assessment process. Such analysis includes initial hazard identification, exposure and dose response assessments, and risk characterization.

Ecology. The relationship of living things to one another and their environment, or the study of such relationships.

Ecosystem. The interacting system of a biological community and its non-living environmental surroundings.

Effluent. Wastewater-treated or untreated-that flows out of a treatment plant, sewer, or industrial outfall. Generally refers to wastes discharged into surface waters.

Emission Standard. The maximum amount of air polluting discharge legally allowed from a single source, mobile or stationary.

Emission. Pollution discharged into the atmosphere from smokestacks, other vents, and surface areas of commercial or industrial facilities; from residential chimneys; and from motor vehicle, locomotive, or aircraft exhausts.

Encapsulation. The treatment of asbestos-containing material with a liquid that covers the surface with a protective coating or embeds fibers in an adhesive matrix to prevent their release into the air.

Endangered Species. Animals, birds, fish, plants, or other living organisms threatened with extinction by man-made or natural changes in their environment. Requirements for declaring a species endangered are contained in the Endangered Species Act.

Environmental Assessment. An environmental analysis prepared pursuant to the National Environmental Policy Act to determine whether a federal action would significantly affect the environment and thus require a more detailed environmental impact statement.

Environmental Audit. An independent assessment of the current status of a party's compliance with applicable environmental requirements or of a party's environmental compliance policies, practices, and controls.

Environmental Equity. Equal protection from environmental hazards of individuals, groups or communities regardless of race, ethnicity, or economic status.

Environmental Exposure. Human exposure to pollutants originating from facility emissions. Threshold levels are not necessarily surpassed, but low level chronic pollutant exposure is one of the most common forms of environmental exposure.

Environmental Impact Statement (EIS). A document required of federal agencies by the National Environmental Policy Act for major projects or legislative proposals significantly affecting the environment. A tool for decision making, it describes the positive and negative effects of the undertaking and cites alternative actions.

Environmental Justice. The fair treatment of all races, cultures, incomes, and educational levels with respect to the development, implementation, and enforcement of environmental laws, regulations, and policies. Fair treatment implies that no population of people should be forced to shoulder a disproportionate share of the negative environmental impacts of pollution or environmental hazards due to a lack of political or economic strength.

EPA Hazardous Waste Number. A number assigned by EPA to waste that is hazardous by definition; to each hazardous waste listed in 40 CFR 261 Subpart D from specific and nonspecific sources identified by EPA (F, K, P, U); and to each characteristic waste identified in 40 CFR 261 Subpart C, including wastes with ignitable (D001), reactive (D002), corrosive (D003), and EP toxic (D004, D017) characteristics.

EPA Identification Number. A number assigned by EPA to each generator; transporter; and treatment, storage, or disposal facility. Identification numbers are facility-specific, except for the transporter who has one number for all his operations.

Estuary. Regions of interaction between rivers and near-shore ocean waters, where tidal action and river flow mix fresh and salt water. Such areas include bays, mouths of rivers, salt marshes, and lagoons. These brackish water ecosystems shelter and feed marine life, birds, and wildlife.

Eutrophication. The slow aging process during which a lake, estuary, or bay evolves into a bog or marsh and eventually disappears. During the later stages of eutrophication the water body is choked by abundant plant life due to higher levels of nutritive compounds such as nitrogen and phosphorus. Human activities can accelerate the process.

Exposure Assessment. Identifying the pathways by which toxicants may reach individuals, estimating how much of a chemical an individual is likely to be exposed to, and estimating the number likely to be exposed.

Extraction Procedure (EP) Toxicity. One of the characteristics, along with ignitability, reactivity, and corrosivity, to make a waste a characteristic hazardous waste. The EP toxic list includes maximum concentrations for 14 constituents which, if exceeded, would make a waste hazardous. Effective September 1990, EP Toxicity was replaced by the Toxicity Characteristic.

Extremely Hazardous Substances. Any of 406 chemicals identified by EPA as toxic, and listed under SARA Title III. The list is subject to periodic revision.

Facility. All contiguous land, and structures, other appurtenances, and improvements on the land used for treating, storing, or disposing of hazardous waste. A facility may consist of several treatment, storage, or disposal operational units (e.g., one or more landfills, surface impoundments, or combinations of them). Under CERCLA §101(9), (1) any building, structure, installation, equipment, pipe or pipeline (including any pipe into a sewer or publicly owned treatment works), well, pit, pond, lagoon, impoundment, ditch, landfill, storage container, motor vehicle, rolling stock, or aircraft; or (2) any site or area where a hazardous substance has been deposited, stored, disposed of or placed, or has otherwise come to be located. Does not include any consumer product in consumer use or any vessel.

Fate and Transport Modeling. A mathematical process for simulating the behavior of contaminants in various environments to predict contaminant concentration and mobility. Models range from relatively simple analytical solutions to complex numerical models.

Feasibility Study. 1. Analysis of the practicability of a proposal; e.g., a description and analysis of potential cleanup alternatives for a site such as one on the National Priorities List. The feasibility study usually recommends selection of a cost-effective alternative. It usually starts as soon as the remedial investigation is underway; together, they are commonly referred to as the "RI/FS". 2. A small-scale investigation of a problem to ascertain whether a proposed research approach is likely to provide useful data.

Fen. A type of wetland that accumulates peat deposits. Fens are less acidic than bogs, deriving most of their water from groundwater rich in calcium and magnesium.

Filter Strip. Strip or area of vegetation used for removing sediment, organic matter, and other pollutants from runoff and waste water.

Finding of No Significant Impact (FONSI). A document prepared by a federal agency showing why a proposed action would not have a significant impact on the environment and thus would not require preparation of an Environmental Impact Statement. A FONSI is based on the results of an environmental assessment.

Floodplain. Lowland and relatively flat areas adjoining inland and coastal waters and other flood prone areas such as offshore islands, including at a minimum that area subject to a 1% or greater chance of flooding in any given year. The base floodplain shall be used to designate the 100-year floodplain (1% chance floodplain).

Formaldehyde. A colorless, pungent, and irritating gas, CH20, used chiefly as a disinfectant and preservative and in synthesizing other compounds like resins.

Friable. Capable of being crumbled, pulverized, or reduced to powder by hand pressure.

Friable Asbestos. Any material containing more than one percent asbestos, and that can be crumbled or reduced to powder by hand pressure. (May include previously non-friable material which becomes broken or damaged by mechanical force.)

Fugitive Emissions. Emissions not caught by a capture system.

Gas Chromatograph/Mass Spectrometer. Highly sophisticated instrument that identifies the molecular composition and concentrations of various chemicals in water and soil samples.

Generator. Any person whose process produces a hazardous waste in excess of 100 kg/month or acutely hazardous waste in excess of 1 kg/month, or whose actions first cause a hazardous waste to become subject to regulation.

Geographic Information System (GIS). A computer system designed for storing, manipulating, analyzing, and displaying data in a geographic context.

Grab Sample. A single sample collected at a particular time and place that represents the composition of the water only at that time and place.

Granular Activated Carbon (GAC) Treatment. A filtering system often used in small water systems and individual homes to remove organics. GAC can be highly effective in removing elevated levels of radon from water.

Greenhouse Effect. The warming of the Earth's atmosphere attributed to a build-up of carbon dioxide or other gases; some scientists think that this build-up allows the sun's rays to heat the Earth, while infra-red radiation makes the atmosphere opaque to a counterbalancing loss of heat.

Ground Water. The supply of fresh water found beneath the Earth's surface, usually in aquifers, which supply wells and springs. Because ground water is a major source of drinking water, there is growing concern over contamination from leaching agricultural or industrial pollutants or leaking underground storage tanks.

Habitat. The place where a population (e.g., human, animal, plant, microorganism) lives and its surroundings, both living and non-living.

Hazard Ranking System (HRS). The method EPA uses to determine which sites should be listed on the National Priorities List (NPL) under CERCLA. The HRS ranks sites by means of a mathematical rating scheme that combines the potential of a release to cause hazardous situations with the severity/magnitude of these potential impacts and the number of people who may be affected. Using the numerical scores from this scheme, EPA and the states list sites by priority and allocate resources for site investigation, enforcement, and cleanup. Sites receiving high HRS scores appear on the National Priorities List. Under SARA, the HRS must be revised by EPA to determine whether it is adequately identifying sites for the NPL (CERCLA §105(c)). Citizens may now petition EPA to conduct a preliminary assessment of a site near them. If the assessment indicates that a release may pose a threat to health or the environment, EPA will do an HRS scoring.

Hazardous Air Pollutants. Air pollutants which are not covered by ambient air quality standards but which, as defined in the Clean Air Act, may reasonably be expected to cause or contribute to irreversible illness or death. Such pollutants include asbestos, beryllium, mercury, benzene, coke oven emissions, radionuclides, and vinyl chloride.

Hazardous and Solid Waste Amendments of 1984 (HSWA). The HSWA greatly increased the complexity of the RCRA regulatory program by imposing restrictions on land disposal of hazardous wastes, authorizing EPA to require corrective action for releases from hazardous waste management facilities, and instituting requirements for underground storage tanks containing petroleum and hazardous substances

Hazardous Substance Superfund. The fund, largely financed by taxes on petroleum and chemicals, and by an "environmental tax" on corporations, which provides operating money for government-financed actions under CERCLA. The fund is a revolving fund in the sense that it enables the government to take action and then seek reimbursement later, or to clean up sites when responsible parties with sufficient cleanup funds cannot be found. Money recovered from PRPs is returned to the fund rather than to the U.S. Treasury.

Hazardous Substance. Under CERCLA §101(14), any element, compound, mixture, solution, or substance which, when released to the environment, may present substantial danger to public health/welfare or the environment. Also includes (1) any substance designated pursuant to section 311(b)(2)(A) of the Federal Water Pollution Control Act; (2) any element, compound, mixture, solution, or substance designated pursuant to section 102 of CERCLA; (3) any hazardous waste having the characteristics identified under or listed pursuant to section 3001 of the Solid Waste Disposal Act; (4) any toxic pollutant listed under section 307(a) of the Federal Water Pollution Control Act; (5) any hazardous air pollutant listed under section 112 of the Clean Air Act; and (6) any imminently hazardous chemical substance or mixture so identified pursuant to the Toxic Substances Control Act. Excludes petroleum (including crude oil not otherwise specifically listed or designated as a hazardous substance under any of the above laws), natural gas, natural gas liquids, liquefied natural gas, or synthetic gas usable for fuel (or mixtures of natural gas and such synthetic gas). The definition of hazardous substances in CERCLA is broader than the definition of hazardous wastes under RCRA.

Hazardous Waste (RCRA). A solid waste which because of its quantity, concentration or physical, chemical, or infectious characteristics may (1) cause or contribute to an increase in mortality or an increase in serious irreversible or incapacitating reversible illness; or (2) pose a substantial present or potential hazard to human health or the environment when improperly treated, stored, transported or disposed of, or otherwise managed. EPA hazardous waste regulations (40 CFR 261) specify that if a material qualifies as a solid waste, and does not qualify for an exemption, it is a hazardous waste if it is listed by 40 CFR Part 261, Subpart D, or if it exhibits any of the four hazardous waste characteristics (ignitability, reactivity, corrosivity and toxicity).

Hazardous Waste Constituent. A constituent that caused the waste to be listed as a hazardous waste under 40 CFR Part 261 Subpart D.

Hazardous Waste Generator. Any person whose act or process produces hazardous waste identified or listed in 40 CFR 261 or whose act first causes hazardous waste to become subject to regulation. Generators are subject to specific hazardous waste management regulations, which apply only to the particular site of generation. The regulations vary by the volume of waste annually generated but include reporting, testing, record-keeping, storage, and shipping and disposal requirements.

Hazardous Waste Management Unit. A contiguous area of land on or in which hazardous waste is placed, or the largest area in which there is significant likelihood of mixing hazardous waste constituents in the same area. A unit may be a surface Impoundment, waste pile, land treatment area, landfill cell, incinerator, tank and its associated piping and underlying containment system, or container storage area. A container alone does not constitute a unit.

Heavy Metals. Metallic elements with high atomic weights, e.g., mercury, chromium, cadmium, arsenic, and lead; can damage living things at low concentrations and tend to accumulate in the food chain.

Hydrogeology. The geology of ground water, with particular emphasis on the chemistry and movement of water.

Hydrology. The science dealing with the properties,distribution, and circulation of water.

Ignitable. Capable of burning or causing a fire.

Indoor Air Pollution. Chemical, physical, or biological contaminants in indoor air.

Interim Status. The period during which the owner/operator of an existing TSD facility is treated as having been issued a RCRA permit even though he/she has not yet received a final determination. An existing facility should have automatically qualified for interim status if the owner/operator filed both timely "notification" and the first part (Part A) of the RCRA permit application. Interim status continues until the permit is issued. Owners/operators of new facilities cannot by definition qualify for interim status, but need a RCRA permit prior to beginning construction of a hazardous waste management facility.

Interstitial Monitoring. The continuous surveillance of the space between the walls of an underground storage tank.

Karst. A geologic formation of irregular limestone deposits with sinks, underground streams, and caverns.

Land Ban. Phasing out of land disposal of most untreated hazardous wastes, as mandated by the 1984 RCRA amendments.

Land Disposal. Includes, but is not limited to, placement in a landfill, surface impoundment, waste pile, injection well, land treatment facility, salt dome formation, salt bed formation, underground mine or cave, or concrete vault or bunker intended for disposal purposes. Land disposal facilities are a subset of TSD facilities. Ground water monitoring is required at all land disposal facilities.

Large Quantity Generator. Person or facility generating more than 2200 pounds of hazardous waste per month. Such generators produce about 90 percent of the nation's hazardous waste, and are subject to all RCRA requirements.

Leachate. Liquid that has percolated through solid and/or hazardous waste and has extracted dissolved or suspended materials from the waste.

Lead Agency. The federal or state agency providing the On-Scene Coordinator (OSC) or the responsible official for a CERCLA response action. Includes the federal (EPA, Coast Guard, DOD, DOI, DOE, etc.) or state agency responsible for collecting data and performing assessments and other studies. The lead agency responsibility may shift during the stages of the Superfund process.

Leak-Detection System. A system capable of detecting the failure of a primary or secondary containment structure or the presence of a release of hazardous waste or accumulated liquid in the secondary containment structure. Detection is based on systemic operational controls (such as visual monitoring) or continuous automatic monitoring of any releases from the containment areas.

Limnology. The study of the physical, chemical, hydrological, and biological aspects of fresh water bodies.

Listed Waste. Wastes listed as hazardous under RCRA but which have not been subjected to the Toxic Characteristics Listing Process because the dangers they present are considered self-evident.

Local Emergency Planning Committee (LEPC). A committee appointed by the state emergency response commission, as required by SARA Title III, to formulate a comprehensive emergency plan for its jurisdiction.

Lowest Achievable Emission Rate. Under the Clean Air Act, the rate of emissions that reflects (a) the most stringent emission limitation in the implementation plan of any state for such source unless the owner or operator demonstrates such limitations are not achievable; or (b) the most stringent emissions limitation achieved in practice, whichever is more stringent. A proposed new or modified source may not emit pollutants in excess of existing new source standards.

Major Stationary Sources. Term used to determine the applicability of Prevention of Significant Deterioration and new source regulations. In a nonattainment area, any stationary pollutant source with potential to emit more than 100 tons per year is considered a major stationary source. In PSD areas the cutoff level may be either 100 or 250 tons, depending upon the source.

Manifest System. Tracking of hazardous waste from "cradle to grave" (generation through disposal) with accompanying documents known as manifests.

Marsh. A type of wetland that does not accumulate appreciable peat deposits and is dominated by herbaceous vegetation. Marshes may be either fresh or saltwater, tidal or non-tidal.

Material Safety Data Sheet (MSDS). Fact sheets required by OSHA on every commercial chemical that must be prepared by the chemical's manufacturer or importer and must include specific information, including its ingredients (1% or more), known or suspected health risks associated with its use or exposure, proper safety precautions and waste disposal, and other information necessary to prevent or minimize a health and safety risk to employees or consumers.

Maximum Contaminant Level (MCL). The maximum permissible level of a contaminant in water delivered to any user of a public water system. MCLs are enforceable standards.

Maximum Contaminant Level Goal (MCLG). The maximum level of a contaminant in drinking water at which no known or anticipated adverse effect on human health would occur, and which includes an adequate margin of safety. MCLGs are nonenforceable health goals.

Mixed Funding Agreement. Allows EPA to reimburse parties for certain costs (with interest) of actions parties have agreed to perform, but EPA has agreed to finance. A mixed funding agreement can be used when some PRPs cannot currently pay for response costs, and other PRPs want to perform response actions and be reimbursed for the non-participating PRPs' shares (CERCLA 122(b)).

Mobile Source. Any non-stationary source of air pollution such as cars, trucks, motorcycles, buses, airplanes, locomotives.

Monitoring Well. 1. A well used to obtain water quality samples or measure groundwater levels. 2. Well drilled at a hazardous waste management facility or Superfund site to collect ground-water samples for the purpose of physical, chemical, or biological analysis to determine the amounts, types, and distribution of contaminants in the ground water beneath the site.

National Ambient Air Quality Standards (NAAQS). Standards established by EPA that apply for outside air throughout the country.

National Contingency Plan (NCP). The basic policy directive for federal response actions under CERCLA Section 105. It sets forth the Hazard Ranking System and procedures and standards for responding to releases of hazardous Substances, pollutants, and contaminants. The plan is a regulation (40 CFR Part 300) subject to regular revision.

National Emissions Standards For Hazardous Air Pollutants (NESHAPs). Emissions standards set by EPA for an air pollutant not covered by NAAQS that may cause an increase in fatalities or in serious, irreversible, or incapacitating illness. Primary standards are designed to protect human health, secondary standards to protect public welfare (e.g., building facades, visibility, crops, and domestic animals).

National Pollutant Discharge Elimination System (NPDES). A provision of the Clean Water Act which prohibits discharge of pollutants into waters of the United States unless a special permit is issued by EPA, a state, or, where delegated, a tribal government on an Indian reservation.

National Priorities List (NPL). A list of sites designated as needing longterm remedial cleanup. The purpose of the list is to inform the public of the most serious hazardous waste sites in the nation. EPA revises the list periodically to add new sites or delete sites following cleanup. Sites on the list are generally slated for EPA enforcement or cleanup. Note that many elements of the CERCLA/SARA program apply to sites regardless of whether they are on the NPL.

National Response Center (NRC). The federal operations center that receives notifications of all releases of oil and hazardous substances into the environment. The Center, open 24 hours a day, is operated by the U.S. Coast Guard, which evaluates all reports and notifies the appropriate agency.

National Response Team (NRT). Representatives of 13 federal agencies who, as a team, coordinate federal responses to nationally significant incidents of pollution and provide advice and technical assistance to the responding agency(ies) before and during a response action.

Navigable Water. Water which by itself, or by uniting with other waters navigable, forms a continuous highway over which interstate or international commerce may be conducted in the customary mode of trade and travel on water.

New Source Performance Standards (NSPS). Uniform national EPA air emission and water effluent standards which limit the amount of pollution allowed from new sources or from modified existing sources.

New Source Review (NSR). Clean Air Act requirement that requires State Implementation Plans go include a permit review that applies to the construction and operation of new and modified major stationary sources in nonattainment areas to assure attainment of the national ambient air quality standards.

No Further Remedial Action Planned (NFRAP). Determination made by EPA following a preliminary assessment that a site does not pose a significant risk and so requires no further activity under CERCLA.

Non-Attainment Area. Area that does not meet one or more of the National Ambient Air Quality Standards for the criteria pollutants designated in the Clean Air Act.

Non-Binding Allocations of Responsibility (NBAR). Determination EPA may make of each PRP's share of responsibility for cleanup. Under SARA, the NBAR is an attempt to require EPA to provide more information to PRPs to encourage settlement (See CERCLA §122).

Non-Point Source. Diffuse pollution sources (i.e., without a single point of origin or not introduced into a receiving stream from a specific outlet). The pollutants are generally carried off the land by storm water. Common nonpoint sources are agriculture, forestry, urban, mining, construction, dams, channels, land disposal, saltwater intrusion, and city streets.

Notice Letter. EPA's formal notice to PRPs that CERCLA-related action is to be undertaken at a site for which those PRPs are considered responsible. Notice letters arc generally sent at least 60 days prior to scheduled obligation of funds for an RI/FS at a designated site. The intent is to give PRPs sufficient time to organize and to contact the government. A notice letter is sent again prior to implementing the remedy.

NPDES Permit. A permit for the discharge of pollutants into navigable waters under the National Pollutant Discharge Elimination System pursuant to the federal Clean Water Act.

On-Scene Coordinator (OSC). Under the NCP, a representative of EPA or the state who directs or coordinates operations at the scene of a removal action.

Opacity. The amount of light obscured by particulate pollution in the air; clear window glass has zero opacity, a brick wall is 100 percent opaque. Opacity is an indicator of changes in performance of particulate control systems.

Open Dump. A land disposal site at which solid (usually municipal) wastes are disposed of in a manner that does not protect the environment, renders them susceptible to open burning, and are exposed to the elements, vectors, and scavengers.

Open Dump Inventory. Under RCRA, EPA's Office of Solid Waste maintains an inventory of open dumps in the United States. The inventory includes all dump sites which do not comply with EPA's "Criteria for Classification of Solid Waste Disposal Facilities and Practices." (40 CFR 257).

Operator. The person responsible for the overall operation of a facility.

Owner. The person who owns a facility or part of a facility.

Ozone (O_3). Found in two layers of the atmosphere, the stratosphere and the troposphere. In the stratosphere (the atmospheric layer 7 to 10 miles or more above the earth's surface) ozone is a natural form of oxygen that provides a protective layer shielding the earth from ultraviolet radiation.In the troposphere (the layer extending up 7 to 10 miles from the earth's surface), ozone is a chemical oxidant and major component of photochemical smog. It can seriously impair the respiratory system and is one of the most widespread of all the criteria pollutants for which the Clean Air Act required EPA to set standards. Ozone in the troposphere is produced through complex chemical reactions of nitrogen oxides, which are among the primary pollutants emitted by combustion sources;

hydrocarbons, released into the atmosphere through the combustion, handling and processing of petroleum products; and sunlight.

Ozone depletion. Destruction of the stratospheric ozone layer which shields the earth from ultraviolet radiation harmful to life. This destruction of ozone is caused by the breakdown of certain chlorine and/or-bromine containing compounds (chlorofluorocarbons or halons), which break down when they reach the stratosphere and then catalytically destroy ozone molecules.

Ozone Layer. The protective layer in the atmosphere, about 15 miles above the ground, that absorbs some of the sun's ultraviolet rays, thereby reducing the amount of potentially harmful radiation reaching the earth's surface.

Particulates. 1. Fine liquid or solid particles such as dust, smoke, mist, fumes, or smog found in air or emissions. 2. Very small solid suspended in water. They vary in size, shape, density, and electrical charge, can be gathered together by coagulation and flocculation.

Pathogens. Microorganisms that can cause disease in other organisms or in humans, animals and plants (e.g., bacteria, viruses, or parasites) found in sewage, in runoff from farms or rural areas populated with domestic and wild animals, and in water used for swimming. Fish and shellfish contaminated by pathogens, or the contaminated water itself, can cause serious illness.

pH. An expression of the intensity of the basic or acid condition of a liquid. The pH may range from 0 to 14, where 0 is the most acid, 7 is neutral. Natural waters usually have a pH between 6.5 and 8.5.

Picocuries per Liter p (Ci/L). A unit of measure for levels of radon gas.

Point Source. A stationary location or fixed facility from which pollutants are discharged; any single identifiable source of pollution, e.g., a pipe, ditch, ship, ore pit, factory smokestack.

Pollutant (Clean Water Act). Dredged spoil, solid waste, incinerator residue, filter backwash, sewage, garbage, sewage sludge, munitions, chemical wastes, biological materials, some radioactive materials, heat, wrecked or discarded equipment, rock, sand, cellar dirt, and industrial, municipal, and agricultural waste discharged into water.

Pollutant or Contaminant (CERCLA). Any element, substance, compound, or mixture, including disease-causing agents that, after release into the environment and upon exposure, ingestion, inhalation, or assimilation into any organism, either directly from the environment or indirectly by ingestion through food chains, or may reasonably be anticipated to cause death, disease, behavioral abnormalities, cancer, genetic mutation, physiological malfunctions or physical deformations.

Pollution Prevention. Any source reduction or recycling activity that results in reduction of total volume of hazardous waste, reduction of toxicity of hazardous waste, or both, as long as that reduction is consistent with the goal of minimizing present and future risks to public health and the environment. Transfer of hazardous constituents from one environment medium to another does not constitute waste minimization.

Polychlorinated Biphenyls (PCBs). Halogenated organic compounds limited to the biphenyl molecule that have been chlorinated to varying degrees.

Potentially Responsible Parties (PRPs). Those identified by EPA as potentially liable under CERCLA for cleanup costs. PRPs may include generators and present or former owners/operators of certain facilities or real property where hazardous wastes have been stored, treated, or disposed of, as well as those who accepted hazardous waste for transport and selected the facility.

Publicly Owned Treatment Works (POTW). Any device or system used in the treatment (including recycling and reclamation) of municipal sewage or industrial wastes of a liquid nature which is owned by a State or municipality. This includes sewers, pipes or other conveyances if they convey waste water to a POTW providing treatment.

Quality Assurance/Quality Control. A system of procedures, checks, audits, and corrective actions to ensure that all EPA research design and performance, environmental monitoring and sampling, and other technical and reporting activities are of the highest achievable quality.

Radon. A colorless naturally occurring, radioactive, inert gas formed by radioactive decay of radium atoms in soil or rocks.

RCRA Facility Assessment (RFA). Usually the first step in the RCRA corrective action process. EPA conducts a comprehensive review of pertinent site information. This may be followed by visual site inspection and if necessary a sampling visit to make release determinations.

RCRA Facility Investigation (RFI). The second step in the RCRA corrective action process. If the RFA indicates a suspected release the regulatory agency prescribes an RFI under a corrective action permit (RCRA §3004(u)) or enforcement action (RCRA 3008(h)). Such investigations can range from small specific activities to complex multimedia studies.

Reasonably Available Control Technology (RACT). Control technology that is both reasonably available, and both technologically and economically feasible. Usually applied to existing sources in nonattainment areas; in most cases is less stringent than new source performance standards.

Receiving Waters. A river, lake, ocean, stream or other watercourse into which wastewater or treated effluent is discharged.

Record of Decision (ROD). Published by the government after completion of an RI/FS, the ROD identifies the remedial alternative chosen for implementation at a Superfund site. The ROD is part of the written administrative record. Judicial review of EPA cleanup decisions may be limited to the administrative record.

Regulated Asbestos-Containing Material (RACM). Friable asbestos material or nonfriable ACM that will be or has been subjected to sanding, grinding, cutting, or abrading or has crumbled, or been pulverized or reduced to powder in the course of demolition or renovation operations.

Release. Any spilling, leaking, pumping, pouring, emitting, emptying, discharging, injecting, escaping, leaching, dumping, or disposing into the environment (See CERCLA §101(22)). Includes the abandonment or discarding of barrels, containers, and other closed receptacles containing any hazardous substance, pollutant, or contaminant. Exclusions include (1) releases solely exposing workers in a workplace, with respect to a claim they may bring against the employer; (2) engine exhaust emissions from motor vehicles, rolling stock, aircraft, vessels, or pipeline pumping station engines; (3) nuclear releases subject to the Atomic Energy Act and financial requirements or the Nuclear Regulatory Commission (also excludes any release of source, byproduct, or special nuclear material from any processing site designated under Section 102(a) or 302(a) of the Uranium Mill Tailings Radiation Control Act); and (4) the normal application of fertilizer. Release also means substantial threat of release.

Remedial Action (RA). The actual construction or implementation phase of a Superfund site cleanup that follows remedial design.

Remedial Action Plan (RAP). This plan details the technical approach for implementing remedial response. It includes the methods to be followed during the entire remediation process--from developing the remedial design to implementing the selected remedy through construction.

Remedial Design. A phase of remedial action that follows the ROD, consent decree, and remedial investigation/feasibility study (RI/FS) and includes development or engineering drawings and specifications for a site cleanup.

Remedial Investigation/Feasibility Study (RI/FS). Extensive technical studies conducted by the government or by PRPs to investigate the scope of contamination (RI) and determine the remedial alternatives (FS) which, consistent with the NCP, may be implemented at a Superfund site. Government funded RI/FSs do not recommend a specific alternative for implementation. RI/FSs conducted by PRPs usually do recommend and technically support a remedial alternative. An RI/FS may include a variety of on- and off-site activities, such as monitoring, sampling, and analysis.

Remedial Response. Long-term action that stops or substantially reduces a release or threat of a release of hazardous substances that is serious but not an immediate threat to public health.

Remediation. Cleanup methods used to remove or contain a release or spill of hazardous substances from the environment.

Removal, Remove, or Removal Action. Under CERCLA §101(23), generally short-term actions taken to respond promptly to an urgent need. With regard to hazardous substances, the cleanup or removal of released substances from the environment; actions in response to the threat of release; actions that may be necessary to monitor, assess, and evaluate the release or threat; disposal of removed material; or other actions needed to prevent, minimize, or mitigate damage to public health or welfare or to the environment. Removal also includes, without being limited to, security fencing or other measures to limit access; provision of alternative water supplies; temporary evacuation and housing of threatened individuals not otherwise provided for; and any emergency assistance provided under the Disaster Relief Act.

Reportable Quantity (RQ). Quantity of a "hazardous substance" considered reportable under CERCLA in the event of a release. Reportable quantities are identified in 40 CFR section 302.5 and may be 1, 10, 100, 1,000, or 5,000 pounds. Quantities are to be measured over a 24-hour period.

Response Action. Any remedial action, removal action, or cleanup at a site under CERCLA §101(25). Includes enforcement-related activities.

Retrofit. Addition of a pollution control device on an existing facility without making major changes to the generating plant.

Risk Assessment. A qualitative and quantitative evaluation performed to define the risk posed to human health and/or the environment by the presence or potential presence and/or use of specific pollutants. Baseline risk assessments are performed as part of corrective action.

Route of Exposure. The avenue by which a chemical comes into contact with an organism (e.g., inhalation, ingestion, dermal contact, injection.)

Run-Off. That part of precipitation, snow melt, or irrigation water that runs off the land into streams or other surface-water. It can carry pollutants from the air and land into receiving waters.

Scrubber. An air pollution device that uses a spray of water or reactant or a dry process to trap pollutants in emissions.

Septic Tank. A watertight, covered receptacle designed to receive or process, through liquid separation or biological digestion, the sewage discharged from a building sewer. The effluent from such a receptacle is distributed for disposal through the soil and settled solids and scum from the tank are pumped out periodically and hauled to a treatment facility.

Site Inspection. The collection of information from a Superfund site to determine the extent and severity of hazards posed by the site. It follows and is more extensive than a preliminary assessment. The purpose is to gather information necessary to score the site, using the Hazard Ranking System, and to determine if the site presents an immediate threat that requires prompt removal action.

Small Quantity Generator (SQG). A regulated facility that generates more than 100 kilograms and less than 1,000 kilograms (about 1 ton) of hazardous waste in a calendar month. However even if a small quantity generator avoids the requirements of full generator status, the facility may still be subject to certain RCRA conditions (e.g., if the quantity of acutely hazardous wastes generated in a calendar month exceeds quantities specified under RCRA).

Sole Source Aquifer. An aquifer which is the sole or principal drinking water source for an area and which if contaminated would create a significant hazard to public health. Sole source aquifers may receive special protective status.

Solid Waste (per RCRA). Garbage, refuse, sludge from a waste treatment plant, water supply treatment plant or air pollution control facility and other discarded material including solid, liquid, semi-solid, or contained gaseous materials resulting from industrial, commercial, mining and agriculture activities and from community activities, but does not include solids or dissolved materials in domestic sewage or solid or dissolved materials in irrigation return flows or industrial discharges that are point sources subject to permits under the federal Clean Water Act or source, special nuclear or byproduct material as defined by the Atomic Energy Act. EPA defines hazardous waste as a subset of solid waste.

Solid Waste Disposal Act (SWDA). The SWDA was amended in 1976 by the Resource Conservation and Recovery Act (RCRA). SWDA has since been amended by several public laws, including the Used Oil Recycling Act of 1980 (UORA). the Hazardous and Solid Waste Amendments of 1984 (HSWA), and the Medical Waste Tracking Act of 1988 (MWTA).

Solid Waste Management Unit (SWMU). Any unit in which wastes have been placed at any time, regardless of whether the unit was designed to accept solid or hazardous waste. Units include areas from which solid wastes have been routinely released.

Source Reduction. Reducing the amount of materials entering the waste stream by redesigning products or patterns of production or consumption (e.g., using returnable beverage containers). Synonymous with waste reduction.

Spill Prevention Control and Countermeasures Plan (SPCCP). Required under Clean Water Act regulations 40 CFR 112.3 for both onshore and offshore facilities that have discharged or reasonably could be expected to discharge oil in harmful quantities.

Spoil. Dirt or rock removed from its original location-destroying the composition of the soil in the process-as in strip-mining, dredging, or construction.

State Emergency Response Commission (SERC). Commission appointed by each state governor according to the requirements of SARA Title III. The SERCs designate emergency planning districts, appoint local emergency planning committees, and supervise and coordinate their activities.

State Implementation Plans (SIP). EPA-approved state plans for the establishment, regulation, and enforcement of air pollution standards.

Stationary Source. A fixed-site producer of pollution, mainly power plants and other facilities using industrial combustion processes.

Storage. The holding of hazardous waste for a temporary period, at the end of which the hazardous waste is treated, disposed of, or stored elsewhere. Facilities are required to have a RCRA permit for storage of hazardous waste for more than 90 days; storage for less than 90 days does not require a RCRA permit.

Subtitle C (of RCRA). A principal regulatory provision of RCRA which establishes a comprehensive "cradle to grave" program to regulate hazardous wastes from generation through disposal.

Subtitle D (of RCRA). Historically, State and local governments have controlled solid wastes (such as municipal waste, mining waste, and other industrial wastes not termed as hazardous). Subtitle D of RCRA provided a minimal federal framework until the 1984 HSWA amendments. With HSWA, both Congress and EPA are advancing a regulatory program to beef up technical regulatory controls over some of the 225,00 solid waste facilities nationwide.

Subtitle I (of RCRA). Regulates underground storage tanks containing petroleum products and substances regulated by CERCLA.

Superfund Amendments and Reauthorization Act (SARA). Signed by the President on October 17, 1986, expanded the scope of CERCLA. SARA is a 5-year extension of the program to clean up toxic releases at uncontrolled or abandoned hazardous waste sites. CERCLA is due for reauthorization again in 1995.

Superfund. The program operated under the legislative authority of CERCLA and SARA that funds and carries out EPA hazardous waste emergency and long-term removal and remedial activities. These activities include establishing the National Priorities List, investigating sites for inclusion on the list, determining their priority, and conducting and/or supervising the cleanup and other remedial actions.

Surface Impoundment. A natural topographic depression, manmade excavation, or diked area formed primarily of earthen materials (may be lined with manmade materials) but is not an injection well. Examples of surface impoundments are holding, storage, settling, and aeration pits, ponds, and lagoons.

Surface Runoff. Precipitation, snow melt, or irrigation in excess of what can infiltrate the soil surface and be stored in small surface depressions; a major transporter of nonpoint source pollutants.

Surface Water. All water which is open to the atmosphere and subject to surface runoff.

Suspended Loads. Sediment particles maintained in the water column by turbulence and carried with the flow of water.

Suspended Solids. Small particles of solid pollutants that float on the surface of, or are suspended in, sewage or other liquids. They resist removal by conventional means.

Swamp. A type of wetland dominated by woody vegetation but without appreciable peat deposits. Swamps may be fresh or salt water and tidal or non-tidal.

Threatened/Endangered Species. Any plant or animal species so listed in section 4 of the Endangered Species Act.

Tidal Marsh. Low, flat marshlands traversed by channels and tidal hollows, subject to tidal inundation; normally, the only vegetation present is salttolerant bushes and grasses.

Total Dissolved Solids (TDS). All material that passes the standard glass river filter; now called total filtrable reside. Term is used to reflect salinity.

Total Suspended Solids (TSS). A measure of the suspended solids in wastewater, effluent, or water bodies, determined by tests for "total suspended nonfilterable solids."

Toxic Release Inventory (TRI). Under SARA Title III, Section 313, facilities that handle certain types of chemicals must report to EPA annually the quantities of these chemicals released to the environment during the year. These releases may be allowed under air or water permits, may be spills of waste or product materials, or may be fugitive smoke stack emissions or product/process tank/oil line losses. EPA is beginning to evaluate TRI data to determine whether facilities have environmentally significant releases that must be addressed under RCRA corrective action or Superfund authorities.

Toxic Waste. A waste that can produce injury if inhaled, swallowed, or absorbed through the skin.

Toxicity Characteristic (TC) Rule. This rule replaced the Extraction Procedure (EP) toxicity test with the TC test to determine whether or not a waste is a characteristic waste based on toxicity. The TC test requires analysis of 25 organic compounds in addition to the eight metals and six pesticides that were subject to the EP test.

Toxicity Characteristic Leaching Procedure (TCLP). The analytical method one must use to determine whether or not a waste is a characteristic hazardous waste based on toxicity. The TCLP is also necessary to comply with provisions of land disposal restrictions as well.

Transporter. A person transporting hazardous waste within the United States which requires a manifest. On-site movement of hazardous waste does not apply. Transporters must comply with 40 CFR Part 263.

Treatment. Any method, technique, or process, including neutralization, designed to change the physical, chemical, or biological character or composition of any hazardous waste so as to neutralize such waste, or so as to recover energy or material resources from the waste, or so as to render such waste nonhazardous, or less hazardous; safer to transport, store, or dispose of; or amenable for recovery, amenable for storage, or reduced in volume.

Treatment Standards. Standards that hazardous wastes must meet prior to land disposal. A treatment standard generally expresses a treatment technology as concentration limits to give generators flexibility in choosing treatment options. Note that concentration limits are based upon the use of best demonstrated available technology (BDAT) for a particular waste or a similar waste.

Treatment, Storage, and Disposal (TSD) Facility. Site where a hazardous substance is treated, stored, or disposed of. TSD facilities are regulated by EPA and states under RCRA.

Trichloroethylene (TCE). A stable, low boiling-point colorless liquid, toxic if inhaled. Used as a solvent or metal decreasing agent, and in other industrial applications.

Turbidity. 1. Haziness in air caused by the presence of particles and pollutants. 2. A cloudy condition in water due to suspended silt or organic matter.

Underground Storage Tank. Any one or combination of tanks (including its connecting underground pipes) used to contain an accumulation of regulated substances, and the volume of which (including the volume of the underground pipes) is 10 percent or more beneath the surface of the ground. Regulated substances include hazardous chemical products regulated under CERCLA and petroleum products. Some tank uses are exempt from regulation, including septic tanks, residential/agricultural fuel or heating oil tanks, and waste water collection systems.

Urea-Formaldehyde Foam Insulation. A material once used to conserve energy by sealing crawl spaces, attics, etc.; no longer used because emissions were found to be a health hazard.

Volatile Organic Compound (VOC). Any organic compound that participates in atmospheric photochemical reactions except those designated by EPA as having negligible photochemical reactivity.

Waste Minimization. Measures or techniques that reduce the amount of wastes generated during industrial production processes; term is also applied to recycling and other efforts to reduce the amount of waste going into the waste stream.

Waste Pile. Any noncontainerized accumulation of solid, nonflowing hazardous waste that is used for treatment or storage.

Waste Reduction. Using source reduction, recycling, or composting to prevent or reduce waste generation.

Water Quality Standards. State-adopted and EPA-approved ambient standards for water bodies. The standards cover the use Or the water body and the water quality criteria that must be met to protect the designated use or uses.

Wetlands. Those areas that are inundated or saturated by surface or ground water at a frequency and duration sufficient to support, and that under normal circumstances do support, a prevalence of vegetation typically adapted for life in saturated soil conditions. Wetlands generally include swamps, marshes, bogs, and similar areas.

INDEX

A

Alabama
  National Brownfields Assessment
    Demonstration Pilots, 186
  Birmingham, 186
  Regional Brownfields Assessment
    Demonstration Pilots, 244
  Prichard, 244

Alaska
  National Brownfields Assessment
    Demonstration Pilots, 187
  Ketchikan Gateway Borough, 187

Appendices, 299
  Brownfields Bibliography, App. F,
    351
  CERCLA Enforcement Against
    Lenders and Government Entities,
    App. E, 343
  Model Prospective Purchaser
    Agreement, App. C, 313
  Sample EPA Comfort/Status
    Letters, App. D, 327
  State Brownfield Program Contacts,
    App. B, 305
  U.S. EPA Brownfield Program
    Contacts, App. A, 299

Arizona
  National Brownfields Assessment
    Demonstration Pilots, 189
  Navajo Nation, 189
  Tucson, 189

Asset Conservation, Lender Liability,
  and Deposit Insurance Protection
  Act of 1996, 28

ASTM Environmental Site
  Assessment Standards
  ASTM Standard E 1527: Phase I
    Environmental Site Assessment,
    152
  Limitations on Use of ASTM Phase
    I Environmental Site Assessment,
    155
  ASTM Standard E 1528:
    Transaction Screen Process, 149

B

Brownfields Assessment Pilots
  Overview, 183
  National Brownfields Assessment
    Demonstration Pilots, 186
  Regional Brownfields Assessment
    Demonstration Pilots, 244

Brownfields Bibliography, App. F,
351

Brownfields Financing Tools
Debt Financing, 172
Bonds, 173
Revolving Loan Funds, 173
Subsidized Low Interest Loans,
172
Equity Participation, 164
Financial Assurances, 181
Bond/Loan Insurance, 181
Loan Guarantees, 181
Grants, 174
EPA Brownfields Assessment
Pilot Grants, 174
Private/Nonprofit Grants, 175
State Grant Programs, 174
Informational/Advisory Services,
177
Brokering, 177
Land Registry, 177
Regulatory Compliance
Assistance, 178
Land Registration and Site
Assessment Fees, 166
Liability Assurances, 178
Certificate of Completeness, 180
Covenant Not to Sue, 179
Liability Release, 180
No-Further-Action Letter, 179
Taxes, 167
Property Tax Abatement, 169

Real Estate Transfer Taxes, 168
Tax Increment Financing, 167
Tax Treatment of Brownfields
Cleanup Expenses, 170

Brownfields Glossary, 355

Brownfields Internet Homepage, 301

Brownfields National Partnership
Action Agenda, 29

Brownfields Programs, See EPA
Brownfields Programs; State
Brownfields Programs

Brownfields Redevelopment
Brownfields Redevelopment
Process, 142
Cleanup Planning and Execution,
147
Detailed Site Assessment or Phase
II Investigation, 146
Economic Assessment, 144
Initial Site Assessment or Phase I
Investigation, 142
Project Development and
Financing, 146
Redevelopment of the Site, 147
Site Identification, 142
Environmental Risk Assessments,
158

Environmental Site Assessments, 147
  ASTM Standard E 1527: Phase I Environmental Site Assessment, 152
  ASTM Standard E 1528: Transaction Screen Process, 149
  Limitations on Use of ASTM Phase I Environmental Site Assessment, 155
  Phase II Environmental Site Assessments, 157
  Liability Protections, 160
  Public Participation, 160

Brownfields Redevelopment Case Studies
  Avtex Fibers Site, Meadville, Pennsylvania, 282
    Applicable Regulations, 284
    Contamination Assessment, 283
    Land Use Planning Issues, 286
    Remedial Planning, 290
  Conclusions, 297
  Redevelopment for Commercial Use, 287
  Redevelopment for Industrial Use, 282
  Redevelopment for Residential Use, 292
  Robinson Brick Company Site, Denver, Colorado, 287

Applicable Cleanup Standards, 289
    Prospective Purchaser and Future Land Use of the Site, 291
    Remedial Planning, 285
    Site History, 287
  Herndon Homes Site, Atlanta, Georgia, 292
    Applicable Regulations Governing Remediation, 293
    Contamination Assessment, 293
    Land Use Planning Issues, 295
    Remedial Planning, 294

Brownfields Showcase Communities, 31

C

California
  Brownfields Initiatives, 49
    Expedited Remedial Action Program, 55
    Prospective Purchaser Policy, 57
    Voluntary Cleanup Program, 53
  National Brownfields Assessment Demonstration Pilots, 191
    Emeryville, 191
    Richmond, 191
    Sacramento, 192
    Santa Barbara County, 192
    Stockton, 194

Regional Brownfields Assessment
Demonstration Pilots, 244
East Palo Alto, 244
Oakland, 246
San Francisco, 247

Case Studies, See Brownfields
Redevelopment Case Studies

Colorado
Brownfield Redevelopment Case
Study, 287
Robinson Brick Company Site,
Denver, 287
Regional Brownfields Assessment
Demonstration Pilots, 247
Englewood, 247
Sand Creek Corridor, 249
Voluntary Cleanup and
Redevelopment Act, 61
Cleanup Verification, 69
Memorandum of Agreement with
U.S EPA, 62
No Further Action Petition, 70
Public Participation, 68
Resources and Capabilities, 67
Site Screening and
Communication, 63
Sites Listed in CERCLIS, 65
Sites Not Listed on CERCLIS, 65
Standards and Risk Analysis, 68

Comfort/Status Letters for Brownfield
Properties
Federal Superfund Interest Letter,
24
No Current Federal Superfund
Interest Letter, 22
No Previous Federal Superfund
Interest Letter, 21
Purpose of, 19
Sample Comfort/Status Letters,
App. D, 351
State Action Letter, 25

Comprehensive Environmental
Response, Compensation, and
Liability Act (CERCLA)
EPA Comfort/Status Letters, Role
in, 20
EPA Enforcement Policy Against
Lenders and Government Entities,
25; App. E, 343
Legislative Reforms, 39
Prospective Purchaser Agreements,
Role in, 6

Comprehensive Environmental
Response, Compensation, and
Liability Information System
(CERCLIS) Database
EPA Comfort/Status Letters, Role
in, 20
Federal Superfund Interest Letter,
24

No Current Federal Superfund
Interest Letter, 22
No Previous Federal Superfund
Interest Letter, 21
State Action Letter, 25
Removal of NFRAP Sites
from, 2

Connecticut
Brownfields Redevelopment
Programs, 71
Community Redevelopment Laws,
76
Comparison of Voluntary Cleanup
Programs, 74
Neighborhood Revitalization
Zones, 76
Tax Increment Financing, 77
Urban Sites Remediation
Program, 75
Voluntary Cleanup Program #1:
Public Act 95-183, 71
Voluntary Cleanup Program #2:
Public Act 95-190, 72
National Brownfields Assessment
Demonstration Pilots, 194
Bridgeport, 194
Hartford, 195
Regional Brownfields Assessment
Demonstration Pilots, 249
Naugatuck Valley, 249
New Haven, 250

D

Debt Financing
Bonds, 173
Revolving Loan Funds, 173
Subsidized Low Interest Loans, 172

Delaware
Voluntary Cleanup Program, 78
Application and Agreement, 80
Site Eligibility, 79
Site Investigation Process, 82
Soil and Groundwater Screening
Levels, 82
Written Assurances, 83
National Brownfields Assessment
Demonstration Pilots, 196
Wilmington, 196

E

Empowerment Zone/Enterprise
Community (EZ/EC) Program
Baltimore, Maryland Empowerment
Zone, 36
Economic Development Initiative,
34
EZ/EC Designations, 35
EZ/EC SSBG Funding, 33
EZ/EC Strategic Plans, 34
Overview, 32

Environmental Risk Assessments, 158

Environmental Site Assessments
ASTM Standard E 1527: Phase I
Environmental Site Assessment,
152
ASTM Standard E 1528:
Transaction Screen Process, 149
Limitations on Use of ASTM
Phase I Environmental Site
Assessment, 155
Phase II Environmental Site
Assessments, 157

EPA Brownfields Program Contacts,
App. A, 299
Brownfields Coordinator Offices,
299
Brownfields Internet Homepage,
301

EPA Brownfields Programs
Brownfields Assessment Pilots, 3,
183
Brownfields Cleanup Revolving
Loan Fund Demonstration Pilots,
4
National Brownfields Assessment
Demonstration Pilots, 186
Overview, 3, 183
Regional Brownfields Assessment
Demonstration Pilots, 244

Brownfields Coordinator Offices,
App. A, 299
Brownfields Internet Homepage,
301
Removal of NFRAP Sites from
CERCLIS Database, 2
Prospective Purchaser Agreements,
6
1989 Guidance on, 6
1995 Guidance, Purpose of, 8
Consideration, 13
Criteria for, 8
EPA Authority for, 7
Model Prospective Purchaser
Agreement, App. C, 313
Model Prospective Purchaser
Agreement, Components of, 15
Public Participation, 14
Comfort/Status Letters for
Brownfield Properties, 20
Federal Superfund Interest Letter,
24
No Current Federal Superfund
Interest Letter, 22
No Previous Federal Superfund
Interest Letter, 21
Purpose of, 19
Sample Comfort/Status Letters,
App. D, 327
State Action Letter, 25
Policy on CERCLA Enforcement
Against Lenders and Government
Entities, 27; App. E, 343

Equity Participation, 164

F

Financial Assurances
Bond/Loan Insurance, 181
Loan Guarantees, 181

Florida
National Brownfields Assessment
Demonstration Pilots, 198
Dade County, 198
Jacksonville, 199
Tallahassee, 201
Regional Brownfields Assessment
Demonstration Pilots, 250
Clearwater, 250
Gainesville, 250
Miami, 251
St. Petersburg, 253

G

Georgia
Brownfield Redevelopment Case
Study, 292
Herndon Homes Site, Atlanta, 292
Regional Brownfields Assessment
Demonstration Pilots, 253
Atlanta, 253

Glossary, 355

Grants
EPA Brownfields Assessment Pilot
Grants, 174
Private/Nonprofit Grants, 175
State Grant Programs, 174

I

Idaho
Regional Brownfields Assessment
Demonstration Pilots, 254
Panhandle Health District, 254

Illinois
National Brownfields Assessment
Demonstration Pilots, 202
Cook County, 202
West Central Municipal
Conference, 204
Regional Brownfields Assessment
Demonstration Pilots, 254
Chicago, 254
East St. Louis, 256
State of Illinois, 256
Site Remediation Program, 84
No Further Remediation Letter, 87
Program Application and Service
Agreement, 85
Site Eligibility, 84
Site Investigation and
Remediation by Licensed
Engineer, 86

Indiana
  National Brownfields Assessment
    Demonstration Pilots, 204
    Indianapolis, 204
  Regional Brownfields Assessment
    Demonstration Pilots, 257
    Northwest Indiana Cities, 257
    State of Indiana, 258

K

Kansas
  National Brownfields Assessment
    Demonstration Pilots, 205
    Kansas City, 205

Kentucky
  National Brownfields Assessment
    Demonstration Pilots, 205
    Louisville, 205

L

Liability Assurances
  Certificate of Completeness, 178
  Covenant Not to Sue, 180
  Financing Strategies and, 163
  Liability Release, 180
  No-Further-Action Letter, 179

Louisiana
  National Brownfields Assessment
    Demonstration Pilots, 206

New Orleans, 206
  Regional Brownfields Assessment
    Demonstration Pilots, 259
    Shreveport, 259

M

Maine
  National Brownfields Assessment
    Demonstration Pilots, 206
    State of Maine, 206
  Regional Brownfields Assessment
    Demonstration Pilots, 259
    Portland, 259

Maryland
  Brownfields Programs, 88
  Brownfields Revitalization
  Incentive Program, 91
    Lender Liability Relief, 92
    Voluntary Cleanup Program, 89
  Empowerment Zone/Enterprise
    Community (EZ/EC) Program, 32
  Baltimore, 36
  National Brownfields Assessment
    Demonstration Pilots, 208
    Baltimore, 208
  Regional Brownfields Assessment
    Demonstration Pilots, 260
    Baltimore County, 260

Massachusetts
National Brownfields Assessment
Demonstration Pilots, 208
Chicopee, 208
Greenfield, 209
Lawrence, 210
Lowell, 211
New Bedford, 211
Worcester, 213
Regional Brownfields Assessment
Demonstration Pilots, 261
Boston, 261
Lynn, 262
Somerville, 263
Westfield, 264

Michigan
Brownfields Initiatives, 95
Amendments to Michigan's
Environmental Cleanup Law,
98
Land Use-Based Cleanup
Standards, 101
Liability Protections, 100
Performance of Baseline
Environmental Assessment, 99
National Brownfields Assessment
Demonstration Pilots, 213
Detroit, 213
Regional Brownfields Assessment
Demonstration Pilots, 265
Kalamazoo, 265

Minnesota
National Brownfields Assessment
Demonstration Pilots, 214
Chippewa County/Kinross
Township, 214
St. Paul Port Authority, 214
Regional Brownfields Assessment
Demonstration Pilots, 266
Downriver Community
Conference, 266
State of Minnesota, 266
Voluntary Investigation and
Cleanup Program, 92
Program Improvements, 94

Missouri
National Brownfields Assessment
Demonstration Pilots, 216
Kansas City, 205
St. Louis, 216
Wellston, 216
Regional Brownfields Assessment
Demonstration Pilots, 267
Bonne Terre, 267

Montana
Voluntary Cleanup Program, 102

N

New Hampshire
Brownfields Program, 103
Eligibility Criteria, 104

Eligibility Determination, 105
Liability Protection, 105
Remedial Action and Certificate
of Completion, 106
Regional Brownfields Assessment
Demonstration Pilots, 268
Concord, 268

New Jersey
National Brownfields Assessment
Demonstration Pilots, 218
Jersey City, 218
Newark, 219
Perth Amboy, 220
Trenton, 221
Regional Brownfields Assessment
Demonstration Pilots, 268
Camden, 268
Voluntary Cleanup Program, 107
Liability Protection, 108
Remediation Loans and Grants,
109
Tax Abatement, 110

New York
Brownfields Programs, 110
Environmental Restoration
Projects Program, 112
Voluntary Cleanup Program, 111
National Brownfields Assessment
Demonstration Pilots, 222
Elmira, 222
New York City, 223

Niagara Falls, 224
Rochester, 225
Rome, 226
Regional Brownfields Assessment
Demonstration Pilots, 269
Buffalo, 269

No Further Response Action Planned
(NFRAP) Sites
CERCLIS Database, Removal from,
2
EPA Comfort/Status Letters and, 20
Prospective Purchaser Agreements
and, 13

North Carolina
National Brownfields Assessment
Demonstration Pilots, 226
Charlotte, 226
Fayetteville, 227
High Point, 227

O

Ohio
Financial Assistance Programs, 116
Brownfield Grant Assistance
Program, 119
Brownfield Site Cleanup Tax
Credit Program, 118
Competitive Economic
Development Program, 120

Ohio Water Development
Authority Loan Program, 117
Pollution Prevention Loan
Program, 117
Water Pollution Control Loan
Fund (WPCLF), 116
National Brownfields Assessment
Demonstration Pilots, 229
Cuyahoga County, 229
Lima, 230
Regional Brownfields Assessment
Demonstration Pilots, 269
Cincinnati, 269
Voluntary Action Program, 113

Oklahoma
Brownfields Program, 120
Regional Brownfields Assessment
Demonstration Pilots, 270
Tulsa, 270

Oregon
National Brownfields Assessment
Demonstration Pilots, 230
Oregon Mill Sites, 230
Portland, 231
Voluntary Cleanup Program, 123
Prospective Purchaser
Agreements, 124

P

Pennsylvania
Brownfield Redevelopment Case
Study, 282
Avtex Fibers Site, Meadville, 282
Land Recycling Program, 126
Financial Assistance, 128
Releases from Liability, 127
Standardized Review Procedures,
127
Uniform Cleanup Standards, 126
National Brownfields Assessment
Demonstration Pilots, 231
Bucks County, 231
Phoenixville, 233
Regional Brownfields Assessment
Demonstration Pilots, 272
Philadelphia, 272
Pittsburgh, 272

Prospective Purchaser Agreements
1989 Guidance on, 6
1995 Guidance, Purpose of, 8
Consideration, 13
Criteria for, 8
EPA Authority for, 7
Model Prospective Purchaser
Agreement, App. C, 313
Model Prospective Purchaser
Agreement, Components of, 15
Public Participation, 14

Public Participation, 14, 68, 160

Puerto Rico
National Brownfields Assessment
Demonstration Pilots, 234
Puerto Rico Industrial
Development Company, 234

R

Rhode Island
National Brownfields Assessment
Demonstration Pilots, 235
State of Rhode Island, 235

S

South Carolina
National Brownfields Assessment
Demonstration Pilots, 236
Cowpens, 236

South Dakota
Regional Brownfields Assessment
Demonstration Pilots, 273
Sioux Falls, 273

State Brownfield Program Contacts,
App. B, 305

State Brownfields Programs, See
Entries for Individual States

T

Taxes
Property Tax Abatement, 169
Real Estate Transfer Taxes, 168
Tax Increment Financing, 167
Tax Treatment of Brownfields
Cleanup Expenses, 170

Tennessee
National Brownfields Assessment
Demonstration Pilots, 237
Knoxville, 237
Memphis, 238

Texas
National Brownfields Assessment
Demonstration Pilots, 239
Houston, 239
Laredo, 240
Regional Brownfields Assessment
Demonstration Pilots, 273
Dallas, 273
Voluntary Cleanup Program, 128

U

Utah
Regional Brownfields Assessment
Demonstration Pilots, 274
Murray City, 274
Ogden City, 274
Provo, 275

Salt Lake City, 276
West Jordan, 277

V

Vermont
National Brownfields Assessment
Demonstration Pilots, 240
Burlington, 240
Redevelopment of Contaminated
Properties Program, 130

Virginia
National Brownfields Assessment
Demonstration Pilots, 241
Cape Charles-Northampton
County, 241
Richmond, 241
Voluntary Remediation Program,
133
Remediated Property Fresh Start
Program, 135

W

Washington
Independent Remedial Action
Program, 135

National Brownfields Assessment
Demonstration Pilots, 242
Tacoma, 242
Regional Brownfields Assessment
Demonstration Pilots, 277
Bellingham, 277
Duwamish Coalition, 278
Puyallup Tribe of Tacoma, 278

Wisconsin
Land Recycling Law, 136
Prospective Purchaser Protections,
137
National Brownfields Assessment
Demonstration Pilots, 242
Northwest Regional Planning
Commission, 242
Regional Brownfields Assessment
Demonstration Pilots, 279
Milwaukee County, 279
Wisconsin Department of Natural
Resources, 279

GOVERNMENT INSTITUTES
MINI-CATALOG

PC #	ENVIRONMENTAL TITLES	Pub Date	Price
585	Book of Lists for Regulated Hazardous Substances, 8th Edition	1997	$79
4088	CFR Chemical Lists on CD ROM, 1997 Edition	1997	$125
4089	Chemical Data for Workplace Sampling & Analysis, Single User	1997	$125
512	Clean Water Handbook, 2nd Edition	1996	$89
581	EH&S Auditing Made Easy	1997	$79
587	E H & S CFR Training Requirements, 3rd Edition	1997	$89
4082	EMMI-Envl Monitoring Methods Index for Windows-Network	1997	$537
4082	EMMI-Envl Monitoring Methods Index for Windows-Single User	1997	$179
525	Environmental Audits, 7th Edition	1996	$79
548	Environmental Engineering and Science: An Introduction	1997	$79
578	Environmental Guide to the Internet, 3rd Edition	1997	$59
560	Environmental Law Handbook, 14th Edition	1997	$79
353	Environmental Regulatory Glossary, 6th Edition	1993	$79
562	Environmental Statutes, 1997 Edition	1997	$69
562	Environmental Statutes Book/Disk Package, 1997 Edition	1997	$204
4060	Environmental Statutes on Disk for Windows-Network	1997	$405
4060	Environmental Statutes on Disk for Windows-Single User	1997	$135
570	Environmentalism at the Crossroads	1995	$39
536	ESAs Made Easy	1996	$59
515	Industrial Environmental Management: A Practical Approach	1996	$79
4078	IRIS Database-Network	1997	$1,485
4078	IRIS Database-Single User	1997	$495
510	ISO 14000: Understanding Environmental Standards	1996	$69
551	ISO 14001: An Executive Repoert	1996	$55
518	Lead Regulation Handbook	1996	$79
478	Principles of EH&S Management	1995	$69
554	Property Rights: Understanding Government Takings	1997	$79
582	Recycling & Waste Mgmt Guide to the Internet	1997	$49
603	Superfund Manual, 6th Edition	1997	$115
566	TSCA Handbook, 3rd Edition	1997	$95
534	Wetland Mitigation: Mitigation Banking and Other Strategies	1997	$75

PC #	SAFETY AND HEALTH TITLES	Pub Date	Price
547	Construction Safety Handbook	1996	$79
553	Cumulative Trauma Disorders	1997	$59
559	Forklift Safety	1997	$65
539	Fundamentals of Occupational Safety & Health	1996	$49
535	Making Sense of OSHA Compliance	1997	$59
563	Managing Change for Safety and Health Professionals	1997	$59
589	Managing Fatigue in Transportation, *ATA Conference*	1997	$75
4086	OSHA Technical Manual, Electronic Edition	1997	$99
598	Project Mgmt for E H & S Professionals	1997	$59
552	Safety & Health in Agriculture, Forestry and Fisheries	1997	$125
523	Safety & Health on the Internet	1996	$39
597	Safety Is A People Business	1997	$49
463	Safety Made Easy	1995	$49
590	Your Company Safety and Health Manual	1997	$79

Electronic Product available on CD-ROM or Floppy Disk

GOVERNMENT INSTITUTES

PUBLICATIONS CATALOG
1997

PLEASE CALL OUR PUBLISHING DEPARTMENT AT (301) 921-2355 FOR A FREE PUBLICATIONS CATALOG.

Government Institutes
4 Research Place, Suite 200 • Rockville, MD 20850-3226
Tel. (301) 921-2355 • FAX (301) 921-0373
E mail: giinfo@govinst.com • Internet: http://www.govinst.com

GOVERNMENT INSTITUTES ORDER FORM

GI GI

4 Research Place, Suite 200 • Rockville, MD 20850-3226 • Tel (301) 921-2355 • Fax (301) 921-0373
Internet: *http://www.govinst.com* • E-mail: *giinfo@govinst.com*

3 EASY WAYS TO ORDER

1. Phone: **(301) 921-2355**
Have your credit card ready when you call.

2. Fax: **(301) 921-0373**
Fax this completed order form with your company purchase order or credit card information.

3. Mail: **Government Institutes**
4 Research Place, Suite 200
Rockville, MD 20850-3226
USA
Mail this completed order form with a check, company purchase order, or credit card information.

PAYMENT OPTIONS

❏ **Check** (*payable to Government Institutes in US dollars*)

❏ **Purchase Order** (this order form must be attached to your company P.O. Note: All International orders must be pre-paid.)

❏ **Credit Card** ❏ *VISA* ❏ MasterCard ❏ AMERICAN EXPRESS

Exp.___/____

Credit Card No. _____

Signature _____
Government Institutes' Federal I.D.# is 52-0994196

CUSTOMER INFORMATION

Ship To: (Please attach your Purchase Order)

Name: _____

GI Account# (*7 digits on mailing label*): _____

Company/Institution: _____

Address: _____
(please supply street address for UPS shipping)
_____

City: _____ State/Province: _____

Zip/Postal Code: _____ Country: _____

Tel: ( ) _____

Fax: ( ) _____

E-mail Address: _____

Bill To: (if different than ship to address)

Name: _____

Title/Position: _____

Company/Institution: _____

Address: _____
(please supply street address for UPS shipping)
_____

City: _____ State/Province: _____

Zip/Postal Code: _____ Country: _____

Tel: ( ) _____

Fax: ( ) _____

E-mail Address: _____

Qty.	Product Code	Title	Price

❏ **New Edition No Obligation Standing Order Program**
Please enroll me in this program for the products I have ordered. Government Institutes will notify me of new editions by sending me an invoice. I understand that there is no obligation to purchase the product. This invoice is simply my reminder that a new edition has been released.

15 DAY MONEY-BACK GUARANTEE
If you're not completely satisfied with any product, return it undamaged within 15 days for a full and immediate refund on the price of the product.

Subtotal_____
MD Residents add 5% Sales Tax_____
Shipping and Handling (see box below)_____
Total Payment Enclosed_____

Within U.S:	Outside U.S:
1-4 products: $6/product	Add $15 for each item (Airmail)
5 or more: $3/product	Add $10 for each item (Surface)

SOURCE CODE: BP01